25 YEARS OF

22
MINUTES

AN UNAUTHORIZED ORAL HISTORY OF
THIS HOUR HAS 22 MINUTES
AS TOLD BY CAST MEMBERS,
STAFF, AND GUESTS

ANGELA MOMBOURQUETTE

NIMBUS
PUBLISHING LTD
nimbus.ca

Nimbus Publishing Limited
3731 Mackintosh St, Halifax, NS, B3K 5A5
(902) 455-4286 nimbus.ca

Printed and bound in Canada

NB1331

Cover & interior design: Meredith Bangay

Library and Archives Canada Cataloguing in Publication

Mombourquette, Angela, author
25 years of 22 minutes : an unauthorized oral history of This hour has 22 minutes, as told by cast members, staff, and guests / Angela Mombourquette.

Issued in print and electronic formats.
ISBN 978-1-77108-540-3 (hardcover)
—ISBN 978-1-77108-543-4 (HTML)

1. This hour has 22 minutes (Television program). 2. Television comedies--Canada--History and criticism. 3. Television and politics--Canada. 4. Political satire, Canadian. I. Title. II. Title: Twenty-five years of 22 minutes.

PN1992.77.T545M66 2017   791.45'72   C2017-904131-2
                                          C2017-904132-0

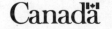  

Nimbus Publishing acknowledges the financial support for its publishing activities from the Government of Canada, the Canada Council for the Arts, and from the Province of Nova Scotia. We are pleased to work in partnership with the Province of Nova Scotia to develop and promote our creative industries for the benefit of all Nova Scotians.

CONTENTS

"That day in the boardroom, I knew it could last forever."

— Rick Mercer

PREFACE

There's a bit of a backstory to how this book came about, and how it ultimately took shape.

It starts in December 2016, when Nimbus Publishing (the publisher of this book) was on the hunt for a non-fiction editor. I'd been working as a writer and editor in magazines for about a decade, and I finagled an interview. While I was preparing for that meeting, a thought occurred to me: "You should probably bring some book ideas."

It might have been a Facebook post or a tweet from *22 Minutes* that set off the little light bulb in my head. That show has been on for—how long now? And nobody has written a book about it? Why not? (This, I would later discover, was a naïve question.)

I dug around a bit; the twenty-fifth season was coming up—a milestone. I had worked at CBC Halifax from the early 1990s to the mid-2000s, and had worked on *This Hour Has 22 Minutes*, so I knew the show, and I knew many of the people. I went into my job interview sensing I had a pretty solid book idea to present, if it happened to come up.

It came up. So here's the bad news part of this story: I didn't get the job. And here's the good news part: the publishers loved the book pitch. (The woman who did get the job, Elaine McCluskey, actually edited this book and did a fantastic job, so, really, it all worked out for the best.)

In order to have this book ready in time for the start of the show's twenty-fifth season, I would only have about six months in which to research and write it. Did I think that was possible? Again, a little naïveté on my part came in handy.

I knew it was important to get the production company that owns the show on board, so I contacted Michael Donovan, once the owner of Salter Street Films (and *22 Minutes*), now the executive chairman of DHX Media, a massive "content and brands" corporation that holds *22 Minutes* as one of its "properties."

Donovan's initial reaction by email was encouraging: "Very interested. Coordinate through my office." A collective "woot!" was raised. The ball was rolling.

Then his company called in its lawyers. (Most recently, these lawyers ne-gotiated a deal to acquire an 80 percent controlling interest in the "Peanuts" brand and 100 per cent of the brand character "Strawberry Shortcake," for $345 million.) Negotiations ensued. Things seemed to be going well until, after months of back-and-forths, DHX abruptly announced that it would not co-operate with the making of this book.

But to quote a popular meme: nevertheless, I persisted. Throughout the negotiations, I had forged ahead. By the time DHX declared it was out, I had already done dozens of interviews; I had collected tons of great stories, and the book was taking shape. The company's lack of co-operation did have one major impact, however: all of the people who were currently working on *22 Minutes* were advised that, well, the company was not playing ball.

So I guess that's why a book about *22 Minutes* hadn't been done before, and that's why we're calling this book an "unauthorized" oral history.

My goal all along has been simply to tell the story of how the show came about, to share some interesting stories from behind the scenes, and to give Canadians a bit of insight into what goes into the making of a show like *22 Minutes*—through the words of the writers, producers, and cast members who were there.

So that's what I've done. God bless the many people who believed in the value of this project, and who found it in their hearts to share their stories about their time on the show.

I will, however, offer up a caution: memories are faulty, and few people remember the same event in exactly the same way. As you'll see, there's no single "true" version of how *This Hour Has 22 Minutes* came to be, or how it has evolved over the years. But that's the beauty of an "oral history" like this one: every person who chose to speak to me was given a chance to tell his or her version of the story—unvarnished, and in their own words.

And keep in mind that this work is not exhaustive. There are a million more stories in the naked studio (and probably a whole bunch about people actually being naked in the studio).

But perhaps we'll save those for the second edition.

INTRODUCTION

These days, fake news is everywhere.

We can probably thank the Americans for that, even though, here in Canada, we've been watching fake news on our national public broadcaster for a quarter of a century now. But our fake news is more properly labelled "satire," not the propaganda-disguised-as-news that some people can't distinguish from fact, and although satirical newscasts are a dime a dozen in 2017, that wasn't the case in the early 1990s.

When the first episode of *This Hour Has 22 Minutes* went to air at 10:30 P.M. on Monday, October 11, 1993, the world was a very different place. For one thing, the internet hadn't yet become a part of daily life in most Canadian homes and businesses. Remember when you had to get your daily news by reading a (cough) newspaper?

The North American television universe was also a very different place. There was no *The Daily Show*, no *Last Week Tonight*, no *Full Frontal*. *Saturday Night Live* had been airing "Weekend Update" since 1975, but spoofing the news hadn't really become a *thing*.

On Canadian TV, we had *Front Page Challenge* and *The Nature of Things*. *The Kids in the Hall* was nearing the end of its run, and the CBC was experimenting (disastrously) with airing the nightly national newscast—renamed *Prime Time News*—at 9:00 P.M.

And now there was this new show. In the months after *CODCO* had aired its final "House of Budgell" in 1992, this thing—possibly a news satire with a bit of *Laugh-In* thrown in for good measure—had been conceived. Mary Walsh had put out some feelers. Over coffee at a Toronto bistro with former *CODCO* producer Michael Donovan and CBC Arts creative head George Anthony, Walsh said she'd been thinking about a news-based comedy show. Did they think that would fly?

They did.

They had pitched it to the CBC. It wasn't a tough sell—Walsh and fellow *CODCO* alum Cathy Jones were tied to this new show, along with a newcomer by the name of Rick Mercer. It would be produced in Halifax, in the studio that had been home to *CODCO*.

It got the green light. The CBC ordered eight episodes—enough to take the show through to Christmas—and then, if the show found an audience, well, they'd see.

I think we all know how that worked out. Fall 2017 marked the start of the twenty-fifth season of the show. *This Hour Has 22 Minutes* has gone on to have an important place in Canadian television history, and to become "must-see" viewing by millions of Canadians.

A whole generation of Canadians grew up with Rick Mercer's incisive "Streeters"; with Mary Walsh's strident Marg, Princess Warrior; with Greg Thomey's scrappy Jerry Boyle, and with Cathy Jones's outspoken Babe Bennett. A whole other generation had Geri Hall's sexy Single Female Voter and Gavin Crawford's gawky Mark Jackson to keep them laughing. Canadian politicians now routinely vie for a chance to endure a good-natured ribbing from Mark Critch, and few people would turn down a cab ride with Shaun Majumder's Raj Binder, no matter how much perspiration is involved.

Twenty-five years on, the show has endured crises, cast changes, and ratings that fluctuate with the seasons. Today's *22 Minutes* bears little resemblance to the show as it was conceived a quarter of a century ago.

It's been a long journey from conception to classic. Here's a peek behind the studio doors into how it all went down.

CAST OF CHARACTERS

Over twenty-five seaons, many people helped create the magic of *This Hour Has 22 Minutes*. Here are the ones whose stories appear in this book.

GEORGE ANTHONY

Montreal-born writer and producer George Anthony has enjoyed a long, successful run at the Canadian Broadcasting Corporation as a network cheerleader for many well-loved television series. He played a key role in bringing Canadians such hit programs as *Royal Canadian Air Farce* and *This Hour Has 22 Minutes*. Before his careers in television, which included a five-year stint hosting his own interview show on Global Television, Anthony made his mark as a founding member of the *Toronto Sun*. He currently serves as CBC's creative point person on *Rick Mercer Report*.

PAUL BELLINI

Paul Bellini is best known as The Towel Guy from *The Kids in the Hall* show, for which he was also a writer, resulting in three Emmy nominations. Other television writing credits include *P. R.*, *Locker Room*, *She's the Mayor*, and *22 Minutes*—which earned him three Gemini Awards. He is the co-author (with Scott Thompson) of the novel *Buddy Babylon*, and currently teaches comedy writing in Toronto.

BILL BRIOUX

One of the leading voices on the North American media and television scene, Bill Brioux has worked as a featured columnist for the *Toronto Sun*, as senior editor at *TV Guide* in Toronto and Los Angeles, and for the last ten years as weekly columnist for The Canadian Press. A regular contributor to national broadcast outlets, his reviews, features, and commentary can be also be found daily at brioux.tv. Currently, Bill is building an advisory board for his TV on Film Project, an initiative to preserve, share, and celebrate Canada's TV heritage.

GAVIN CRAWFORD

Gavin Crawford was born at the ripe old age of zero in Taber, Alberta. He joined the cast of The Second City in 1998, then went on to co-create (with partner Kyle Tingley) and star in *The Gavin Crawford Show* on the Comedy Network. He was lured to Nova Scotia by an opportunity to fill in for Mary Walsh on *This Hour Has 22 Minutes*. A two-week guest spot turned into eight seasons. He is currently host/producer of *Because News* on CBC Radio One.

GEOFF D'EON

Geoff D'Eon left his straight CBC newsman job in 1993 and took *22 Minutes* on the road, producing and directing hundreds of ambushes, celebrity headlocks, sleepovers, and *Talking To Americans*. Bossed around no fewer than four Canadian prime ministers on location. Was euphoric when *22 Minutes* regularly started beating *The National* in the ratings. Considers himself to have had one of the "best jobs ever" at the CBC.

BILL DONOVAN

Bill Donovan, a New Brunswick broadcast journalist, first appeared in Newfoundland as the CBC's regional news supervisor in the early 1970s. After other postings with the corporation, he returned to St. John's in 1980 as director of television. In 1985, he moved to Halifax as the CBC's regional director for the Maritime provinces, where he oversaw the arrival of *CODCO* and *This Hour Has 22 Minutes*.

COURTESY ROB ALLEN

JOHN DOYLE

John Doyle has been the *Globe and Mail*'s television critic since 2000. In 1991, after working briefly in radio and in television, he began writing a column for *Broadcast Week*, the *Globe*'s television magazine, and from 1995 to 2000 he was the critic for *Broadcast Week*. His book *A Great Feast of Light: Growing Up Irish in the Television Age* was published to acclaim in October 2005. His book about soccer, *The World is a Ball: The Joy, Madness and Meaning of Soccer* was a national bestseller in Canada on publication and listed for the William Hill Irish Sports Book of the Year. John's favourite TV show of all time is *Fawlty Towers* and he supports Toronto FC when he's feeling optimistic.

IVAN FECAN

Ivan Fecan is a Canadian media executive, producer, and philanthropist who boasts titles such as VP Creative Affairs at NBC, Head of English TV at CBC, and CEO and President of CTVglobemedia. He built CTV into a multibillion-dollar conglomerate with Canada's top-rated broadcast and cable networks, and the number one programs in news, sports, and entertainment.

GERI HALL

Geri Hall waitressed until she got angry inside, then auditioned for The Second City and became a professional actor. She has starred in so many commercials that for a while, the mere sight of her face would make people want to buy random stuff—like plane tickets, or shredded cheese. She has appeared in TV shows and films; she's been handcuffed by one of our prime ministers (but not by the one she would have chosen, if given an option); and that raspy voice that got her teased in public school—it's turned out to be a good thing.

EDWARD KAY

Edward Kay is a showrunner, writer, and author who enjoys creating works that are funny or dark, and frequently both. He was a staff writer and producer for *This Hour Has 22 Minutes* for four seasons, then went on to co-create three popular television series: *Olliver's Adventures*, *Jimmy Two-Shoes*, and *Finding Stuff Out*.

JACK KELLUM

Jack Kellum was a singer and guitarist who performed regularly in clubs and resorts around Toronto and Southern Ontario in the early 1960s before beginning his career in television. In 1973, he moved with CBC from Toronto to St. John's to produce *Land and Sea*, a local version of *This Land*. He produced and directed the program *Ryan's Fancy* before creating the *Wonderful Grand Band* series. From 1986 to 1992 he was senior producer on the *CODCO* series, and in 1993 became senior producer of *This Hour Has 22 Minutes*. He has also produced numerous other musical, comedy, and variety programs for the CBC. He now lives in Fergus, Ontario, where he is enjoying grandchildren and retired life.

PENNY LONGLEY

Penny Longley worked at CBC Halifax for more than thirty-five years in television production and programming. She retired in 2004.

GERALD LUNZ

Gerald Lunz is an award-winning television writer and producer who began his career in live theatre. He worked on the national tours of the legendary Newfoundland comedy troupe CODCO, which consisted of Andy Jones, Mary Walsh, Greg Malone, Tommy Sexton, and Cathy Jones. When *CODCO* launched as a half-hour CBC television show, Lunz served as associate producer. While working with CODCO he met another young Newfoundland comic, Rick Mercer, and they formed a creative partnership. When *CODCO* ended in 1992, most of the company continued on with *This Hour Has 22 Minutes*, where Lunz served as a producer. He is currently executive producer of *Rick Mercer Report*.

ED MACDONALD

Ed Macdonald was born and raised on Cape Breton Island. The youngest of five children, Macdonald had little interest in anything other than comedy and aliens. He can be seen in episodes of *Trailer Park Boys*, *Hatching, Matching and Dispatching*, *The Bette Show*, and, briefly, in *The Jon Dore Television Show*. In the mid-'90s, he began writing on *22 Minutes* and many other TV shows. He has won three Gemini Awards for excellence in writing, a Writers Guild of Canada Award, and a Golden Sheaf Award, among others.

ALAN MACGILLIVRAY

Alan MacGillivray is a native of Halifax, where he has spent most of his life. He began working at Salter Street Films in 1986, and over the next twelve years performed roles of general manager, producer, executive producer, and treasurer, as well as senior vice-president of production. He left Salter Street in 1998 and freelanced for the next five years. In 2003, he became the supervisor of production and business affairs for *Rick Mercer Report*.

PETER MANSBRIDGE

Peter Mansbridge was the long-time chief correspondent of CBC News. He anchored *The National,* CBC's flagship nightly news program, and all CBC News specials. In almost fifty years with CBC News, Mansbridge interviewed countless international leaders. He remains the only Canadian journalist to have been to the White House to interview the then-US president, Barack Obama.

FRED MATTOCKS

Fred Mattocks played a key role in fostering collaboration between CBC TV and independent producers in the Maritimes between 1986 and 1999. Through this time he supported, enabled, and eventually led changes that resulted in CBC Maritimes being the largest single collaborator with independent film and video producers outside of Toronto. Fred continues to value the broader creative community and views partnerships with artist and creator communities as keys to the success of his latest venture, CBC Local Services.

TIM MCAULIFFE

Tim McAuliffe is a writer and producer, known for *This Hour Has 22 Minutes*, *The Office*, *Last Man On Earth*, *Late Night with Jimmy Fallon*, *Corner Gas*, and *Up All Night*.

RICK MERCER

Rick Mercer began his career in comedy performing and writing in his hometown, St. John's, Newfoundland, with a series of one-man stage shows. His solo *Show Me the Button: I'll Push It (or, Charles Lynch Must Die)* debuted at the National Arts Centre in 1990 followed by a national tour. He launched his television career in 1993 as one of the creators, performers, and writers on *This Hour Has 22 Minutes*. In 1998, he joined Gerald Lunz and Michael Donovan to create the satirical dramatic series *Made in Canada*, where he again starred and contributed as a writer. In 2001, his CBC special *Talking To Americans* became the highest rated Canadian comedy special ever, with 2.7 million viewers. He currently hosts the *Rick Mercer Report* on CBC Television.

COLIN MOCHRIE

Colin Mochrie joined *This Hour has 22 Minutes* in 2001, where he came up with fifty-four different characters, two of whom made it to air. He now tours the world doing improv, which is so much easier than writing and remembering jokes. Still accepts awards for Peter Mansbridge.

MARK MULLANE

Before Mark Mullane started his current career in real estate, he spent fourteen years as an award-winning film and television producer, director, and writer for some of Canada's most beloved shows, including *This Hour Has 22 Minutes*, *The New Music*, and *Street Cents*. He has also produced a number of music videos, most notably for the Grammy Award-winning band Arcade Fire. In addition, he was in the indie-famous band North of America that released six albums and toured extensively throughout Canada, the US, and Europe.

PHYLLIS PLATT

Phyllis Platt has worked extensively as a journalist, producer, and broadcast executive. She has served as a television executive in the roles of CBC executive director of TV arts and entertainment, and network program director, supervising the development and production of some of Canada's most popular programs, including *This Hour Has 22 Minutes*, *The Newsroom* and *Da Vinci's Inquest*, as well as television movies such as *Million Dollar Babies* and *The Arrow*. She is a recipient of the Women in Film and Television Outstanding Achievement Award and has served as jury chair of the international Rose d'Or Television Festival.

STEPHEN REYNOLDS

Stephen Reynolds is an Emmy and Gemini Award–winning director and producer. He is perhaps best known for his contributions to Canadian comedy shows *This Hour Has 22 Minutes*; *Hatching, Matching and Dispatching*; *CODCO*, and *Made in Canada*. He has just finished directing his second season of the Emmy-winning PBS Kids' series *Odd Squad*, his first season on Family Channel's *The Next Step*, and a second season on CBC's *Mr. D*. Reynolds, and is currently helping to develop three television projects and two feature films.

HENRY SARWER-FONER

Henry Sarwer-Foner has won numerous Canadian Screen Awards, Geminis, Directors Guild of Canada Awards, and Canadian Comedy Awards as the director of *This Hour Has 22 Minutes*, *The Industry* (aka *Made in Canada*), *Corner Gas*, and *Rick Mercer Report*. In addition to directing the comedy series *Living In Your Car*, *Less Than Kind* and *Hatching, Matching and Dispatching*, Sarwer-Foner has also directed dramas such as *Traders* and *The Associates*.

PETER SUTHERLAND

Peter Sutherland has been a camera operator at CBC Halifax since 1989, and has been shooting video for *This Hour Has 22 Minutes* since the very first episode. He has been behind the camera for more than four hundred political ambushes. You can find his signature in the basement of the White House in Washington, DC, and on the ceiling of the Peace Tower in the Parliament Buildings in Ottawa.

JENNIFER WHALEN

An alumnus of Second City Toronto, Jennifer Whalen is a co-creator, executive producer, writer, and star of *Baroness von Sketch Show,* airing on CBC in Canada and IFC in the United States. She was head writer for the award-winning satirical comedy *This Hour Has 22 Minutes.* She developed long-running shows *Little Mosque On the Prairie* (CBC/Mind's Eye) and *Instant Star* (CTV/Epitome). She has also worked on *The Ron James Show* (CBC), *The Jon Dore Show* (Comedy Network/IFC) and the critically acclaimed *Gavin Crawford Show* (Comedy Network/Shaftsbury). She has won a Canadian Screen Award for Best Show, and one for Best Writing for her work on *Baroness von Sketch Show* and has been nominated for three Geminis and four Canadian Comedy Awards. She has won both a Writers Guild of Canada Award and a Canadian Comedy Award for her work on *This Hour Has 22 Minutes.*

DANNY WILLIAMS

Danny Williams is a lawyer, businessman, and community leader who served as premier of Newfoundland and Labrador from 2003 to 2010. Under his leadership, the province's economy experienced unprecedented growth and prosperity. Since then, Danny has stepped back from public life, focusing on his various business interests. He has lost count of the number of times he's appeared on *22 Minutes.*

The Pioneers

1979–1992

The biblical account of the lineage of *This Hour Has 22 Minutes* might go something like this: CODCO the theatre troupe begat Wonderful Grand Band the troupe, which begat *Wonderful Grand Band*, the TV show, which begat *CODCO* the TV show, which begat 22 Minutes, the institution—given that it has survived now for twenty-five seasons on Canadian television.

Both the *Wonderful Grand Band* and *CODCO* television shows had something in common, in addition to cast members Tommy Sexton, Greg Malone, Mary Walsh, and Cathy Jones: an unassuming guy by the name of Jack Kellum.

Kellum was an Ontario-born musician turned television producer who had moved to Newfoundland in the mid-1970s to produce and direct shows like *Land and Sea* and *Ryan's Fancy*. He was one of a handful of people who played an instrumental role in the events that ultimately led to the birth of *This Hour Has 22 Minutes*.

BILL DONOVAN

Director of Television, CBC Newfoundland, 1980–85; Regional Director, CBC Maritimes, 1985–1997

I was a regional news supervisor in Newfoundland in the mid-1970s. They had recruited a few people to salt the place, and one of them was Jack Kellum.

Jack came to me one day and said, "I want to take you to a local emporium." I can't remember the name of it; it was a big barn of a bar in a shopping mall.

I had no idea what I was getting into, except that I knew Jack, and I trusted him. So in we went, and we saw the Wonderful Grand Band, and of course, not only had I never seen anything like it—neither had anybody else. It was quite unique and astounding. At the end of the evening, Jack said, "What do you think? I think we could do a show with these guys," and I said, "So do I."

So it was Jack who brought the Wonderful Grand Band to the CBC, or he brought the CBC to it.

JACK KELLUM

Senior Producer, 1993–2002; Executive Producer, 2002–2011

Wonderful Grand Band came after CODCO—not *CODCO* the television series, but CODCO the troupe. Nothing out of Newfoundland had ever really been done with CODCO because of the control and the influence of the Catholic Church—they were always attacking the church.

They were *persona non grata* at the CBC, but with me being a newcomer, and with the strength of the traditional music in the WGB show—and with the support of Bill Donovan—we were able to get WGB into the studios in Newfoundland. It was not easy, though. It was painful.

....

The *Wonderful Grand Band* television show—a mix of musical performances and comedy sketches—aired regionally on the CBC from 1980 to 1983. The original cast featured Tommy Sexton and Greg Malone (often playing the much-loved characters Mr. Budgell and Nanny Hynes). Cathy Jones and Mary Walsh joined in the show's final year. The band played a mix of traditional and original comedic songs, and included Newfoundland musical stalwarts Sandy

Morris and Ron Hynes. The show became a cult hit in Newfoundland and Labrador, drawing enormous audiences across the province.

RICK MERCER
Cast Member, 1993–2001
Wonderful Grand Band had the biggest influence on me—more than any television production in my lifetime. I was obsessed with *Wonderful Grand Band*. It was everything to me. I thought it was the funniest show ever made. I thought the music was brilliant. And the whole thing was being shot down the street—that was what was amazing.

BILL DONOVAN
It was very much under-budgeted. It ran as a regional show; it was my dream to get it to the network. There were those in the establishment in Newfoundland and those in the CBC in Newfoundland who were not comfortable with it even being produced, never mind being produced for the network, because it was pretty rough stuff. I thought it was hilariously funny.

JACK KELLUM
Wonderful Grand Band got the highest television ratings of any show ever in Newfoundland. Newfoundland had a population of, let's say 500,000. Our ratings for the three years we were on were consistent, and they were in the 250,000 range. That means that half of the population every Monday night was watching the show.

GERALD LUNZ
Creative Producer, 1993–1998
It was the biggest show in Newfoundland. It would clear the streets. A whole province was sitting in front of the TV, because it was theirs—it was about them. They knew the characters. If they don't get it in London, Ontario—fuck 'em. It ain't for them.

BILL DONOVAN

Wonderful Grand Band was hugely successful in Newfoundland. It had an audience that compared to full network shows—just in Newfoundland.

It was successful right across every demographic you could think of, from young people—because it had a folk rock musical foundation—to as old as you can get.

RICK MERCER

The biggest television stars of the day weren't coming from Los Angeles; they were coming from St. John's, Newfoundland—that's where they all lived. And that's not an exaggeration. If you look back at the ratings—like, the biggest shows of the day, *Dallas*, or *Knots Landing* or what have you—*Wonderful Grand Band* always outdrew those shows. Literally, everything stopped, and those people were superstars.

Mary and Cathy were featured heavily on that show. They weren't cast members per se—Tommy Sexton and Greg Malone were—but Cathy and Mary were often there on the show, so they were a big part of the show that had a bigger influence on me than anything else.

So, they were my idols to begin with.

Around the same time, during the early 1980s, brothers Paul and Michael Donovan were struggling to keep their fledgling production company, Salter Street Films, afloat in Halifax. The company's early feature films—*South Pacific 1942*; *Siege*; and *Def-Con 4*—had not been big money-makers, and the company was on the hunt for a more consistent way to generate income.

ALAN MACGILLIVRAY
General Manager/Senior Vice-President of Production/Producer,
Salter Street Films, 1986–1998

It was Michael's idea to get into television at that point. They had only done feature films, and the feature film business in Canada was even harder then than it is now. It was hard to make any money. So Michael thought, from a business perspective, television was much more reliable.

One story was that he was driving by CBC one day, and he noticed a lot of the technicians sitting outside. He drove by a couple of hours later and they were still sitting outside, so he thought, "Hmmm. Maybe we can work something out here."

JACK KELLUM

A filmmaker named Charlotte Harper made Michael Donovan aware of *Wonderful Grand Band*, and he really took notice. Michael started to familiarize himself with them and with CODCO—not *CODCO* the television series, but CODCO the comedy troupe.

Michael started a dialogue with Bill Donovan in Halifax, who was then regional director of CBC in the Maritimes. Michael and Bill started to chat about the possibilities of doing a television show.

BILL DONOVAN

I came to Halifax in 1985. Shortly after I got there, I was approached by Michael Donovan—who is no relation, I should point out. We had never met before I arrived in Halifax with CBC.

Michael approached me and said—and I'm pretty sure this is exactly what he said—"If I can get a contract with the CODCOs, would you be willing to produce them with CBC facilities?"

It was an unusual request. CBC Halifax's Bell Road studios had once been the home of several much-loved series, including *Don Messer's Jubilee* and *Sing-along Jubilee*, but those shows had been produced entirely in-house.

A partnership between an independent producer—like Salter Street Films— and the nation's public broadcaster—the CBC—would be among the very first experiments anywhere in the country in that kind of co-operation. The CBC would provide the infrastructure—studios, equipment, and crews—while the producer would bear the costs of the performers and production staff.

BILL DONOVAN

I said yes. Now, that was a fairly big "yes," because at the time, the CBC's situation was that we had facilities, but very little cash. The above-the-line costs would be the writers, the singers, the dancers, the performers—what you see on the screen. That's all cash, and the CBC's cash had been depleted by budget cuts and so on, and part of it had been used to form a fund for independent production.

So the funds that had once been within the CBC, which would have allowed us to theoretically produce what was on the table, no longer existed. So my "yes" was conditional on Michael getting a contract with the CODCOs, and getting cash from the independent production fund, which meant that he had to get a network deal. All of those pieces had to come together.

There was a lot riding on this potential deal, and not just for Salter Street Films. CBC Halifax—the "plant," as the building was known to employees—had not produced any significant amount of prime-time network content in nearly a decade.

FRED MATTOCKS
Plant Manager, CBC Halifax, 1986–1994; Director of Television, CBC Maritimes, 1994–1995; Regional Director, CBC Maritimes, 1995–1999; currently General Manager, Local Services, CBC English Services

Frankly, while CBC Halifax had a very rich heritage, the station, when I arrived in '86, was in deep trouble. We were producing, I think, a total of four hours of network programming, and two of those were a weekend church service called *Hymn Sing*. This was a very big descent for a station that, ten years before, had been producing the bulk of, or a lot of, the network's Canadian content—successful Canadian content. Things like *Singalong Jubilee*.

I used to say, in those days, that we had a whole bunch of talented people in that station who had their eyes firmly fixed on the past. At one point, I remember a great friend of mine, Rosalee Wood, who worked with me—this was in the summer of '86—burst out in a meeting after somebody went into a long speech about the "good old days" and said, "Oh, for fuck's sake. I wish we'd had Don Messer stuffed and put on a cart, and we could drag him through the hallway once a day!"

JACK KELLUM

Michael was able to put together a deal with the CBC network, with Bill Donovan's support and the support of a number of other people in Halifax at the CBC. People don't realize it, but these things don't happen without support in the most unlikely places. I know Fred Mattocks was a big supporter. At that point, I was not involved, but what it turned into was the *CODCO* series.

FRED MATTOCKS

The station had been written off by the network. You know, one of my first meetings, when I was plant manager, with the network—I was brought to Toronto by a guy named Frank Phillips, who was then called the network production manager. He called me up and said, "Come to Toronto."

I went to Toronto, and he sat me down and said, "Fred, you're a nice guy, and you're very talented, and you're at the start of your career. Don't get too invested in Halifax, because we are going to write it off. It's just going to be a news-only station. We're not going to do any production there."

I remember saying to him, "I've just been hired to make sure that doesn't happen."

He said, "Good luck to you, but the network's already decided."

So Bill Donovan's leadership was critical. Bill had the vision and drove the network relationships. And I was his guy making this happen.

BILL DONOVAN

As part of the package, we recruited Jack Kellum to come [from St. John's to Halifax] with the *CODCO* project, because running a show with the CODCOs was exciting, to put it mildly. But Jack had done it. He had been there. I trusted him.

JACK KELLUM

It was the fall of 1986 when we began production on *CODCO*. Bill had asked my boss in Newfoundland if he could borrow me, and my boss said yes.

I got involved when we had to pick a director. My first contact with Michael was when we flew out to Vancouver in 1986 to see the CODCO group performing at a World's Fair and to meet a potential director, John Blanchard. He became the first director of the *CODCO* series.

I hadn't known Michael before, but we had the flight to Vancouver to get to know one another. The CBC offered my services at no cost to Michael, and I think Michael was somewhat comforted by that, because I had known these performers and I'd known that they weren't the easiest people to work with. Everybody had hang-ups. I often looked at my job as more of a babysitter than a producer.

BILL DONOVAN

This was the first co-production with an independent producer ever, I believe, in that particular location. And that was a major piece of business. So we were operating with a mixed crew of CBC staffers and independent freelancers. That was basically unheard of.

It wasn't an easy fit. Independent producers like Salter Street were in the habit of making shows as quickly and as cheaply as possible. Old-school unionized crews at the CBC had been doing things their way—with strictly controlled workdays and generous overtime allowances—for decades. It took creativity and flexibility on both sides to find ways to make the relationship workable.

FRED MATTOCKS

Strictly speaking, it wasn't the first co-production, but it was the first successful co-production. It was the first network-funded co-production. There was a co-production before that, which happened just before I arrived in '85, with an independent producer, and I'm told it was a failure—certainly a creative failure. But when I say it was a failure, the relationship between the indepen-dent producer and the CBC was terrible. And that wasn't the independent producer's fault. It was CBC's fault.

PENNY LONGLEY
Manager of Program Services, CBC Halifax, 1986–2004
Dealing with an independent producer, and operating a design department with independent producers, we learned a lot—and it was good. We had to.

I had to learn that the way we had been doing things for the last whatever number of years was not necessarily the good way. And when these outside people came in who had worked on films and so on, they brought an entirely different perspective, and it was a perspective I didn't know at all. I learned a lot from how they did things.

First of all, they were used to doing things for a nickel. And they were used to doing things really fast. And I think the old CBC—we kind of had a culture that you take your time and you don't ever…"rush" isn't the right word. It was just an entirely different way of looking at things. No sense of urgency.

FRED MATTOCKS
What you need to know about that time—and this is ancient history now—was that up until '84, the CBC had been the producer of record in television in this country. And in '84, Telefilm Canada, or whatever its predecessor was—the Canadian Film Development Corporation—was set up, and it announced government support for an independent production industry in the country.

That was taken very hard at the CBC, and it was taken very hard in Halifax. The notion that somebody outside the CBC would actually be producing CBC content was a very, very difficult one. Difficult for the unions, difficult for many people who had been at the CBC a long time and who were very, very proud of their heritage. There were few places in this country that had as rich a heritage of in-house production as CBC Halifax.

Having said all of that, my job—and Bill Donovan hired me to do this—was to create successful independent production in CBC Halifax. That was my job, and we succeeded spectacularly. You know, by the middle '90s, we were producing more network production with independent producers than any other region in the country. We had, at one point, I think, three network shows that were number one in their particular category.

PENNY LONGLEY

Fred Mattocks is one of the smartest people I've ever met in my life; he was smart enough to realize that we'd better get on this train and we'd better damn well learn how to do it. And we'd better damn well learn that change is good, because there was a lot of resistance, as you can imagine, from inside. People said, "I've done my job this way for twenty-five years, and you assholes think I'm going to change, and I'm not." There was a lot of that.

So we had to all work to say, "Listen, you know what? You want to survive, you'd better learn." And most of them did.

FRED MATTOCKS

At the time when *CODCO* was being established and then being produced, I was the person responsible for operations, and the challenge with *CODCO* was producing sketch comedy—television sketch comedy—in a plant that was not built for sketch comedy.

We had a trailer city out back with containers we used for set storage and so on. I mean, we actually pioneered a kind of production process to be able to do that, because with *CODCO* we were shooting, typically, if I remember correctly, for two or three months, but we were doing hundreds of sketches. And each sketch, potentially, could have its own set, could have its own costumes. To shoot efficiently, we had to shoot a number of sketches every day.

So it was very, very design-intensive, very process-intensive. It was a big production challenge for that plant. That plant had never done sketch comedy before; we hadn't designed it, we hadn't built it, and we hadn't shot it, and all of those things were new.

And as history shows, we got very good at it, very quickly.

JACK KELLUM

CODCO used humungous resources. It was a factory, running 24/7, with sets being built and designed and installed and then taken out again.

The regular routine was that the director and myself would go into the studio, probably at seven o'clock on Monday morning. We would go through the day's schedule and what we planned to get through that day, and then we would walk into the studio to see what shape the sets were in. It could be one, two, or three sets at a time in the studio, and often when we went in, the last touches of paint were just going on.

We would work probably from eight in the morning until seven at night, and as we were wrapping up the day, the old sets were on their way out and the new sets were on their way in. Next day the same thing. And on it went. It was really labour-intensive on the part of CBC.

But there were bumps, and it often fell to Kellum to smooth the relationships between Salter Street, the cast, and the CBC.

RICK MERCER

Jack's legacy is huge in Canadian broadcasting, and he had a great capacity to deal to with the eccentric behaviour of showbiz people. He'd seen it all.

FRED MATTOCKS

Any kind of troupe performance medium, whether it's television or theatre or whatever, is going to be chaotic at times. It's just the way it is. You've got creative, passionate human beings who each have a very strong vision, because they wouldn't be doing it otherwise.

So it's always chaotic, and *CODCO* was particularly chaotic, partly because, when we first started it up, we had no idea the size of the tiger we had by the tail. And when I say, "we," I include Michael Donovan in that. I actually include the CODCOs in that, too, because I don't think they had any idea. So it was a lot of learning.

JACK KELLUM

In my whole life working in the broadcast industry, I never felt I was working for a production company or for the CBC. I was always working for the show. It used to drive Fred Mattocks crazy, because we would have knock-down, drag-out, nasty arguments: "Who the fuck are you working for? Are you working for the CBC, or are you working for Salter Street?"

And then I used to have the same kind of things with Salter Street, with Alan MacGillivray. The fights were about equal for me. So I said to myself, "I guess I must be doing my job okay, because they're both unhappy with me."

FRED MATTOCKS

Well, you know, in the moment, he might be right. I always appreciated Jack's role, because that's what was required. He was the honest broker, and he was the single person there who was thinking about the creative possibilities, and thinking about the cast and talent, and who had his eye on the creative ball.

Not to say that CBC didn't, and not to say that the independent producer, Salter Street Films, didn't, but on both sides of Jack there were different agendas. With the CBC, it was, "We have to deliver this thing. We have to deliver it to a certain schedule, and in a certain framework—a creative framework, and a budget framework."

On the independent producer's side, it was very similar topics, budget being one that was absolutely in common, but a very different view. I mean, Michael Donovan needed to make money. His company couldn't survive if he didn't make money.

Jack was firmly in between them, and Jack was very much, at points, the heart of the show.

ALAN MACGILLIVRAY

Jack describes that pretty well, I think. I didn't know—and he didn't let me know—the extent to which he was having arguments with Fred Mattocks, but it's pretty easy for me to believe that was going on, because this was when the CBC was introduced to the whole idea of co-production—what they called a co-production.

We didn't see it as a co-production. We were producing the show with help from them. It wasn't a co-production from my point of view, because we were responsible if we went over budget.

· · ·

Elsewhere in the country, at the start of the 1990s—while *CODCO* was in production in Halifax—another young Newfoundlander was beginning to make his name on the national stage.

RICK MERCER

I had done my one-man show, which was called *Show Me the Button: I'll Push It (or, Charles Lynch Must Die)*. It was a one-man show about, believe it or not, the Meech Lake Accord, and Newfoundland's position in Canada. It was directed by Gerald Lunz.

GERALD LUNZ

That show started with me asking Rick if he had the chutzpah to say what he was saying—in downtown St. John's in late-night cabarets—on a stage at the National Arts Centre in Ottawa, right in their faces.

And he was like, "Let's do it." Bold.

RICK MERCER

It's a story unto itself how the show became as big as it did, because we went to Ottawa to do this one-man show at the National Arts Centre, and it became quite the *cause célèbre*—it was a real sensation in Ottawa. You know, cabinet ministers started showing up for it, national media people started showing up. Charles Lynch himself showed up. He loved it because he called himself "the Salman Rushdie of Newfoundland" and I had put a fatwa on his head.

So the show was a big hit, and then a series of events occurred. I didn't understand at the time that they were as extraordinary as they were, I guess, because I was young and naïve.

At the same time that I was doing my show, there was another production happening out west, a one-person show. It was a much bigger show, and that show collapsed in its opening run somewhere on the Prairies. Suddenly these theatres—they had a hole in their season and they needed something. And there I was, this nineteen-year-old, yelling at this old man about the Constitution.

So Gerald did a deal with these theatre companies, and I left the National Arts Centre and rolled right into a national tour. I played Toronto for a month, I played Vancouver for a month or three weeks, went back into Ottawa, held over a run there, went to Newfoundland, did a record-breaking run at the LSPU Hall [*the former Longshoremen's Protective Union Hall, now a performing-arts centre in downtown St. John's*], then moved uptown to the Arts and Culture Centre, which was unheard of, and then we toured Newfoundland.

Now, all those things occurred, I'm not sure in what order. But someone who also came to that initial show at the National Arts Centre was [CBC creative head] George Anthony. And George Anthony said, "You should be on the CBC," which was very exciting to me, of course.

We started talking about doing the one-man show as a television show and then also, barring that, developing some project for me at the CBC. And that's when *22 Minutes* came along—further down the road, but not that long after.

GEORGE ANTHONY

Creative Head of CBC Television Arts, Music, Science & Variety, 1990–2003; Director of Special Projects, CBC, 2003–2007; Creative Consultant, CBC, 2007–present

I came to CBC in November 1990. [Director of television programming] Ivan Fecan basically brought me in. Looking back, I realize he had the guts of a cat burglar, because at the time I was a small "c" celebrity because I used to write about celebrities in the *Toronto Sun*. I was a columnist and entertainment editor at the *Toronto Sun*, which was a tabloid paper.

The idea of bringing anyone into the CBC from a tabloid newspaper was not favourably regarded. But to bring someone in from a tabloid newspaper to run two departments—because Ivan had merged two departments: the Arts, Music, and Science department, and the Variety department—in theory, made no sense, but it worked out really, really well. So, as usual, he knew what he was doing.

So I came in in '90, and I inherited a whole lot of shows between the two departments. Everything from *Adrienne Clarkson Presents* to *Kids in the Hall* and *CODCO*. So that was really where I met Michael and most of the gang, was during my time with *CODCO*.

• • •

JACK KELLUM

CODCO ended in '92, and there was a big hole in the studio schedule in Halifax. Michael was told, I believe by Bill Donovan, that if he could fill it, the facilities would be his.

GEOFF D'EON
Editorial Producer, 1993–2003; Executive Producer of CBC Arts and Entertainment, Atlantic Region, 2003–2008

CODCO, by all accounts, had been a bit of a three-ring circus. It was sort of bedlam by the end, with the entire cast in the edit suite screaming and shouting about what should and shouldn't be in the show. It became sort of dysfunctional.

GERALD LUNZ

CODCO had just wrapped up its tent, I think, a year before, and Michael and Jack Kellum—CBC Jack and Michael independent—were trying to create something. How are we going to fill this hole now that we have this Halifax production thing going? We should keep this going. It's employing a lot of people, it's having a voice from the East Coast. Michael was very strong on that, and Jack of course had come out of Newfoundland with *Land and Sea* and all kinds of early work with *CODCO*. So they were constructing something.

BILL DONOVAN

And that's when *22 Minutes* was hatched. And there are many versions of how that happened.

2

Series Concept Created By...

1992–1993

JACK KELLUM

At some point along there in the spring of '93, Mary Walsh approached Michael and said, "Michael, I think I could get myself and Cathy and maybe Andy." [*Mary was referring to Cathy's brother, Andy Jones, an actor and writer who had been an outspoken cast member on* CODCO, *and who had left that show over a controversial sketch that presented a scathing critique of the Catholic priesthood.*] It was starting to be known at that point that Tommy Sexton had AIDS and was dying. Mary and Greg weren't talking, so Greg was not on the list.

She said, "I think I can get them together to do a fake news show."

GEORGE ANTHONY

In the old days, Michael was incapable of having a conversation with you without somewhere inserting a pitch. You could just bump into him on the street in Halifax and he would say, "Oh, hi. Listen, have you ever thought of…?" And he was wonderful. Just a great pitcher. He also had great ideas. So when we got together—which was quite frequently—he would pitch me on different things.

After *CODCO*—which I loved—came to an end in '92, Michael called me and said that he and Mary Walsh wanted to meet with me about something. I can't remember exactly why, but we met at [now-defunct Toronto restaurant] Bistro 990, and it was afternoon. It was like four in the afternoon or something, before the busy dinner rush. This is how I remember it, anyway.

Mary said that she had an idea for a new show, and it would be different, in that it would be actually organized and well run. She said, "We've tried anarchy, and that was fun, but it doesn't really get you where you want to go." So I was intrigued, and she suggested doing a weekly news-based show. I don't know if she mentioned *That Was the Week That Was*, but there was something on in Britain or somewhere that was a news spoof.

So I thought it was a good idea, and they should go away and develop a scenario and come back with it. And that was kind of the first thing.

RICK MERCER

This is how I understand the genesis of *22 Minutes*: *CODCO* came to an end, and Salter Street, like so many companies of that size, they had come to the conclusion that the way you keep your doors open is you have a television series. I mean, Salter Street was successful in the movie business, but the thing about the movie business is, there's nothing consistent about it. So, you do a movie, or two movies one year, but then how do you keep the lights on for the year that you don't make a movie, and how do you pay the people? A series allows that to happen.

So, I think Salter was probably very eager to carry on the series work, and I know that Salter Street had developed, with Jack Kellum, a fairly substantial proposal for a show that would feature [Halifax comedian] Bill Carr. At the last minute, Michael Donovan decided, "No, I'm not going to do that," and he pitched a Mary Walsh vehicle.

I don't think they had very much else. And at the same time, I was discussing with George Anthony where I would land on the CBC, because he wanted me on the CBC. So I don't know how my name ended up in the mix. Gerald had a relationship with Michael Donovan, because Gerald was the associate producer of *CODCO*, and I know Michael was very intrigued at the amount of media that we had generated with this one-man show, *Show Me the Button.*

JACK KELLUM

The CBC had offered my services; I think that was a comforting factor again, because I had worked with these people, and I knew some of their quirks and how to help out when trouble struck—and it used to strike fairly frequently.

BILL DONOVAN

I'm not sure I would have been brave enough to try it without Jack Kellum there, because Jack had been there at the ground level, and he was a supremely good producer. He understood—he had a real feel for this kind of program.

JACK KELLUM

Michael just told me that Mary had come to him with an idea to satirize the news, and that she thought that she could bring Cathy and Rick Mercer, and she thought she could bring Andy Jones. In the end, she didn't bring Andy.

So with that thread of an idea, Michael and I met, probably every other day for two weeks, fashioning a program proposal for the network on this fake news show that became *This Hour Has 22 Minutes.*

GERALD LUNZ

Michael and Jack wrote the pitch, obviously. Mary was busy. She was doing *A Moon for the Misbegotten* in London with Colm Feore, directed by Martha Henry. It must've been spring of 1993, because I remember going to London to talk to Mary, which is where we had the first conversation about this potential series pitch: What is it—chalk or cheese?

Mary said, "I don't know."

I said, "Mary, you are going to have to get involved. If you want to be involved in the creation of this show, you should get in touch with Michael." But of course she couldn't, because she was up to her eyeballs doing O'Neill. So that truck went ahead of itself with Michael and Jack.

JACK KELLUM

The original proposal that went in was not what you see on *This Hour Has 22 Minutes* today, but there were basic elements of it that are in the show still today.

GERALD LUNZ

I think Andy's name was also on the pitch. Andy Jones. I remember the quote from Andy: "You can use my name for bait as long as I don't have to do the series." Because Andy had just come off six harrowing years, taxing years, on *CODCO*. He was so tired of living in a quasi-apartment in Halifax and not in St. John's, where he wanted to be. He wanted to get on with other things.

BILL DONOVAN

Early on, when the idea was going forward with the network—I'm not sure what exact state it was at, but it was pretty well accepted that we were going to do this show—I got a call from the network boss, a chap named Ivan Fecan.

He said, "I understand Andy Jones has dropped out," and I said, "I hear the same thing."

Fecan said, "Well, it strikes me that—no Andy, no show."

I said, "I don't think that's the case. I think maybe Rick Mercer might be a game changer. Andy has his own genius. He likes complicated sketches and he likes them long, and if he doesn't feel that he fits into this format, be that as it may. Rick Mercer has the best editorial mind I have ever met, including all of the news people I've worked with. He sees the story that should be done, and he sees exactly the angle as well as anybody does. He also works extremely hard."

So Fecan accepted that. It went forward.

IVAN FECAN
Director of Television Programming, CBC; 1987–1991, Vice-President of Entertainment Programming, 1991–1992, Vice-President of CBC English Television, 1992–1993

I don't remember that specifically, but it has a ring of truth. You know, Andy had proven himself as a satirist, for sure, and I don't think I knew Rick Mercer particularly well at the time. So I would certainly have leaned on Bill's advice.

JACK KELLUM

So we went to Toronto with this program proposal. We had a meeting set up with the head honchos in Toronto, and the first time we went, the meeting was scheduled for nine o'clock, and we arrived at ten, and they all had other things, so the whole thing was cancelled. We went up there for nothing, because Michael got the times wrong.

The next time we went, several weeks later, I was living in Halifax and I didn't have a car, so Michael was going to pick me up to go to the airport. The flight was to leave at eight o'clock, and at 7:55 we arrived at the airport, and Michael didn't have a ticket. So I ran ahead and he said, "Just don't let them close the door!"

I got there and I said to the guy at the door, "I've got a buddy who is on his way, but we are just a bit late." And he said, "Don't worry, I won't close it until he gets here."

So we went to Toronto, and we made our pitch for what later became *22 Minutes*.

IVAN FECAN

My memory is really that this show came out of *CODCO*, which sort of came out of *Wonderful Grand Band*. So, for me it goes back to the early '80s when I was in charge of variety at CBC—the position that George Anthony ultimately had in the early '90s—and I saw *Wonderful Grand Band*. It gave me an appreciation of East Coast humour that stayed with me. Then I ended up putting *CODCO* on, and out of *CODCO* came *This Hour*, with not all of the same people, but many of the same people. So there is a continuum here.

PHYLLIS PLATT

Network Program Director and Executive Director for CBC Arts and Entertainment, 1992–1996; Executive Director, CBC Arts and Entertainment, 1996–2000
I was the network program director at that point. It means that you oversee essentially all final programming decisions in collaboration with the vice-president, who was Ivan Fecan at that time. But he gave me a lot of leeway, and we tended to have the same kind of tastes in what we thought would work and appeal to a Canadian audience.

GEOFF D'EON

They pitched this weekly topical variety sketch show to the CBC and it received a favourable reception, because the CBC was in desperate need of new programming—edgy programming—and Michael by now had a proven track record, having successfully produced *CODCO* in Halifax.

PHYLLIS PLATT

I didn't really know Michael that well. I liked the pitch a lot, because, as is often the case when you are sitting in that chair, people come in and decide they have to really sing and dance and be exciting and all that. And Michael is not a singer and dancer. He's not that kind of guy, and I was intrigued by him. I liked the approach that they were coming at it with—but also, I could tell how smart they were.

ALAN MACGILLIVRAY

Michael is a very, very bright individual. When he focuses on something, there's very little that can stop him from achieving his goal. He learns very quickly, and he has a fascination with the creative. He sees a lot of opportunities that other people don't see.

GERALD LUNZ

I have nothing bad to say about Michael Donovan, ever. He is the absent-minded professor. You think he isn't plugged in at all, but then you realize it's that his mind is at a different level of chess than what you are playing.

JACK KELLUM

I like to call Michael the absent-minded professor, because he is notorious. Michael, in my estimation, has made his fortune and his success because he surrounds himself with good people. He surrounds himself with people who know what they're doing and know how to do it, and I guess that is the story of a successful businessperson. In those days, he had Alan MacGillivray. Alan MacGillivray deserves huge credit for starting Salter Street films.

ALAN MACGILLIVRAY

I think Jack is giving me too much credit. I think the first part of what he said is true: Michael can spot people who will help him do what he wants to do, and Michael is very smart.

JACK KELLUM

We pitched it to George Anthony, Phyllis Platt, and George's assistant at the time, who later went on to become Ivan Fecan's head of comedy at CTV.

We made our pitch—and it was a decent pitch. I think out of that came, "Well, we will give you eight." It was enough to get a start.

ALAN MACGILLIVRAY

We had this strange contract with CBC for twenty episodes, but they could bail after eight. So that would take us to Christmas, and then they could say, "No more," and we would be out of luck.

IVAN FECAN

I, personally, had a long-running interest in doing satirical newscasts, from my time in radio. I was one of the producers on [CBC Radio news and information program] *Sunday Morning*, and we did a satirical newscast and cabaret show on radio. I was a big fan of *Spitting Image*, the British puppet show, which was viciously satirical. And I was casting around, hoping to find such a show in Canada. So when Michael Donovan came in with this idea, there was a willing buyer there.

PHYLLIS PLATT

One of the many things I liked about the pitch was that I thought the Newfoundland sense of humour—and the willingness to hoist anybody on their own petard—could turn it into a kind of pan-Canadian thing that would look at the centres, like Toronto and Ottawa, through a different set of eyes, but with a sensibility that belonged to a lot of other Canadians as well.

GEORGE ANTHONY

It would have to be a terrible idea before I wouldn't go for something that involved Mary and Cathy, and I really enjoyed working with Michael. Michael was fun and he was really smart, and it was a very important thing for a lot of people to keep that show in Halifax at CBC. There were all sorts of different benefits to it for the region.

GEOFF D'EON

They were given an order. They got a green light to develop a show—a yet-to-be-named show.

GERALD LUNZ

Is what was pitched what occurred on television and what you finally saw at the end? Not even close.

• • •

GEOFF D'EON

So Mary Walsh and Michael Donovan and Jack Kellum put together a team of people who could execute this as-yet-unnamed weekly satirical variety show. They pulled together the creative team in the spring and summer of 1993, and the first order of the day was the cast.

Mary, obviously. A no-brainer, being the show's prime motivator. Cathy Jones. Again, a no-brainer, being a brilliant, comedic, gifted actor.

GEORGE ANTHONY

Having Michael was a real reassurance for me. It wasn't just Mary and the gang going off on their own, because that would've been a harder sell, frankly, as much as I love them. But Michael was there, so we were going to have at least one grown-up in the mix, and he had the experience of working with them. Then he brought in Gerald, so that was—okay, not only do we have a showrunner; we have someone running the show.

The term "showrunner" is relatively modern parlance for a hybrid position that exists only in the world of television production. The showrunner is generally the most senior writer who is also an executive producer, and who is ultimately responsible for guiding the creative vision of the show and for controlling the financial aspects of the production.

JACK KELLUM

We were able to bring in Gerald Lunz. At that time, Gerald was just starting his relationship with Rick Mercer. And Gerald came with Rick. Gerald had wandered into the Newfoundland drama scene; I don't know where he came from, but he ended up being a good friend of Cathy's. And then he ended up working for us on the *CODCO* series, not in any great position, but he endeared himself. Gerald is a very sharp character. He endeared himself to enough people, and by the time *22 Minutes* came around, he was in deep enough that everybody was comfortable with him and he actually became the first creative producer of the show.

GERALD LUNZ

We started to try and frame it. Who would the people be? Then George Anthony came into it. George had just seen Rick's and my work. I was producing and directing Rick's first play at the National Arts Centre, which made kind of a bang. So George was very much in our camp when Mary said, "I want to get together."

It was me and Cathy and then Rick, of course, and George said, "Very good—of course Rick, and Gerald's going to be the show producer." And Michael said yes, of course, because I had already worked with *CODCO* and I knew how to work with this talent.

GEORGE ANTHONY

Rick was on *Midday* in those days; he used to do the "Rant" on *Midday*. I had no idea how he would be in the long haul, but Mary was completely sold on him, and that was honestly enough for me.

GEOFF D'EON

So Rick Mercer was a known entity to a limited extent. All people knew was this young guy, Rick whoever he is, is pretty good on TV, and he is sharp as a tack.

RICK MERCER

So through the jigs and the reels, I ended up being asked whether I would be part of this project, and of course I leapt at the opportunity, because everything I had done up until that point was to get on television. I'm not one of those people who started in the theatre and then went into television and now bemoans the fact and likes to wax on about, "Oh, I can't wait to get back on the boards."

It was the exact opposite. I went into theatre because I saw it as a way to get on television, because that is what *CODCO* did. So the plan I saw ahead of me, by these pioneers: if you want to get on TV, you go and do comedy onstage; that's how it happens. So that is exactly what I did.

I leapt at the opportunity to be part of this show, because the word was, it was going to be political, and my one-man show was very political—I mean, it was about Meech Lake. So I was obviously super-intrigued about being a part of it.

GERALD LUNZ

All these things came together, and Rick of course, being the youngest of the troupe—he was only nineteen at the time—had the fire to get on that stage. He was as bold as brass.

Michael formed the group of us. We were all huddled together in downtown St. John's. Cathy, Mary, and Rick and I all lived within a block. It was just so tiny that we could keep this conversation going.

RICK MERCER

I had never done television before, so I was brand new. In the room was Mary and Cathy and myself and Gerald, and Jack was around, and Michael was around. And very quickly, and very evidently, I thought this was a nightmare like nothing I could ever experience, because we were just in a room, and it was like, "Okay, now we're going to do a TV show."

GERALD LUNZ

The important thing to understand is how this collective formed itself. Everyone had different things. Rick and Mary were more the political junkies. Cathy is one of the, if not *the* most versatile comic actresses you have ever seen on television, since the likes of Carol Burnett—just absolutely can spin it any which way. She is perfect in everything. It really wasn't her thing to get into politics. She was like, "Oh my God, do we have to? Why can't we just do stuff about, you know, social commentary?" Just to have fun. She was more sketch.

Greg Thomey, of course—very funny cat.

Thomey was as mad as a hatter and thinking so much outside the box that he was absolutely a gem. He would just make us laugh. I've never laughed so hard in my life as in the early days with Greg Thomey. Comic genius. And then you want to say, how close to madness is comic genius? Absolutely brilliant.

In St. John's, we all knew Tooms; we had done theatre with him and he had done a few spots on *CODCO* as well. So that was the new core; that kind of gelled itself.

GEOFF D'EON

So that was the cast that they settled on: Mary, Cathy, Rick, and Greg. Then they set about the business of assembling the production team.

GERALD LUNZ

The search for directors started before we had the thing formed. This was before anything had actually been set—was it fish or fowl? We were just talking. It was open; it was great.

We would fly directors out to St. John's and have a meeting with them, then take them out drinking to see if they had any valour. [*Laughing*] And then—this is my favourite thing about St. John's—there were stories like, "I've got to go, man, I am on the seven o'clock flight tomorrow morning," and we would say, "Don't worry! We'll drop you off."

That's how we ran into Henry Sarwer-Foner, in that process of looking for directors. That's why Henry has been with us forever—because he fit in with that crowd.

HARVEY SARWER-FONER
Director, 1993–2003

I had directed [CBC youth consumer show] *Street Cents* for two years [in the late '80s and early '90s]; that's the show I cut my teeth on, and where I learned how to direct multi-cameras.

The network in Toronto needed people who could do that. They had me on the *Friday Night! with Ralph Benmergui* show as an observer, kind of an apprentice, if you will. When the second season came up, I was being considered to direct it, but at the same time, I got the call about this comedy show in Halifax with some people from *CODCO*. I don't remember exactly how it went down. It seems like an obvious choice in retrospect, but at the time, you know, I had a new baby, three months old—my first child. So that only added to the surreality.

RICK MERCER

Then there was this proposal. And this proposal, which was what we were going to follow along—it didn't look anything like *22 Minutes*. There was a country song every week—like, a novelty song about the news. There was this sketch that was going to be ongoing, starring all of us as members of a Rosedale family. We were going to satirize [the wealthy Toronto neighbourhood of] Rosedale, which is something Mary always wanted to do, and she was going to work with [author] Timothy Findley on this.

Now, that may be a very good idea, but I was horrified, because I was getting my chance to be on television, and suddenly—I mean, I was young enough and arrogant enough—I was like, "I don't need Timothy Findley to write for me. I'll write my own stuff, thank you very much!"

And plus, all I knew was, I didn't sound anything like anyone from Rosedale. At that point in my life, I had never even walked through Rosedale. So

I had no interest in satirizing the people who lived there, because the first rule of satire is, you have to know what you're talking about. I didn't know anything about WASPy rich people in Toronto.

GEOFF D'EON

Mary had a different idea about what the show should and could be than Rick and his partner Gerald did.

Gerald was the showrunner. The creative producer. They had a pretty clear idea as to what this show should be, and it didn't include some of the elements that Mary had in mind. For instance: Mary thought that it should have a weekly musical sketch, much in the way that *This Hour Has Seven Days* had. [This Hour Has Seven Days *was a newsmagazine that appeared on CBC television from 1964 to 1966.*] So people like Ron Hynes or members of the Wonderful Grand Band would be commissioned to write a song and would appear on the show in a musical segment. But in Mary's mind it was more of a variety show. It would have music and it would have sketches and it would have news desk segments, but it was very much a variety show.

RICK MERCER

Those meetings in St. John's, they were a real eye-opener. What was evident was—no one knew what this show was going to be. There were a lot of ideas bandied about that were highly unlikely to come to fruition. So I stopped worrying about that, because I would say to Michael, "Is there going to be a country singer every week?" And, Michael would just say, "Absolutely not. That's not happening."

And, then, at the same time, I knew there were negotiations going on to make this happen. But Michael would say, "No, no. That's not happening. Ignore those negotiations," and I realized that, well, television is a pretty shifty business, isn't it?

Likewise, we met a television director that Mary liked very much and had worked with years before on *Up at Ours*, which is a landmark television show. [Up at Ours *was a continuing drama shot in 1979 and set in a St. John's board-*

ing house, starring Mary Walsh.] But at this point he was a news director; he hadn't directed anything like what we were talking about in a very long time. And, in fact, he had no interest in doing it, because he liked doing the news.

So he was brought to this room, and everyone begged him to take this job. And I could tell the last thing he wanted to do was go to Halifax. He was like, "Mary, I haven't done anything like this in, you know, twenty years or whatever." This is nothing against this individual, because by all accounts, I'm sure he's a great guy. But I also heard there was this other guy, Henry Sarwer-Foner, who had directed *Street Cents*. And, to me, *Street Cents* was a great kids' show, and also it moved really fast, and it was very modern, and it was a lot of different things that I thought you needed in television.

And I can remember saying to Michael, "Are we really going to get this news guy?" And he's, like, "Oh, no, no. Absolutely. That's not happening." I'm like, "He's being brought in, we're having these conversations, and he's not going to get the job?" And he's like, "Well, CBC wouldn't have him. Oh, don't worry about that."

So it was like, "Oh, okay."

GERALD LUNZ

My job was a hybrid; we were all learning. We didn't know dick about what we were doing, which is probably why it was so funny and so raw.

I was the showrunner. We didn't have a name for it at the time, because we didn't know there was such a word as "showrunner," so they called it "creative producer." I worked with the talent. As Rick says, when he tries to explain who I am to people, he says, "This is Gerald; he speaks fluent crazy."

I have worked with actors my whole life—trying to get them to the stage to do their best, all that stuff. That's why I once had lovely brown hair and now it's all white.

It was crazier when people were all ragged out on drugs back in the days of the '80s. That was more difficult, but now we are all sober. *22* wasn't as crazy as the earlier shows. *CODCO* was pretty nuts, but they all were at the time. If you talk to anybody who was working in showbiz in the '80s, I don't know how anybody got anything done. It was really like self-abuse. Ridiculous.

RICK MERCER

It was Gerald who said, "You have to fight for your piece of this show." Every idea was freaking me out. I mean, every time I turned around, someone else in St. John's was on the show—that was the other thing. People I knew would call me up excitedly and say, "Oh, my God! I'm doing a new show, with Salter Street, with Mary Walsh!" I was already in meetings about it. I'd be, like, "Oh, congratulations, I guess."

So suddenly all sorts of people thought they were on the show, including my dear, dear friend Lois Brown, who I love, and probably owe my entire career to, because she was my drama teacher. But she was going to come on the show and do a poem. She is a very accomplished performance artist and poet, but, she is that—a performance artist and poet. I mean, she used to sit on a stage in a wedding dress and recite long poems.

I'm Lois's biggest fan. There's no such thing as a Lois show I wouldn't go see. But I knew—I didn't know much about television—but I knew that wasn't prime-time television at eight o'clock, and I knew it wasn't about politics, so I was very afraid.

GERALD LUNZ

It was like high school a lot of times. That's what made it fun. The stakes were high and everyone hadn't had this opportunity yet, so they worked a lot.

RICK MERCER

And then, I guess, we all went to Halifax, and it was perhaps the most—it absolutely *is* the most exciting thing that has ever happened to me in my entire life.

I was terrified, because I just did not believe that I had the talent to be in a room with Cathy and Mary. I mean, these were my comedy idols. I was terrified at the idea of being in a sketch with these people. Cathy Jones can do accents and voices and characters like nobody's business. I did characters a little bit, but my one-man shows were essentially me standing on stage, or sitting and talking. It wasn't stand-up, but there wasn't a lot of brilliant character work, like Cathy and Mary. So the idea of being put in a sketch with these two people was so intimidating.

The next person hired was a veteran news producer who made the radical—some would say crazy—choice to join a show that had a guaranteed run of only eight episodes.

FRED MATTOCKS

One of the bits of genius of the early *22 Minutes* was that we actually had a CBC news producer, Geoff D'Eon, at the heart of the unit. The whole purpose of that was that *22 Minutes* was topical sketch comedy, so the question was, at the beginning, how does a group of people who are performers and comedians and satirists—what is it that brings the topic of the day to them?

It was a bit in reaction to *CODCO*. Some of *CODCO*'s sketches were very philosophical and very sort of societal—and it's not a criticism of *CODCO*. *CODCO* was never designed to be topical. *CODCO* was about great truths, and *22 Minutes* was designed to be topical. So, how did we get the "T" in topical? Well, we thought we'd put a news producer in the middle of it, so Geoff D'Eon was hired for that.

GEOFF D'EON

I was the executive producer of local news. I had been doing the job for five years, and the fun had gone out of it for me. I had been working in local news for more than ten years, and what started out as a religious pursuit for me—with all of the zeal that that entails—gradually dissipated, so I began to look around to see what else was out there.

I let that be known to my boss at the time, [CBC Maritimes director of television] Saleem Ahmed. Saleem knew that I wasn't enjoying it that much anymore. So Saleem called me into his office one day and said, "There's a new show starting here in Halifax that might be suitable for you," and I asked him what it was. He told me that it was a weekly satirical show, news-based, with a very talented cast from Newfoundland, and it was due to go into production in September 1993.

I was intrigued by this. I was intrigued by the fact that Cathy and Mary were in it, and I was intrigued by the fact that it had a *CODCO* pedigree. So I called Phyllis Platt, an old colleague, then a big mucky-muck at the network, and I said, "There's this show starting in Halifax." And she said, "Yes—and you should do it."

I said, "But Phyllis, that would involve leaving news. That would be a big, big step to take."

She said, "Geoff, I guarantee you if you take this job, you will thank me one day."

So I thought about it, and it didn't take too long to decide. I had a meeting with Michael Donovan and I asked him why somebody like myself should work on a show such as the one that they were creating. And it became clear that the network wanted the comfort of having a news person embedded in *This Hour Has 22 Minutes*. So it was really, I think, Phyllis's initiative more than anyone else's.

FRED MATTOCKS

It was a kind of revolutionary thing. Here we have an arts and entertainment show, and at the heart of it is a hard-bitten journalist. And it was a great thing. You know, tensions are the lifeblood of creativity in many situations, and we had lots of tensions and lots of crises, with a small "c," around those tensions. But I think the evidence shows that they were healthy for the product, and healthy for the program, and healthy for the audience.

GEOFF D'EON

The thinking was that this show was going to speak in the vernacular of television news. It was going to have a news desk. It was going to have four "anchors," and it was going to make fun of the news, the way the news was delivered, and also people in the news. And because it was going to make fun of people in the news, that would necessarily involve politicians, and this was potentially dangerous ground for CBC, because CBC is governed by journalistic policies. There is a perceived need for balance, and the journalistic programs are all done under the auspices of this journalistic "bible," or policy handbook.

But this new show wasn't. This new show was not going to be considered a journalistic enterprise—and yet it very much had its tentacles in the world of news and current affairs. So Phyllis and Michael and Jack, I believe, agreed that it would be sensible to have somebody who spoke the language of news embedded in the unit.

RICK MERCER

Geoff D'Eon was a flashpoint, because some people didn't want a news show to begin with, but then they felt that this guy, Geoff D'Eon, was being brought in because he knows how news is done. "He's going to make us do this show like it's a news show."

I was of the school, of course, that I wanted it to be a news show. I couldn't believe we were getting the executive producer of a news hour to stop doing news, to come and do what we were going to do.

JACK KELLUM

Geoff became very important in this whole process. I don't count myself the person who brought him in, but I sure worked on it, I'll tell you, because I knew his knowledge would help us greatly—because we were trying to duplicate a news show, and none of us had any experience in news except Geoff. So he became a very integral part of it.

GEOFF D'EON

I quit my job as the executive producer of news, surprised a lot of people around me, including my wife, and embraced this new challenge.

I was given the glorious title of Editorial Producer. My job was essentially to keep the show on track journalistically, to ensure that the show was topical, and to help ensure that the show was dealing with subjects that would be in the news.

PETER SUTHERLAND
Road and Studio Camera, 1993–present
I thought it was pretty brave of him to jump ship out of the newsroom and go into a completely different platform. But he was good at it. He's a good leader. I followed him to Afghanistan twice; it's something that you don't take lightly, to go into a war zone, if you don't believe in the guy's ability to lead.

GERALD LUNZ
Geoff came out of news and we were circus people. He must have felt like, "Oh my God, I've dropped out of news and joined the circus."

But his mid-life crisis was our gain.

• • •

GEOFF D'EON
So this cast of people gathered in the writers' room, which was the old Radio Room at CBC Sackville Street [in Halifax]. The meetings were focused on what this show could be, because the show didn't exist at this point.

GERALD LUNZ
You know how they kind of keep things away from you, like the money? You come up with ideas—okay, it's an aircraft carrier—Michael was fabulous that way, you could call it devious if you want, to never expose you to the actual financial limitations of what you can and can't do.

And when you have a broad canvas, you will just paint big, and I think Mary was led astray on that front, because she was really painting big.

ALAN MACGILLIVRAY

I was always involved with *22 Minutes* as, kind of, the watcher of the money. We had a very small budget, initially. I think I can tell you this, now that it's twenty-five years later: it was $100,000 an episode, $35,000 of which was CBC services and $65,000 of which was cash. That was a very, very small amount of money, even in those days. But the way I looked at it was—unlike other shows where you can spend weeks and months in post-production, this was a show in which we only had one week to spend the money. So that was a real plus, as far as I was concerned.

GERALD LUNZ

Then it came together. I think Michael said, "I'll do this for ten cents," just to get it started. So we didn't have money; it wasn't a production-y thing. It had to be done smart—and that's writing, and that's performance and characters—because we didn't have sets.

I think we had three wigs when we started; it was that poorly funded. We had to beg and borrow stuff off Judi Cooper-Sealy in Toronto who did wigs and make up for *Second City* and for *CODCO*, and was now working on *Kids in the Hall*.

So we were just begging, borrowing, and stealing. We didn't have any money. The salaries were better than anybody was making off UIC [Unemployment Insurance], I'll tell you, but it wasn't really star shit.

HENRY SARWER-FONER

Liftoff is always the most dangerous part of launching a new series, and especially this one, because we didn't have any time or money. It was a real pressure cooker, because nobody really knew what it was, or whether it was going to work, you know?

I only came on board two weeks before we produced the first show, which is not a lot of time—in fact, it's an insane amount of time, especially when you've got no money and limited production resources. I knew there was a group of very talented people involved, but nobody knew what the show was yet—and back then, you have to remember, there were no other shows to compare it to. So we had to make it up on the fly, and the cast was made up of four very strong personalities, all with different visions of the show.

GERALD LUNZ

In Mary's mind, I think it was more like a *Smothers Brothers* kind of thing. She wanted to have a broader show, which in my mind would be an hour-long show. You can't cram all that shit into a half hour. There would be a sketch component and there would be a music component—Ron Hynes would sing something from his newest album. There would be something odd, an art performance—Lois Brown would do one of her pieces of poetry in her sad bride costume. Rick and maybe Andrew Younghusband would do some of their sketches from their late-night cabarets at the LSPU Hall. And then Mary and Jonesey—they were already a natural fit. They could do anything. They had been working together for so long, and were so talented.

GEOFF D'EON

I think it's true to say that in the minds of Rick and Gerald, it was much more of a fast-paced parody of a news program. And that was what I thought it should be, too.

RICK MERCER

I wanted a news desk. I'm not saying that because that's eventually what happened. I wanted a news desk for a couple of reasons: I had seen a pilot out of Los Angeles one time, and it was essentially an extended version of the "Weekend Update" style of news, and I thought, "I could do that." I didn't have a lot of faith in my abilities as a performer, but I thought, "I can do 'news anchor,' right? I know I can do that. I can't, necessarily, compete with anyone else, but I can do 'news anchor.'"

So I wanted the news desk, and there was certainly pushback. Some people didn't want a news desk at all. They wanted much more sketch, and covering the news in different fashions.

What I quickly figured out—and it's a lesson that has served me well in my entire television career—is that you have to embrace your budget. I could tell that there was no money. There was literally none. So the news desk was doable.

GERALD LUNZ

Mary's impression was that she was going to be head writer and it was going to be a show called *Mary*, which was one of her ideas for a title, long before Michael came up with the name.

RICK MERCER

Then there were people at the network who were coming up with all sorts of weird questions, like, "Who's going to do sports? Rick or Greg?"

I don't know anything about sports. Greg, I guess, follows sports a bit, but Greg wanted to do odd songs. Greg's sense of humour—I mean, he's a genius, there's no one funnier—but he's very absurd in his outlook on life and comedy. So that kind of question—who's going to do sports?—just sent Greg over the edge.

I also remember one time someone came from the network with these photographs of these puppets, and they were *Spitting Image* puppets. Remember *Spitting Image*, in England?

And there we were. These puppets cost a fortune, we were told over and over again. Cost a fortune! Thousands and thousands of dollars, and somewhere at the CBC people were very excited about this project, because *Spitting Image* was a huge hit in England.

And here it was, the Mulroney *Spitting Image* doll, and the Kim Campbell, and whoever else were the political figures of the day. Potentially, they could be on the show every week. And we all just looked and said the same thing: "Oh, so—less of us, you mean?"

I thought it had some potential, because I thought, well, this could be like *The Simpsons*. I mean, *The Simpsons* became *The Simpsons* because they were in *The Tracey Ullman Show*. That was how one of the greatest comedy shows of all time was created. So I could see that this could actually work.

I remember I could see Greg, and in his head, he's like, "Yes, yes, this is very interesting; very interesting." And Greg looked like he was sold on this idea of these puppets every week.

And then Greg was like, "Can we catch them on fire?"

And the network was like, "Oh, no! These are very, very expensive puppets!"

"Oh, then," Greg said. "Oh, no. Not interested. Thank you. Please take them away."

GEOFF D'EON

So there was no unanimity on what this show should be, but there was tremendous excitement in everybody, because we understood that we had a blank canvas here that we could create a show on. People were really energized and there were great ideas floated. It was a fantastic time. It was just fun to go to work because you knew that when you went to work every day, somebody was going to have a really good idea.

GERALD LUNZ

For me, this was the most exciting time in television I have ever, ever had, because I've never been in a situation where it's a complete blank page. And God love the network at this time; they just went with it.

GEOFF D'EON

It was intoxicating. To work on the show at that time was intoxicating. The first season was figuring out what it could be. "What are we doing with this thing? Is it a variety show, what is it?"

HENRY SARWER-FONER

It was stressful. Everybody was sticking their neck out, and it was chaos. We had no graphics or resources or money. I had to just sort of cobble something together very quickly.

RICK MERCER

What I started advocating for was that I was going to do the "Rant," which I called the "Streeter." I had already done them for *Midday*. I thought, "Whatever else happens with this Rosedale sketch and the singer and the poetry, I'm going to have this 'Rant' that I do." And at the end of this, at least I'll be able to take the tape of me doing the "Rant," and I'll be able to say, "This is what I want to do. This is the show I want to invent," right?

So very quickly, everyone—and by "everyone" I mean the money and the network—they immediately were like, "Well, yes, of course. We'll do that," because it's still to this day perhaps the most affordable two minutes of television that you can get. There's no costume, there's no set, there's nothing except me and the camera. It's not a tough sell.

When you're in a room and people are saying, "We'll have to build a house that looks like Rosedale, with a grand, sweeping staircase and a giant dining room," and then I'm like, "I just need a camera for half an hour to go down and run around by the harbourfront," it's an easy sell.

HENRY SARWER-FONER

I quickly realized I'd better come up with a way to tie all these disparate elements together: sketches, rants, satirical news, commercial parodies, mockumentary, or whatever we came up with—some kind of modular format that would allow the show to flow seamlessly, and prevent the series from being painted into any corners.

I think that's what's special about the show to this day: that you never really know what's going to come down the pike. I mean, sure it's a news parody, but there's always other elements as well. So, my first job was to figure out a way to stitch it all together.

RICK MERCER

I could argue that all of my ideas managed to make it into the show, but I honestly felt that what we ended up with was a show that I could see myself in. Some of the other ideas, perhaps they were great ideas, but they just weren't a fit for me, personally, and the show, very much, was about four people fighting to create a show that they could shine in.

I mean, it's why Cathy Jones wanted to do characters—because she's the best in the world at that, whereas I wasn't interested in a show that was all about doing characters, because I knew that wasn't my high suit.

At the end of the day, it wasn't a matter of my ideas winning the day; it was what was affordable—and what was affordable was that news desk. We were, literally, creating a show where people said, "Okay, but Greg and Rick can only have one tie!" Money was that tight. Plus, the show had to be shot in a week.

GEOFF D'EON

I had been out of the news business for a month and I could tell already that this thing was going to fly. These people were really funny. They were really gifted, really talented, and they were interested in the news—everyone except Cathy.

RICK MERCER

Anytime anyone mentioned the news, Cathy would burst into tears, because the news makes Cathy sad.

She would be like, "Why would anyone want to do anything about the news?" And then she decided she would be the Good News Fairy, and she would only talk about good things, which makes no sense, but still it made her happy, because she just wants to tell jokes and be funny, you know? That's all she's ever wanted to do.

• • •

JACK KELLUM

There's an interesting story. One thing that we learned in the *CODCO* years was how difficult it was to deal with five very intelligent, very opinionated, very strong personalities. You would hit a point of contention, and you would have to go to war, but it wasn't going to war with one person. It was going to war with five people.

"War" is too strong a word, but it was difficult, and it made life difficult. And these situations were not always rational. They were sometimes quite irrational.

So Michael and I, as we were talking about the possibility of starting up this new fake news show, we realized that somehow or other we had to break the collective. We had to break it down into individual elements so not everyone was dealt with equally.

RICK MERCER

It was a stressful time creating the show, and obviously the show, to a very large extent, was sold because Mary Walsh was going to be part of it.

JACK KELLUM

This is where we get into the controversial part. On every show, Mary Walsh has a "[series concept] created by" credit.

Mary Walsh didn't create that show. All of us created that show. Greg Thomey created it. Michael created it. I created it. Mary Walsh created it. Rick Mercer created it. Gerald Lunz created it. Everybody had their own finger into the creation of that show.

But Michael and I decided that if we were to break the power of the group—it wasn't a draconian thing, it was just logical to make it move smoother—we decided, why don't we make Mary the head writer? That would break it. That could rationalize paying her more and it would give her a responsibility beyond that of the group. Not to the point that she would be management, but she would be head writer and all of the other writing would have to go through her.

So we started off like that, but before long, with things like getting scripts in on time, Mary was the biggest offender. Here was a head writer who didn't give a shit about the writing and was always late in handing in her scripts. So it went to pieces. It was a reasonable idea, but Mary was not playing the game.

RICK MERCER

That was in the early days, and I don't blame her for having that credit, because when you're creating television, you negotiate the credit that you can negotiate. And I think that when the show was green-lit, it was conceivable that Mary would fulfill a role that is comparable to head writer, but, as the show progressed, she didn't fulfill that role. I mean, that's just not a role that she did. She wrote her material, and I wrote my material, and Greg wrote his material, and Cathy wrote her material; that's the way the show was.

I don't want to rehash old battles, and I don't know how Mary felt about not retaining the title of head writer. Perhaps Mary felt that that was appropriate, you know, given the nature of the way the show evolved. But at least as long as I was there, no one else ever had that credit, because no one ever fulfilled that role.

JACK KELLUM

She was quite angry about losing her head-writer credit, and Michael said, "Okay, I've got an idea. Let's give her a "series concept created by" credit and that will keep her happy.

So Mary's credit still hangs on there.

3

Countdown
to Launch

1993

As the team hashed out the look and feel of the show, one important issue remained outstanding: what were they going to call this thing?

GERALD LUNZ

It was Michael who came up with the title *This Hour Has 22 Minutes*, although now, as time has fled, I think they have reduced it just to *22 Minutes*, because nobody knows what *This Hour Has Seven Days* was anymore. Originally you had to know that to know the joke.

The joke was a reference to *This Hour Has Seven Days*, a weekly newsmagazine that ran on CBC Television from 1964 to 1966. The show was known for its outspoken hosts, and for its satirical tone, which often tested the boundaries of CBC journalistic policies.

....

GEORGE ANTHONY

Michael phoned me, because he was struggling to come up with a name. I can't remember what some of the others were, but he said something like, "Well, *This Hour Has Seven Days* is taken."

Then he said, "We could always call it *This Hour Has 22 Minutes*," and he laughed, and I laughed, and I said, "That's it! That's the title."

He said, "No, no, no; I'm just kidding."

I said, "No, Michael, that title is great," and he protested. Then he told someone else that the crazy network guy thought *This Hour Has 22 Minutes* was a good title and they said, "Yeah, that's good."

So then he thought, "Okay—maybe." I had a feeling that the moment he had said it, he was sorry he'd said it. He didn't think I would think it was such a great title.

That's how I remember it, but I'm sure there are many versions of that story.

GEOFF D'EON

The first time I heard it, I had a brain freeze. I wasn't sure if it would catch on at all.

I always thought it was a very clever title, because it spoke to the DNA that it was going to draw from. And why "22 Minutes?" It's a half hour, minus the eight minutes for commercials.

Anyway, that was the name of the show. I remember distinctly running it by one of the senior managers at CBC Halifax, who said, "What is this new show you're working on?"

I said, "It's called *This Hour Has 22 Minutes*," and she shook her head and said, "No—that is a terrible name. That will never catch on. That will never last. Surely that's a working title."

PHYLLIS PLATT

To me, it was the kind of title that would make people think, "What does that mean?" And the minute you get somebody interested in checking out what the show is, you've got a plus. So I thought it was an interesting enough name for a show, and not like the names of most television shows, to attract attention.

GERALD LUNZ

I thought it was a winner, I thought it was so CBC. It was foolish; it meant nothing.

JACK KELLUM

I didn't really like it. It was too much *This Hour Has Seven Days*. I just wasn't crazy about it.

GEOFF D'EON

The show was very much in the spirit of *This Hour Has Seven Days*, which was, of course, a hugely celebrated television show in Canada, massively popular, known for its edgy commentary and for breaking rules, such as an anchor in tears on air one night. This would be unthinkable in the world of news, but on *This Hour Has Seven Days*, the commentators and the anchors were human beings, first and foremost. But they were also journalists, so they also dealt with difficult subjects of the day in a variety of ways: comedic, interview, satirical.

This Hour Has Seven Days was quite scathing, and eventually it ran afoul of the taste of the politicians in Ottawa. There was so much incoming heat directed at the CBC because of the outlandish behaviour of *This Hour Has Seven Days* that it was cancelled. But that was the tradition that Michael wanted to model this new show on. He wanted a show that was irreverent, that would rock the boat, that would say things that weren't being said on other CBC platforms. He wanted to say things that weren't generally being said in the world of Canadian television at the time.

With the name issue resolved, it was then decreed that the performers would play characters instead of using their own names on the show. That decision didn't sit well with everybody.

HENRY SARWER-FONER

They were all given pseudonyms, which was really odd. That was something I wasn't too crazy about, because I knew, eventually, they'd get to be known as who they were. But, nonetheless, we stuck to it for many years.

GEOFF D'EON

A decision was made, I can't remember by whom, that the actors would not be playing themselves; they would be playing newscasters who had to be named. So Rick Mercer became J. B. Dickson; Greg Thomey became Frank MacMillan; Cathy Jones had no idea what she wanted to be called, except that there was an anchor on *Midday* at the time called Tina Srebotnjak and Cathy liked the musicality of the name, so Cathy became Sydney Dubizzenchyk. And Mary became Molly Maguire.

RICK MERCER

That was a battle I lost, for sure. Everyone had their own interests, obviously, and some people are more comfortable in a character. For some actors or sketch comedians, what they find the most frightening is being themselves. So, some people would much, much rather be a character. Someone like myself, I would just rather be myself.

GERALD LUNZ

That was Michael being nefarious. They all had character names, because Michael is very smart and he realized one thing: it's like a radio station. They own the names of the jocks. Like, Rockin' Stu—that's owned by CFRB, so if you leave the station you can't be Rockin' Stu over at CFRA.

RICK MERCER

There was also a very early conceit that people had backgrounds. So I was J. B. Dickson, which was kind of loosely based on J. D. Roberts. People's initials in a name—how '70s or '80s was that? Sydney Dubizzenchyk—she had the unpronounceable last name, which is wildly politically incorrect now. But that was based on Tina Srebotnjak—which was pretty WASPy to suggest that Srebotnjak can't be pronounced—but anyway, it always got a laugh. Molly Maguire, of course, you can Google the Molly Maguires, that's a group of revolutionaries. And Frank MacMillan, I don't know where that name came from, but Thomey did very much like the notion of the characters and, early on, I guess, there was the suggestion that maybe there would be behind-the-scenes conversations, almost sitcom-esque, among the news anchors, and I think we might have played with that a little bit. So Frank MacMillan had his brother, Tim MacMillan. He was our roving correspondent who always went to the wrong place. "I'm not in Amsterdam, Frank. There was a mistake at the airport!" Every time. It used to kill me.

But very quickly, I stopped saying, "I'm J. B. Dickson." I just refused to say the name, because I was, like, "I'm Rick Mercer, damn it!" And eventually, one of the biggest fights that I ever had at *22 Minutes*—and, you know, for all the business that I did with Michael Donovan, we exchanged words only a few times—but one of the biggest offences that I made was in an edition of "Talking to Americans." I said, "I'm Rick Mercer. Welcome to 'Talking to Americans'" and he had it removed from the show when he found out that I used my real name.

And, again, when we eventually did the *Talking to Americans* special, it was branded and titled with my name in the title—not J. B. Dickson. It was a real sticking point with the owners of the show.

Now, of course, everyone uses their real name on the show.

Things were falling into place. The show had a news desk and four "news anchors"—anchors who knew very little about how a real newscast was made—but on this point, the show had its ace in the hole.

GEOFF D'EON

I didn't have to teach Rick and Mary to think like journalists. I think I taught Rick how to craft a story as a journalist might. I remember being on a shoot once with Rick and Peter Sutherland, and Rick was doing an on-camera. I noticed the way he was holding the mic. He did one take, and he said, "Any notes?" And I said, "Yeah, for God's sake, hold the mic like a man." And then he took a real grip on the mic [*laughing*].

I taught them the behavioural tics of newscasters and reporters in the field. I was able to show them the craft—not the ideas, because they already had the ideas, and certainly not the funny because they were the funny—but somebody needed to show them the structure; somebody needed to point out the architecture of the world of news: the way people stood, the way they held microphones, the way they might phrase something, which often involved pomposity—or which didn't always involve the rhythms of natural speech, let's put it that way.

I like to think that I was helpful in that way. Having someone who spoke the vernacular of news was helpful in creating this quasi-news environment that *22 Minutes* lived in. But no one on *22 Minutes* considered themselves journalists. I think I considered myself a lapsed journalist.

RICK MERCER

It's like anything—a great resource is put in your shop and you can utilize it, or you can not utilize it. I never felt threatened by Geoff's presence, because I just thought that was what the show needed.

In order to parody something, in order to satirize something, you have to know your subject matter in and out. And the fact that we had a news guy there who would tell me my sentences were too long—and that news sentences were this long—that's not something that you know as a layman watching the news. It doesn't really sink in.

GEOFF D'EON

I was able to do things that I wished I could have done in edit suites in news.

If Boris Yeltsin appeared to be drunk on a piece of news tape, in news you might have to be very careful about the way you couch that. At *22 Minutes*, you could revel in it. You could glory in the fact that the leader of the Soviet Union was pissed as a newt at an official function. You didn't have to hold back, and the effect of that for me was incredibly liberating. It was very freeing—it was like the chains had come off; I was out of the cell. So for me personally, there was a sense of euphoria that we were able to tell stories in a new and satirical way.

PETER MANSBRIDGE

Chief Correspondent, CBC News, 1987–2017

The brilliance of Geoff was, he had a natural sense of humour. He could see what could work. But he also understood the news system—how to get tape. And, initially, he used to get stuff out of our department without us even knowing it was going, and then suddenly we'd see it the next week on his program [*laughing*].

Some of us were going, "Hey! You can't do that. That's not right. That's news material! We're going to have all kinds of problems." Of course, we never had problems.

But it was his brilliance of knowing how to use the system, and use our archives, in a way that could be really funny. And it worked out exactly that way.

RICK MERCER

I remember talking to Geoff early on, and saying, "Can we take raw footage—steal it basically, from the CBC—and re-edit it for our purposes?"

And I remember him saying, "Yes! We can do that! I'll never work in news ever again!"

And, I thought, "This guy's joined the circus." So I was a big fan from day one.

GEOFF D'EON

Mary was passionately interested in the news. Mary had worked in a radio newsroom in Newfoundland for a while. Rick was sharp as a tack and keen as mustard. He devoured the newspapers. Every day, a stack of newspapers would arrive. This was pre-internet. This was pre-Google. So our raw material was newspapers, and we got every daily published in Canada delivered. Everyone's desk would be piled high with clippings. It was literally, clip the newspapers, find a story that had an interesting set-up, and then look for the twist—look for the punchline at the end.

RICK MERCER

I can't understate how important Geoff was to the show, because he was a real newsman and he knew how it worked. I mean, he taught me how to write news copy.

GEOFF D'EON

Rick is simply a brilliant mind, and one who is not afraid to speak truth to power, which is a foundational belief for a good journalist. He already had that. He had that instinctively. In Newfoundland, they call it "saucy." Rick was really saucy, and was not afraid to say what he thought.

Newfoundlanders have a particular relationship with Canada which is unlike the other provinces'. It has everything to do with them living on a rock in the middle of the Atlantic and not really feeling part of the country until 1949—and even after 1949. So Newfoundlanders brought an outside perspective to what was going on in Canada. I do not think that *This Hour Has 22 Minutes,* or another variation of it, could have been written by a writing team and actors from Ontario, for instance. This troupe of Newfoundlanders was not deferential in any way to anybody. They were saucy.

And I think in order to be a good journalist, you need to have a little bit of that sauciness. You need to not be afraid to say the thing that is going to piss some people off. You know that aphorism—one of journalism's jobs is to comfort the afflicted and afflict the comfortable? Well, we didn't really put that on T-shirts, we didn't have it chiselled in marble on the wall, but that was part of our ethos. That was part of what drove us.

RICK MERCER

There was a real push-back from news people. Lots of people thought it was great—Linden MacIntyre always loved the show, but he's a bit of a trouble-maker himself—but some people were aghast, especially in the early days. You know, we were taking footage.

I remember me and Greg—you would be flicking through the TV channels at the CBC, and you would see video getting fed from one end of the country to the other. So you would see a politician getting ready to be interviewed somewhere; they could be going, "Hey, Harry! Do you ever need to get your car fixed?" Like, talking to a cameraman, or talking to the reporter in another city—they're going to interview him and they're shooting the shit for a couple of minutes. And we would look at it, and we would pick up the phone and say, "Can you roll on this?"

And they would roll on it, then we would take it, and we would edit it, and we would put it on television. It was outrageous! A lot of news people had a lot of ethical questions about what we were doing. It's hard to believe that *22 Minutes* was as radical a TV show as it was, now, because it's twenty-five years later. Everything has changed.

GEOFF D'EON

Cathy was a little bit out on a limb, in the sense that she wasn't much interested in news. She didn't like watching the news; she found the news upsetting. Cathy would deal with news the best she could, but it didn't really matter, because what she brought was this incredible comedic gift. She is one of the funniest women on Canadian television ever, in my mind. A brilliant comedic actress.

She didn't understand anything about warlords in Somalia, but she created Debbie Aideed, who was the Newfoundland wife of the warlord. "Sure, he's a dictator and he kills people, but he don't drink." She was able to pull off brilliant comedic performances, and at the end of the day, *This Hour Has 22 Minutes* wasn't trying to change the world, it was trying to entertain people in an interesting and new way. It appealed to news junkies such as myself, because we were able to skewer people who needed to be skewered, using the world of and the techniques and the methods of news, but our primary function was to make people laugh and to entertain them.

RICK MERCER

I learned all these news tricks from Geoff; he was a great resource. And, of course, he also knew how to field-produce. Like, we didn't know how to go ambush!

Remember, when we started, there were no ambushes. Then, one time, we decided we were going to Ottawa. And then it was suddenly, "Okay, we're all going to Ottawa." And the next thing you know, everyone had ideas that involved costumes, and involved all these different things. Thomey, I remember, needed a canoe, but that was Thomey's sense of humour, you know—"I need a canoe!"

And then, very quickly, all of these ideas were thrown out because it broke the bank. There was barely money to put one person and the cameraman and Geoff on the plane, so that was it. There was no hair, no makeup; there were no costumes, no props; there was no renting of this space or that space—nothing.

And, again, that's where Geoff came in, because that's how news operates.

GEOFF D'EON

The topicality was an area I focused on, so I would look ahead, not so much to what was happening on Monday and Tuesday, but to what was going to be happening on Wednesday and Thursday and Friday in the country.

I was helped by a raft of assignment editors from across the country; I had relationships with assignment editors in all the newsrooms because of my ten years in news. You develop a Rolodex; I had the assignment editor for *The National* in my Rolodex, and I could phone assignment editors at most regional newsrooms and ask for field tapes—not just edited items, but field tapes, so we were able to look at footage that hadn't actually made it to the news.

RICK MERCER

I started winning some battles based entirely on practicality. I could do a news anchor, there could be a news desk. Whoever was in charge of budgeting realized, very quickly, that *CODCO* had been an expensive television show—big sets, big crews, big makeup bill, big everything. There just simply was no money for that type of show, so I started winning a number of those battles.

And then Mary's back went out.

4

Season One: Hot, Sweaty, and Energized

1993

GERALD LUNZ

Mary had had a bad back all her life. Forever. It's a Newfoundland thing. But it got worse and worse, and then when she was drinking, she became an acrobat, which probably exacerbated the whole thing.

Mary is sober as a judge, and she got there pretty well around this time. But the damage was done, and she had to have back surgery.

This all happened probably a month or three weeks before curtain, and it was like, "Holy fuck."

RICK MERCER

The two creative forces in that room that were at loggerheads the most—and I don't mean that in a bad way, but we just had different visions—would have been myself and Mary, and she is a formidable person to have an argument with about anything. All I had was youthful moxie. Mary had a lot of experience doing a lot of amazing television, including the stuff that influenced me more than anything else.

So I was never entirely comfortable being in that situation with Mary, but then, I also viewed it as a matter of life and death, because I saw this was my chance to be on television. Whereas for Mary, I think it was just one project that was coming on the heels of other very successful projects that she had been involved in—namely, *CODCO*. I mean, they were superstars.

So Mary's back went out seriously. She was completely incapacitated and couldn't move. That's why, in the first number of episodes, she's not at the news desk.

GERALD LUNZ

We are opening in three weeks and she is on a board and she is probably medicated and frustrated. So it was very testy times.

GEOFF D'EON

Mary was suffering chronic back pain and was holed up in the Cambridge Suites. She literally could not get out of bed. She was in agony, and we were having these meetings in the Radio Room where all of the aspects of a news show template were raised and discussed.

GERALD LUNZ

We were trying to put this together and Mary was laid out in a bed in the Cambridge Suites. I remember this one meeting—bizarre.

HENRY SARWER-FONER

She was bedridden, so we'd have to trek over to wherever she was staying at the time and have our meetings in her bedroom, because she literally couldn't get out of bed.

GEOFF D'EON

There would be this ceremonial trooping of the guard, where we would all march down Sackville Street to the Cambridge Suites and assemble around Mary's bedside, and these meetings were extraordinary! I had never been to meetings like these ones. Mary was in pain; she was angry most of the time because she was in pain, and she was frustrated because she couldn't be at the production meetings.

GERALD LUNZ

So, okay, we are opening in a week, and Mary is pretty fucking off at this point. It's all running away without her, and it's all because of her back. And she had this character, Marg Delahunty. I don't know where Marg was first done, but I knew her character of Marg, and I said, "Mary, I will bring the camera to your house. Let's shoot Marg in bed, like she is so despondent with whatever is going on in the world that she just can't get out of bed"—which was the perfect way to get her into the show.

"That's how we can do this!" It was great. So Mary was actually popped into the show when she wasn't in the show.

Mary's bespectacled, housecoat- (and occasionally swimsuit-) clad Marg Delahunty made an indelible mark on the show with her scorching commentaries on politics and society.

RICK MERCER

Mary, being Mary—being literally crippled, I mean, essentially, with the movement ability of a quadriplegic at that point—she created Marg Delahunty, and created one of the most famous segments in Canadian television history. That's what she did while her back was out. Most people just lie there in agony.

HENRY SARWER-FONER

Well, you see, that's the thing about that show. I mean, you have no other choice; you just try to make it work. You can't fight it.

GEORGE ANTHONY

Mary was a key part of the show, obviously. They had already risen to the occasion, but now they really, really did, in finding creative ways to deal with that. I was concerned about Mary's health, obviously, but from the show point of view, it just became a great challenge where people had to sort of double down. And they just were brilliant.

It was just amazing to see it happen that way. It just established Marg Delahunty instantly as one of the best characters on the show.

RICK MERCER

Well, she had to be in the show. She was the big star. Cathy was as well, but there was no doubt about it—the show was being hung off Mary Walsh, to a large extent. I was like this whippersnapper that was getting attention, but I was coming from stage, and some television. But Cathy and Mary—this was the extension of *CODCO*, which was a critical darling. Critics loved *CODCO*, so there was going to be a lot of eyeballs—at least, critical eyeballs—looking at this show.

• • •

GERALD LUNZ

So then we kept tuning it, and then we realized—oh fuck, it's a half hour; this has to be concise.

GEOFF D'EON

The pacing was really important. Gerald was very hawkish on this. It was established very early on that pacing would be one of the gods that we would worship. Nothing was to last longer than sixty seconds. This show had to move like a bullet. So if there was a sketch, or if there was a piece that you didn't like as a viewer—no matter, hang in there, we are going to keep it moving.

GERALD LUNZ

Well, yeah, the big thing we said was because we had four people and twenty-two minutes, you couldn't do a buck [*a minute*] and a half. Try to keep everything under ninety seconds. And it became so difficult. So difficult, mostly for the girls, because they were so used to the theatre beat.

What Geoff and I had to do a lot was cut, trim, cut. Reduce, reduce, reduce. And that process, because we were moving at light speed, was done on the fly, constantly.

HENRY SARWER-FONER

I loved *CODCO*, but it was too…I mean, the sketches were long sometimes. And I particularly felt that for this show, we wanted to have a rapid-fire pace. It needed to grab the short attention span of TV viewers, and the format pretty much allowed us to do anything we wanted, depending on what was happening that week.

BILL DONOVAN

There is a discipline that's attached to the half-hour television format. If you were to run the program without commercials—in other words, twenty-nine minutes and thirty seconds or whatever—it wouldn't necessarily improve the program. It might just give somebody an extra two minutes to drag on about something that had already been used up.

Not everything on the show has to be hilarious funny, but in the world of satire, you have to have a point. And you can dull the point by going on and on about it.

GEOFF D'EON

We kept it moving with bumpers that Henry Sarwer-Foner designed, and we kept it going with short jokes, short sketches. The show moved at a blistering pace, and this was unusual at the time. This was actually an innovation. I think this was one of the things that *22 Minutes* taught showrunners: that audiences would respond to a show that moved like a bullet. And this one did. It cracked like a whip and it moved like a bullet, and I think that was one of the keys to its success.

It drew from Rowan and Martin's *Laugh-In* in that regard. We had all watched it. Just keep a breathless pace, keep people laughing. If they didn't get that joke—no matter, they'll get the next one. Just keep it moving.

GERALD LUNZ

Michael ran the show economically because there wasn't enough time to spend a lot of money. You had to have this thing done by eight o'clock on Friday night, so you couldn't blow it out the way film productions and sitcoms can really just kill you. Time is your enemy. That's why it always worked really well.

JACK KELLUM

Henry was the first director, and actually Henry created the style, the on-air look of it. He was very into brisk camera moves and stuff like that, and he is very much responsible for what turned out to be the general look of the show. And he did a good job.

HENRY SARWER-FONER

What I tried to do was come up with a distinct shooting style for each segment and each character. So if you think about Rick's "Rant," which was the very first thing I shot—I remember thinking it would be most impactful if it was all one continuous hand-held take, shot in a kind of grainy black-and-white, to capture the raw energy and immediacy of this rant.

So we went down to the dilapidated part of the harbour at sunset with our cameraman, Peter Sutherland, and shot what has become this iconic signature piece, mostly because of Rick's razor-sharp writing and performance. But I like to think the shooting style added to the intensity and impact of the rants.

And then, let's say, a Joe Crow, which I don't think Cathy does anymore, for obvious reasons. But there, I kind of wanted a more filmic style—shot in the woods, by a lake, with a campfire. I wanted to feature the elements, you know—fire, and water, a testament to the indigenous peoples' connection with the land. You just try to find the best way to capture what the performers were writing at the time.

What makes it interesting is that you get to do all kinds of different styles. Sometimes you're parodying a commercial, or a movie, or a trailer. And sometimes you're coming up with something fresh. So it's always exciting.

RICK MERCER

The other thing that made the show famous, I think, that came about as a necessity, was this philosophy that we were going to move like a news unit, and that meant we could go outside. So we were a cheap show that looked like a million bucks. I mean, my "Rants"—the location was fantastic, but I had to travel there and go do it. It was on the harbourfront in Halifax with all those containers around, and in Pier 21 at the time, which was empty.

The "Mrs. Enids" would go for a walk, and they would walk through the Public Gardens in Halifax, which was just up the street. They were in these glorious, beautiful locations. So the show actually looked great, but our set was the great outdoors.

Myself and Greg, we would do these ice-fishing guys, and we would be on an actual lake, with trees and snow and ice. I mean, if I wanted to produce that in Toronto—I can't even imagine the time and the money that would cost.

Halifax looked great, and people were so generous. I don't know if things have changed, but very quickly, people would throw you the keys to their house in a heartbeat to shoot there.

These were phenomenal spaces in terms of art direction, but it was all found.

• • •

JACK KELLUM

I think I can take some credit for the idea of taping in front of a live audience, because when we used to do the *Wonderful Grand Band* show, the first year we did it, we did it in the studio without an audience. Given the fact that it was the first year, it was all kind of experimental anyway. But there was a certain flatness to the performances.

Then in the second year, we did it we did it in front of an audience, and all of a sudden—holy moly, new dynamics were coming out of the performers. There were big embarrassments when you had to do things over in front of an audience. It was embarrassing for the performers; it was embarrassing, I guess, even for the audience. But we noticed that the audience seemed to bring the performance to a higher level.

GEOFF D'EON

Michael Donovan insisted that the show have a live audience. The director, Henry Sarwer-Foner, wasn't sold on this idea. Henry knew the studio because he had directed *Street Cents* in it, and he felt it was too small, and it would be impossible to make the show look good.

I think also in Henry's mind was that it would be very difficult to bring precision timing to the show. Henry it is an incredibly gifted director; he's also a drummer, and he has an amazing acuity with timing. Henry wanted the show to be put together with the precision of a Swiss watch, and you can't really do that when there is an audience in there, laughing.

Taping in front of a live audience didn't really lend itself to the kind of precision approach that Henry wanted. But Michael insisted, and to his credit, he was dead right about that. Michael was absolutely right that the live audience would keep the show moving, and that the performers would get energy from the audience. It would also preclude the ability to stop and do endless retakes to get the perfect take.

Having a "live" audience didn't mean the show would go live-to-air in the same way a newscast did. A typical taping went like this: the cast members would each deliver jokes from the news desk in front of the live audience, stopping and starting for gaffes—both verbal and technical. They would throw to segments that had been recorded and edited earlier, which were played back on monitors scattered around the studio, and the audience's reactions would be recorded. After the desk portion was complete, a couple of sketches would then be performed and recorded live, using sets that had been assembled that day. Over the subsequent days, all of the show's elements would be packaged together in an edit suite, and the show would be fed to Toronto for broadcast.

HENRY SARWER-FONER

The number of sketches shot each week always exceeded what was needed to fill that twenty-two minutes that could be used on the show, and there were four actors—and four mouths to feed, so to speak—so we needed to try to make it somewhat fair, in terms of what got to air.

There was a bit of competition there, you know, like a natural competition. We tended to overshoot by, I think, at least ten minutes, usually. Basically—produce anything that might work, and then see what sticks. It was kind of a Darwinian process. The audience got to decide what got aired and what got fed to the comedy goat.

ED MACDONALD
Writer, 1994–1997; Showrunner, 2008–2009
Henry is a fucking brilliant TV director, and you can so tell the difference when it's him or someone else. He's difficult, because he demands everything

be perfect. A lot of people can't swing with that, but a lot of people can. I dig that. I like it when someone really won't settle, and that's Henry.

HENRY SARWER-FONER

You don't really have time to overthink things. I'm a detail-oriented individual. I enjoy sweating the small stuff, so it's kind of ironic that I ended up working in a genre where there's simply no time. But you have to learn to go with the flow and not overthink things. Trust your first instinct, because there's no other choice, you know? And I think everybody, in every department, had to embrace that approach.

But it's funny. I eventually came to the realization that the frenetic pace was probably healthy for me, in a weird kind of way. I guess it's kind of more like jazz than a studied composition. You just blurt it out on instinct, and then you move on to the next tune.

I mean, it can be frustrating and imperfect, but sometimes you can express a feeling and reflect what's happening in the moment in a more visceral way than you could otherwise. You just have to sort of be open to that.

JACK KELLUM

And the other thing about the live audience—this is going to sound terrible, but it's a fact. When you do it in front of a studio audience, you can only repeat it so many times, and then you have to either scrap it or live with it, because you have to be respectful of your audience. But when you're doing it in an empty studio with no audience, it can go on forever and ever and ever, and you run yourself into overtime like crazy because there is no control on the end of it, other than the producer's control.

You always want to leave the scene with the performer being happy, so the tendency is that if the performer is not happy, you do it again, even if the director is happy. As the producer, I guess because of my old performing background, I was always sympathetic to the performer rather than to the other side. So it was a means of limiting, putting a definite end to it, so you wouldn't to lose control of the budget, basically.

So number one, it sharpens the performance, Number two, it puts a limit on the time that you can spend on any particular thing.

Of course, not the whole show was done in front of the audience. There was all the pre-taped stuff. But the live stuff in front of the audience is just gravy to me. It was what gave the show its look and feel.

GERALD LUNZ

There are different schools of comedy in this country: there's Second City, which is sketch and improv; there's the stand-up school; and then there is the theatre company. We were really out of the theatre stuff, so we knew how to play live.

Michael knew, as did I, that the performers will really come alive with an audience. If you take that away from the performers—the last thing we all had was technique. Working to the camera is different. It's a different performance speed than playing live.

So we knew that was our strength. It was also about creating the natural laugh, because there was no sweetening. We didn't have that kind of technology.

HENRY SARWER-FONER

I had mixed feelings about the live audience, because I knew, on the one hand, it would energize the performers, but you always have to be careful, when you're shooting something for television, that it doesn't get too "big." And you have to be careful that your performers aren't playing too much to the room.

But at the same time, I guess the audience at home gives you some licence when they hear the live audience, so the fact that the performances are a little bigger and broader is fine. But what was nice about this particular show was that we got to pre-record pieces that were a little more intimate, that had a different tone to them, a different pace to them. So I think it's the mix of all those elements that makes the show very, very special.

GEOFF D'EON

Bleachers were built, which accommodated about eighty to a hundred people, jammed in. There was a news set, and then there were bleachers, and then there was a very small area off to the side where we could put flats [*movable set walls*] to create rudimentary living rooms or "locations" where sketches could unfold.

HENRY SARWER-FONER

The audience was stuffed into every crevice and, literally, inches away from the cameras.

GERALD LUNZ

I think most people's rec room is bigger. There was no backlight; you couldn't light anything from the back. The audience was like, sixty people. They looked like *Howdy Doody*'s gallery in these wooden flats. It was tiny.

That's when they decided they were going to have to make a real studio—and Halifax got a new studio out of it.

FRED MATTOCKS

Well, it was a tiny studio: 2,400 square feet, a 13-foot grid—which means the lights are close to the floor—and if you had walked in after the audience was in, what you would have seen was a place that was absolutely packed. The audience was packed in, the cast was within touching distance of the audience—you couldn't swing a cat in the space.

And we had full houses. I mean, *22* never taped, in my day, where we didn't fill every seat in the house. It was kind of a "must-do" in Halifax, to go to a *22* taping. You would have seen the cast there, you would have seen the crew there, everybody wedged in cheek by jowl, doing television and live sketch comedy in a space that was never designed for it.

GEOFF D'EON

So the first episode was written, and on October 8, 1993, a Friday night, a live audience was invited in. The room was hot. Sweaty. Energized. I remember being really excited, and we performed a live show with taped inserts. We would take news footage—which was part of my job, to gather the news footage that would be required—and then we would manipulate the news footage and somehow make it absurd or try and make it funny. There were taped playbacks in the studio, and Gerald was the ringmaster. The audience was whipped through a two-hour assembly of the show, and I was completely intoxicated by the process.

I was used to making television that simply went out on television. You might watch it in the company of two or three other people; sometimes you heard back it was good, sometimes you heard back it wasn't so good, but most of the time you never got any feedback about the television shows you were making, really. This was instant feedback. It was live. People roared with laughter, and you could see the lift that it gave everyone associated with the show.

We would all crowd around the side door and watch the taping. A joke that had been laboured over for a day was run in front of the audience, and they roared with laughter. The effect on the writers and the cast was real and immediate. I looked forward to those tapings every week; they became the highlight of my week—standing in the back of the room, behind the bleachers, listening to the audience react to pieces we had worked on that week. When they roared with laughter, it was the most satisfying feeling. And when they didn't laugh, you learned—okay, that's not the way to do that.

HENRY SARWER-FONER

And then it would be my job to edit the episode and bring it to time over the weekend. It was a gruelling schedule. I was working seven days a week.

GEOFF D'EON

The beauty of *This Hour Has 22 Minutes* was that it wasn't live to tape, in that exactly what we did was what went to air. After every taping, there was what was called the producers' meeting, and we would review each and every item and how it played. The audience was our guide. Sometimes we would defy the audience and put in pieces that we just felt were the right things to put in. Maybe this audience didn't get it; maybe it doesn't play as well live as it will on television; other criteria came into play. But the audience was our focus group. It was an instant focus group on whether a given piece was going to work or not.

So we would have the producer meeting, and at the end of that, a paper lineup [*indicating which elements were going in the show and where*] would be created.

HENRY SARWER-FONER

I was fortunate in that [the editing process] was left to me, and I think ultimately it was best for the show for someone to do it, and everybody could then shift gears onto the next episode.

There was no time. That applies to network notes and even notes on scripts and stuff. So, in other words, to survive this process, rather than people micromanaging, everybody got to kind of piss out their territory and they were left to do their jobs with full autonomy in all the different departments.

GEOFF D'EON

Henry would take it into the edit suite, he would edit the show Saturday and Sunday, and we would polish it on Monday. The pacing of the show was incredibly quick, and it was really well cut by Henry. So it was a satisfying watch.

It was fed by satellite to the network, and by Monday night it was on television. The turnaround was breathtakingly quick.

HENRY SARWER-FONER

I was so stressed and exhausted. I remember my first weekend on the show, going to Halifax Harbour with the family to chill out. We arrived just in time to see a cruise ship pulling away—and I so badly wanted to jump on board to escape.

RICK MERCER

I'll tell you the greatest moment of my life, and I don't know if I've topped it yet, is when we went into what was called "the boardroom" at the CBC— which was, you know, a fancy word because it was just a room with this table with, like, twelve or fourteen chairs in there. I remember we were going to watch the edited version of the first episode....

We watched the show, and I remember thinking, "This is the best show ever! I cannot believe I'm on this show! I love this show. I would watch this show. If this show happened and I wasn't part of it, I would want to jump off a bridge. This is, like, amazing!" And I thought, "This show is going to go forever."

It was one of the greatest moments ever.

• • •

The first two episodes went to air—at that point, on Mondays at 10:30 P.M. The ratings were decent—468,000 and 535,00—but not extraordinary. And then opportunity knocked, in the form of a federal election.

GEOFF D'EON

It was the end of the Mulroney era. Kim Campbell was the prime minister. Everybody fully expected that the Mulroney years would soon be coming to an end, and the Tories were going to get a shellacking. It was October 25, 1993.

JACK KELLUM

I don't know if it was Geoff, but I suspect that it may have been, who arranged to have a live feed into the national election coverage.

GEOFF D'EON

Through my work in news, I knew the executive producer of the election night special; his name was Arnold Amber. I had an idea—it was kind of the flip of me running *CODCO* sketches on the supper-hour news—that *22 Minutes* should be in the election-night special, so I phoned Arnold Amber. Cranky old news guy, really good programmer. Sense of fun. Fearless.

I said, "Look, I have this new job. I'm working with a bunch of comedians; we are doing a satirical news show called *This Hour Has 22 Minutes*. You haven't seen it yet, but I think it's going to be really good. We do political satire, and I think it would lighten the density of your election-night coverage if you let us come on board and do some sketches."

To everyone's amazement, including mine, he said yes.

GERALD LUNZ

God love Geoff D'Eon and his connections with news. This is why the show worked: it was the most fabulous collective of people with the greatest talents that complemented each other.

RICK MERCER

At this point, we're only on the air two weeks, and we're a sensation. You could just sense it. People were like, "What is this show?" And it was late-night, but everyone was talking about it. To me, it was the culmination of anything I could ever imagine. And then when Geoff said, "You're going to be on the election live," I mean—even now, I'm getting excited—the idea of doing that, the hair went up. "What do you mean we're going to be on live? Reacting to the news, so there's no scripts? We can say whatever?"

I don't know who allowed it to happen, but thank God they did; it was amazing.

GEOFF D'EON

22 Minutes had had two airings—two episodes in October—but we were given live access to the airways—and we are talking *really* live now. We were standing by in the studio in Halifax, and there were certain spots where they were going to call on us. Sketches had been written, news copy stories had been written. The cast were nervous. This was really live and this was to the country. This would be a top-rated show and an amazing opportunity for *This Hour Has 22 Minutes* to get its name out there. A marketing opportunity.

HENRY SARWER-FONER

You have to realize that nobody had, like, grand expectations. We were just trying to survive. And I remember being very nervous. "Oh, God! We're going to go *live*-live," and I'd never done that before.

GERALD LUNZ

We had this hit, I guess it was a buck—that's what Geoff would say, because it's the language of television, a buck, a buck and half—a minute and a half.

GEOFF D'EON

So they came to us and we did some funny bits. I got great feedback from the master control room in Toronto: "That was great; we are going to come back to you."

GERALD LUNZ

[Peter] Mansbridge threw to us, and they had already announced the election results. [Kim Campbell, Mulroney's successor] had been defeated. Slammed.

GEOFF D'EON

We kind of knew which way the election was going to go; everybody did. Everybody knew the Tories were going to lose. So they came back to us for a second hit.

And in one of *22 Minutes*'s greatest moments, when the show was still in its infancy, the segment ended with Cathy, Rick, and Greg conga dancing in the studio in a circle, chanting, "Mulroney is no more—hey! Mulroney is no more—hey!"

GERALD LUNZ

They did a conga line! "Mulroney is no more—hey!" It was so sophomoric, but it was so funny and full of life.

RICK MERCER

We did the conga line around the desk, and the idea that the CBC, in its national election coverage, would have people dancing—news anchors dancing in a conga line—is so wild and off-the-charts. I can't imagine it happening now, in a million years.

GEOFF D'EON

Everyone seemed to enjoy it, and I remember my head was exploding, because chanting "Mulroney is no more—hey!" is what so many people I knew were thinking. Pretty much everyone I knew in the world of news was thinking it, but they weren't allowed to say it.

We could say it. We were like the court jesters. We were like the fool in *King Lear*. We were allowed to say the bad thing. That was so liberating and so intoxicating.

RICK MERCER

Nine people out of ten, turning on the CBC—they thought we were news people! People didn't know who I was. I was just a guy at a news desk; so was Greg, and Cathy looked like a news anchor. So the idea that we started doing a conga line and singing, "Mulroney is no more…!" Hysterical!

PETER MANSBRIDGE

That was a bizarre night. I mean, pretty well everybody knew the Conservatives were going to lose, but to win just two seats? And that's what they ended up with. They went from a majority government to two seats, and, you know, people were pretty happy that they'd done that on that night. So these guys captured the mood. There was a conga line going on in the country that night. They just put a real face to it.

HENRY SARWER-FONER

I think it went well. It was very exciting. I remember—you get this sort of adrenaline high after, when it goes well. I can see why some people are addicted to live TV, because they're adrenaline junkies, you know? I'm not really in that category [*laughing*].

IVAN FECAN

At that time, the CBC news was the number one news in the country. I mean, today, it's the number three news nationally, but at the time, it was number one. And that was a huge opportunity for audiences to sample the talents of these people.

PETER MANSBRIDGE

It was different. It wasn't, you know, the sort of Wayne and Shuster show that some of us go back to. I can't remember what my actual thought was at that moment, but it was probably—this is good, this has potential. It looked a little amateur-hour in the whole way it was done, compared to what you see them doing now, but it was something that had potential for the future, and it delivered on that potential.

JACK KELLUM

That was quite significant in getting the word out that this thing was happening in Halifax.

GERALD LUNZ

I guess the reach was monstrous, and outside the usual people that would be tuning in to this kind of thing. And that's when the show took off. It. Took. Off. We were renewed immediately for the full season. Numbers started to crawl up higher than anybody had ever seen.

HENRY SARWER-FONER

Well, it was a shot in the arm. We had a captive audience who were interested in current affairs, so it kind of launched the show into the Canadian zeitgeist pretty quickly.

RICK MERCER

We were late-night, right? So we were a sensation, but in that way that, like, we were a really cool band. There's lots of cool bands, but it's hard to get downtown to see them.

People hadn't had time to get to know us. We were so far from household, it's not funny. So that particular election was historic, and, back in those days, there was only one game in town for election night—that would be the CBC, right? Everyone in the country was watching.

PETER MANSBRIDGE

In those days, they would ask to come on our show. Today, we ask them to come on our show, right? That's the difference. And, you know, they attract viewers, they are legitimately funny—yet, at the same time, they're making a point about our system.

Since then, they've always been on our election night programs in one way or another. And as far back as I can remember now, they've always been there at our insistence—begging, basically, for them to be a part of the program in some fashion, because it's good.

GEOFF D'EON

That's when I knew we were really onto something. If we could conga dance around the studio, singing, "Mulroney is no more," this show was going to fly.

5
A Place in the TV Universe
1993–1994

The next hurdle was to figure out where this new show might fit on the CBC's complicated new schedule. Initially, network programming executives presumed *22 Minutes* was better suited to late-night than to prime time—but the ratings would not bear this out.

GEOFF D'EON

Political satire was not new, but political satire in prime time television didn't really exist. It existed in late-night television. And when *22 Minutes* was ordered, that was, in fact, the plan.

The CBC schedule had just been retooled in a well-meaning but disastrous way. The news had been moved to nine o'clock. The old *National* and *The Journal* were abolished, and this program called *Prime Time News* was created.

The then-head of English Television, Ivan Fecan, wanted to put the news at nine o'clock and have an "Early Prime Time" before the news. The news would unfold between nine and ten, and after the news was finished at ten o'clock they would have what was called a "Late-night Prime" for adult content.

So that was the television universe, and it wasn't really working that well.

IVAN FECAN

Actually, it was the president's [Gèrard Veilleux's] initiative, and [director of News and Current Affairs] Trina McQueen and I were there to implement it.

ALAN MACGILLIVRAY

Prime Time News. What a silly experiment that was. Everybody except the news people knew that wasn't going to work.

GEOFF D'EON

22 Minutes was born in a world where *Air Farce* could be in early prime but *This Hour Has 22 Minutes* would be a late-night show. So the first two broadcasts were at 10:30 on a Monday night, and then it bounced around a little bit. Sometimes it was on at 10:30; sometimes it was on at 11.

It actually did really well in its first two broadcasts. I think it got 468,000 viewers in its first broadcast. There were high-fives in the *22 Minutes* meeting rooms at that point. But it got bounced around pretty dramatically, and then there was a Christmas hiatus, and then in early 1994 it was moved to eleven o'clock. And eleven o'clock turned out to be a bit of a graveyard. Its ratings went down to 200- and 300,000. Still considered decent for a late-night show at the time, but not a ratings hit.

JOHN DOYLE

Television Critic, The Globe and Mail, 2000–present
One could say the circumstance of the dire ratings late at night were mitigated

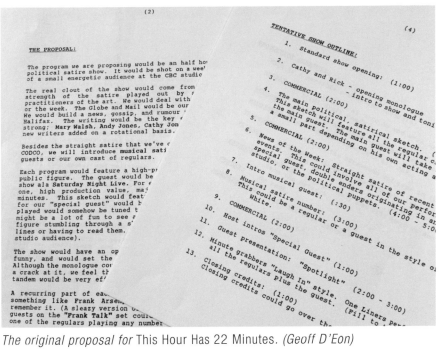

THE PROPOSAL:

The program we are proposing would be an half ho~
political satire show. It would be shot on a wee~
of a small energetic audience at the CBC studio

The real clout of the show would come from
strength of the satire played out by ~
practitioners of the art. We would deal with
or the week. The Globe and Mail would be our
We would build a news, gossip, and rumour ~
Halifax. The writing would be the key ~
strong; Mary Walsh, Andy Jones, Cathy Jon~
new writers added on a rotational basis.

Besides the straight satire that we've ~
CODCO, we will introduce musical sati~
guests or our own cast of regulars.

Each program would feature a high-p~
public figure. The guest would be
show a la Saturday Night Live. For ~
one, high production value, ma~
minutes. This sketch would feat~
for our "special guest" would ~
played would somehow be tuned t~
might be a lot of fun to see ~
figure stumbling through a s~
lines or having to read them.
studio audience).

The show would have an op~
funny, and would set the
Although the monologue co~
a crack at it, we feel t~
tandem would be very ef~

A recurring part of ea~
something like Frank Arse~
remember it. (A sleazy version ~
guests on the "Frank Talk" set cou~
one of the regulars playing any number

TENTATIVE SHOW OUTLINE:

1. Standard show opening: (1:00)

2. Cathy and Rick - opening monologue
   - intro to show and toni

3. COMMERCIAL (2:00)

4. The main political, satirical sketch. (
   This sketch will feature all the regular c~
   the main guest. The main guest will take
   a small part depending on his own acting a

5. COMMERCIAL (2:00)

6. News of the Week: Straight satire of recent
   events. This could involve all of our perfor~
   special guest, double enders originating in a~
   studio, or the political puppets. (4:00 - 5:0~

7. Intro musical guest: (:30)

8. Musical satire number: (3:00)
   This could be a regular or a guest in the style o~
   White.

9. COMMERCIAL (2:00)

10. Host intros "Special Guest" (1:00)

11. Guest presentation: "Spotlight" (2:00 - 3:00)

12. Minute grabbers "Laugh In" style. One Liners pe~
    all the regulars plus the guest. (Fill to ~

13. Closing credits: (1:00)
    Closing credits could go over th~

The original proposal for This Hour Has 22 Minutes. *(Geoff D'Eon)*

Peter Mansbridge, who made numerous appearances on the show, was CBC's chief correspondent and anchor of The National *until July 2017. (Peter Mansbridge)*

Mary Walsh, in character as Marg, Princess Warrior, kisses Stephen Harper after his announcement that he would run for the leadership of the newly created Conservative Party in 2004. Walsh ambushed politicians of all stripes as the unstoppable warrior. (Jonathan Hayward/CP PHOTO)

Gavin Crawford's two-week guest spot on 22 Minutes *eventually turned into an eight-season run.* (Liam Sharpe)

Rick Mercer made his mark on 22 Minutes with his famous "Streeters" (later known as "Rants"). Mercer was also known for the extremely popular "Talking to Americans" segments. (Jon Sturge/Mercer Report)

Henry Sarwer-Foner, the show's first director, created the look and feel of This Hour Has 22 Minutes. *(Henry Sarwer-Foner)*

Cape Breton performer Ed Macdonald was one of the show's first writers. He also did a stint as showrunner in Season 16. (Ian Brown)

Gerald Lunz was the show's first creative producer. He is now executive producer of Rick Mercer Report. *(Mercer Report)*

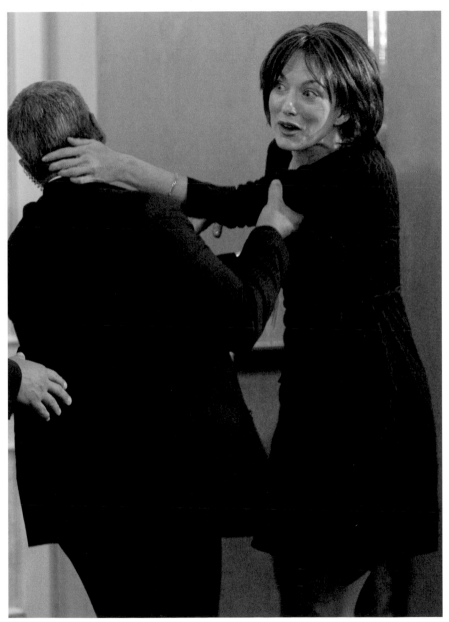

Geri Hall was taken into custody and handcuffed when she tried to ask a question at a Stephen Harper news conference in Halifax in 2008. Hall was in character as Single Female Voter, but security did not appreciate the joke.
(Peter Parsons/CP PHOTO)

Former CBC executive Phyllis Platt witnessed the original pitch for the show; she oversaw the birth and development of what became This Hour Has 22 Minutes. *(Peter Moss)*

Tim McAuliffe was a 22 Minutes writer and producer who has also worked on The Office *and* Late Night with Jimmy Fallon. *(Tim McAuliffe)*

Ivan Fecan is a Canadian media executive, producer, and philanthropist. He was vice-president of CBC English Television from 1992 to 1993. (Don Dixon)

Paul Bellini was a writer and showrunner on This Hour Has 22 Minutes. *(Andre Tardif)*

Former regional director Fred Mattocks was instrumental in fostering collaboration between CBC TV and independent producers in the Maritimes. (Fred Mattocks)

Paul Martin is surrounded by Mary Walsh, left, and Cathy Jones, in costume as Eulalia and Mrs. Enid. Martin, who later became prime minister, was in Halifax to take part in a public session at Dalhousie. (Andrew Vaughan/CP PHOTO)

Jack Kellum was a CBC staffer who served as the show's first senior producer. (Maj Kellum)

by the fact that nobody was watching CBC after nine o'clock. They insisted on showing this strange version of the news at 9 P.M., and then after that, it was a wasteland for CBC.

GEORGE ANTHONY

I think the intent of the eleven o'clock time slot for *22 Minutes* was all part of establishing the show and seeing how it could perform in different ways. And a lot of that was dictated by the nine o'clock news thing. Adult Prime kind of threw off our traditional concept of scheduling.

IVAN FECAN

We would try different shows out at different times, as a programming strategy. I recall I did the same thing with *Degrassi*; it used to be an afternoon kids' show, and I think in '87 or something, I moved it into prime time, and it took off. It's part of the programmer's bag of tricks that you move stuff around a little bit on a trial basis, to see whether you can connect with an audience. So this would be entirely consistent.

PHYLLIS PLATT

When you start a new show, you are not necessarily going to get an instantaneous huge audience, but it really came out of the gate quite well, because it was a different perspective for a lot Canadians on how Newfoundland, which is such a unique part of the country, could—in a very spot-on kind of way—take the piss out of a lot of politicians and big business people.

ALAN MACGILLIVRAY

We were in three or four different time slots in the first eight shows. It was almost like they didn't want us there. But the audience followed us, and they stuck with us.

GEOFF D'EON

The show started to gain traction with viewers. It became a critical darling. All of the television reviewers at the time—people that we were afraid of, people who had led reigns of terror, like John Haslett-Cuff in the *Globe and Mail*— he identified it as the freshest and best television show of the 1993–94 season, and he was followed very quickly by other television critics who adored *This Hour Has 22 Minutes* because it was fresh. It was different. And Phyllis Platt had an idea—she just had a hunch that it might work well in early prime.

So for three episodes in that very first year, in 1994, she moved it to early prime as an experiment. To eight o'clock. And the ratings went through the roof. The third time it aired at eight o'clock, it got 923,000 viewers or some-thing, and at that point it was clear that *22 Minutes* had found an audience. It was a critical darling, and it was going to be a huge success.

PHYLLIS PLATT

That was my job: to try to figure out flow, which Ivan Fecan was very good at. He taught me how to look at the flow of a schedule. So I had this book—this was when we still did things on paper—where you could take one sticker that says *This Hour Has 22 Minutes* and move it somewhere, while at the same time taking a different show's sticker and putting it someplace else. You just kept working it and working it and working it, essentially all the time. I didn't move shows around unless I had managed to convince myself and others that this would create a better flow.

I did think that the show would catch on in Canada; we just needed to be sure of when the best timing was and how we could attract the biggest audience.

JOHN DOYLE

For CBC, their ratings benchmark is probably still a million. That tells you that the show's having a real impact and you can probably do better with selling ads around a show that consistently does a million. But that's a hard figure to reach in Canada.

If you're getting below 500,000, I think you're in jeopardy. And if you go below that, to somewhere in the twos, you're definitely in a situation where the broadcaster should reconsider what the hell is going on if you have that small an audience in prime time.

IVAN FECAN

There's less of an audience in late-night. That's the trade-off, and the fact that it has survived this long, and is still pretty popular, to me suggests that putting it in the earlier time period was the right decision.

GEOFF D'EON

And don't let anyone tell you we didn't care about ratings. We were really consumed with ratings. The first time we beat *Royal Canadian Air Farce* in the ratings, we were really proud of that, and then *22 Minutes* went on to become one of the highest-rated shows on the network.

It was a sobering moment when *This Hour Has 22 Minutes*'s ratings beat the ratings of *Prime Time News*. That was actually slightly worrying for a news junkie like me—when more people were watching the satirical news than were watching the actual news. Michael Donovan actually had a quote about it in the *Toronto Star*, about how satisfying it was when the satirical news was drawing higher than the real news.

Lots of people have talked about that in subsequent years. Jon Stewart would say how worrying it was that college students were getting their news from *The Daily Show* and not from the real news, but I don't think that really worried us too much.

GEORGE ANTHONY

It was a very sobering moment, and very schizophrenic for some of us. I was thrilled with the numbers—and then I was not thrilled with the numbers, because it was the news! We want news to be the top thing on the air. That was why it was moved, to give it that shot.

But it *was* a great moment.

IVAN FECAN

One of the banes of CBC as a public broadcaster is that commercials matter, and therefore, ratings matter. Hopefully, one day the CBC can be commercial-free, but as long as it's not, ratings matter. It's always a balance between what is popular, what has quality, and what has commercial value.

GERALD LUNZ

I think within a year, we had over 1 million viewers. And then over the next three years it built to 1.4, 1.5—just crazy stuff.

GEOFF D'EON

Ratings solve everything, as the old expression goes. Higher ratings brought more cash to the show: bigger budgets, more money for travel, bigger salaries for the writers and staff.

But good ratings hadn't solved everything. In the first season, just as the show was beginning to gain traction with viewers, the show's producers—who were responsible for securing the money to finance the show from various provincial and federal film funding agencies, such as Telefilm Canada—were on the verge of running out of cash.

ALAN MACGILLIVRAY

We weren't fully financed at that point. We had expected money from the Province of Nova Scotia to come in, and that didn't happen.

What saved our butts was that Ralph Holtz, the local Telefilm guy, watched the first few episodes of the show. He called us and said, "We think this is great. We would like to be a partner in this." So they invested money after the show was on the air! It was unheard of.

That was a big sigh of relief, because we didn't have any interim financing. We were basically going with what we had in the bank, which wasn't much, and CBC cash and services. But I was biting my nails. I think Ralph called us maybe four weeks into the show, and then we started thinking, "Oh my God, this might actually work. We might actually be able to pay people."

That wouldn't happen now, because you just wouldn't be able to proceed without being fully financed. And I'm not sure why CBC allowed it—maybe they just didn't understand financing at that point.

GEOFF D'EON

Nobody knew for sure that it would be renewed the following season, but everybody was taking bets that it would be. It was a pretty safe bet that it would be renewed—and it was.

When it came back for its second season, it was a prime-time show, and then I think the show just went from strength to strength and it just built. The first five years of that show was like riding a rocket ship and hanging on for dear life, because it achieved so many successes and broke so many barriers.

• • •

Now the show had to find its legs. Its Halifax home base—far away from the executives at the CBC's national headquarters in Toronto—turned out to offer an unexpected advantage.

GEOFF D'EON

People have asked me, "Was there ever anything that the CBC was uncomfortable with and shut down?" The answer is—almost never. The CBC gave a huge creative licence to *22 Minutes* and were brave. They allowed the show to take risks, and protected and defended the show. That's the big picture, and that was the case 99 per cent of the time.

HENRY SARWER-FONER

I think the show was lucky to be based out of Halifax. We were kind of left alone. It was kind of a grand experiment. I guess the equivalent, these days, would maybe be a web series or something. And with no time for network notes, we could basically do whatever we wanted, as long as it was fast and cheap.

GERALD LUNZ

That was the greatest thing about being in Halifax or being in the regions: they were not there. A lot of times I talk to people here in Toronto, and they say, "Didn't you have any network interference?" And I say no.

Because they can be like, "Why does she have to wear a red hat? Can't it be a blue hat?" You go, "What the fuck is the difference?"

But then I realized it's because we had George Anthony, and George got it, because he had been working in entertainment—he had been the entertainment editor of the *Toronto Sun*, he had been in Los Angeles, done junkets for years, he knew all the people. Great friends with Joan Rivers. He knew all about comedy and style and personality.

GEORGE ANTHONY

I saw myself as a cheerleader, if you will, for those shows. I championed a lot of shows over the years and I was lucky, because they were very successful. I would not have been championing them for as long, if they had not been.

So I really felt that it was my main job, to a great extent, to effect a cordial separation of Church and State. I wanted to keep the talent away from the network, and I wanted to keep the network away from the talent. And I *was* the network, so I was in a position to do that.

FRED MATTOCKS

George Anthony was an absolutely critical supporter—and not just in the kind of blind sense. George wasn't a fan boy, although he was a fan. George would come down periodically and give people a shake when they needed a shake. But he was, and is, to this day, a consistent supporter of *22 Minutes*. The show would not have succeeded without him.

He ran air cover for Jack a number of times, because Jack, you know, was in the middle between the plant and the independent producer. There were points at which Jack would get on the network's bad side, and George would make sure that, you know, stupid things didn't happen.

GERALD LUNZ

George was very much behind us. He was central in letting us go, and probably battling the big fight up along, if there was one to be had. It didn't filter down to the creative, so we still had the playpen.

GEORGE ANTHONY

What I felt Ivan and Phyllis were counting on me for was to get them the very best shows that I could, so my philosophy was basically to create a safe place for the artists to deliver their very best work. That was my modus operandi, and that was basically what I did.

I designated myself as the one who would take the bullets. I felt my obligation was to get the very best show possible out of the investment that the CBC had in these shows.

When you are investing in a show, that means another six shows aren't happening because you are putting your money there, so I felt it was my role to protect the business investment of my boss—the CBC. And the way to do that would be to get the absolute very best work out of everybody.

You couldn't get the very best work out of everybody if someone didn't like the colour of the set, or someone thought we were going too close to the edge or whatever, because then you start inhibiting the creative, and you are starting to kill your own investment.

I don't remember having to stop that many bullets for *22*; a couple, maybe. For my bosses it was—a) was the show working? And b) was it delivering what it was supposed to deliver? And c) did they have to be on the phone every week defending it? And since it was yes, yes, and no, they were happy to let me do it.

GEOFF D'EON

There might have been Tories at the board of director level who didn't like what we were saying about Brian Mulroney, and there might have been Liberal board members who didn't like what we were saying about the Liberal government, but we never got interference on that level. We were protected really well. So I would have to give kudos to the CBC top management for protecting the show and giving the show what it needed to become successful.

FRED MATTOCKS

I can remember a conversation that I think ended with me, where I got called by a group of network executives who had overall budget responsibility for the show. They told me that my job was to cut the CBC part of the budget of *22* in half, and their helpful suggestion was that I actually take *22* and *Street Cents* and make them one production unit.

I think I was regional director when that happened, and I just said, "That's not happening." And they said, "Well, we may have to cancel the show." And I said, "Well, go ahead, then. Go ahead and cancel it."

It is a tough card to play, but at the end of the day, it was one of the network's most successful shows and I was pretty confident that wasn't happening. And it didn't.

As the show's advocates held the network at arm's length, the cast in Halifax was busy working out the kinks. This group wasn't nearly as volatile as the cast of *CODCO* had been—but it wasn't all smooth sailing.

HENRY SARWER-FONER

Once the show had its identity and the format, then it was the day-to-day, just trying to make the pieces work and trying to keep a positive energy on set.

JACK KELLUM

I had worked with these guys for a long time, since way back in the '70s. I understood, in many instances, what was going on.

Both Cathy and Mary—I hate to say it, but I have to—they are both very insecure people. I can't understand it. My own mind has great difficulty getting around this. Both of them: two of the most talented people in this country. But they both have very, very low self-esteem. And Cathy goes into these crying jags. Somebody puts her off just a tiny bit, just a hair, before the show, she would break into tears. The makeup women would go crazy, because she would be crying her eyes out.

HENRY SARWER-FONER

They were all anti-authoritarian by nature, as was I [*laughing*]. But at the same time, as the director, I was the authority on set, so the first season was quite, you know, stressful—sort of trial by fire, until we got to know each other, and I eventually earned their trust.

PETER SUTHERLAND

Cathy used to cry a lot during the first take of sketches. I'd go over to Michael Donovan and say, "I'm a little worried about Cathy." He'd say, "Trust me, after she cries, the performance is much better."

HENRY SARWER-FONER

Nothing kills comedy like stress while it's being performed, you know? I mean, there might be stress behind the scenes in trying to figure out the writing process, and what the art department needs to build, and all those kinds of things. But once you're on set, I always try to make it calm, and create a positive atmosphere for the performers to work in.

Cathy Jones's masterful characters—Babe "I'm just goofin' around" Bennett, Joe Crow, Mrs. Enid, and Sandy Campbell, among many others—quickly became staples of the show.

RICK MERCER

Cathy just wants to laugh. It's always been a tough fit for Cathy. It's funny that she's the last one standing.

Every one of her characters laughs, if you notice. Every single one of her characters, they all have a laugh. That's all she wants. She just wants people to laugh, so it's a tough gig for her.

PAUL BELLINI
Writer, 1994–97; Showrunner, 1998–1999

Cathy's a brilliant sketch comedian. The thing with Cathy is that, you know, she can make a big hem and haw, and she was never certain about anything, and she was always in trouble. I mean, all this stuff. And then she'd get before of the cameras and do something that no one else could do, and we'd all look at each other and go, "Gee, that's it! You just can't top that!"

I've worked with a lot of sketch comedians over the years, and she might be the best, just in terms of pure talent. Cathy was a real chameleon. And she committed to her characters in a way that a lot of people just can't or won't.

HENRY SARWER-FONER

I think probably the biggest lesson I learned then was that each actor has a different process. No two performers are the same; they all need different things from a director at different times. You just try to be as empathetic and constructive as possible with your feedback, and you try to feel out what they need from you, to help them achieve their best.

By Episode 5, Mary Walsh had recovered from back surgery and was ready to make her first appearance at the news desk with the rest of the cast. Mary's early sketch characters included chatty uber-Canadian Connie Bloor and man's-man Dakey Dunn—and, of course, Marg Delahunty.

GERALD LUNZ

When Mary did finally come back, we could finally fill out the desk. Rick was holding together the body politic with these two fabulous comics, but the show had to be more newsy. We were trying to hit that ball. So when Mary came in, that kind of focused it more, and the writing became sharper.

That's when it came into what it was, which was a real collective.

ED MACDONALD

Mary was just sort of Mary. She is formidable and fun, and I did like writing with Mary, but sometimes you just had to sit there while she did it. She really wouldn't listen to anything you said. You were just there to be a sounding board.

HENRY SARWER-FONER

She has a lot of strengths. She's a brilliant performer. When she's in the moment, when she's on her game, she embodies the character. She is that character in the moment. And if you do different takes—some actors are more studied, and once you've rehearsed it and they've made the decision that this is what they're going to do, they kind of stick to that.

With Mary, it's often that each take is completely different, because she's just feeling it out in the moment. It's a very emotional thing for her. I mean, she's got a brilliant mind, but it's interesting; when she's performing, it comes from her gut.

Greg Thomey was making his mark—literally ("If you can mark an X, you're my kind of people!")—with Jerry Boyle of the Newfoundland Separation Federation, and with his hapless journalist Tim MacMillan, brother to Thomey's Frank MacMillan persona.

RICK MERCER

The genius of Greg Thomey—I don't know if there's anyone who's worked on the show who is not entirely in awe of the genius of Greg Thomey.

The success that he deserved didn't quite come. There's a guy in my office right now who told me that when he was in university, he had all these *22 Minutes* tapes, because he did a film and television degree. He and his friends would drink and watch *22 Minutes*, and they would hit "mute" anytime anyone but Greg was on.

ED MACDONALD

I remember Thomey being so funny. I would literally almost pee, he was so funny. In the room where we were writing, for the first month, he said nothing. He would just kind of stare at me. And I was like, "Oh God, that guy hates me."

He came in one day as this character from *Boys of St. Vincent*, Brother Glackin, and I remember almost choking, I laughed so hard. And I remember Rick Mercer being the colour of a fire engine, because he was dying.

HENRY SARWER-FONER

He had a wonderful sense of the absurd. I think that's perhaps one of his strengths. In person, as well, he's a very funny guy.

GERALD LUNZ

I remember this moment: Greg went into [costume designer] Patti Parsons's trailer, put on a skullcap, put on a neck brace, and grabbed a saxophone. And he started playing that guy from [Canadian jazz-funk band] the Shuffle Demons, when he had hurt his neck. Well, Cathy had to run to the bathroom; she was going to wet herself. And of course he wouldn't let up, once he got into it, just to make us laugh.

HENRY SARWER-FONER

One of his iconic characters was Jerry Boyle, which we'd always do in front of a live audience. That was something he was not necessarily always that comfortable with, but he did it. He was a real trooper.

In the rehearsal, he would always be very particular about the blocking—when he'd get up from his desk, when he'd turn to the camera—much more so than any of the other actors. Most of them wouldn't really care that much about that stuff. But he really wanted to know what he was he was doing, and rehearse it very precisely before the audience arrived. And then, sometimes, when it was time for him to come out for the audience, all the blocking would go out the window. He'd be so in the moment that he'd just be channelling Jerry—and those would be the best ones.

And then there was Rick. Not entirely comfortable as a character actor—although he regularly appeared as one of the (four) Quinlan Quints, and as a conservative commentator in "The Right Answer"—Rick found other ways to express himself, particularly through his signature "Rants."

ED MACDONALD

Mercer. I went to a taping the week before I started on the show, I think, and you could tell right away that he was a star. It was obvious that he had other fish to fry, even then. He was very smart, very politically astute, and he was really into it. That's the difference right? Obviously if you really love it, you're going to be better at it, and he really does. He's really interested in that shit, and I'm like, "How do you stay awake listening to them?" They're Canadian politicians. Holy shit, every one of them has the personality of a dead librarian. They're just so dull. The only way they're even interesting is if they're crazy, right? And that only comes along once in a while.

BILL BRIOUX
Veteran Television Columnist, TV Guide/Sun Media/The Canadian Press, 1985–present
Right from the get-go, Rick was somebody you had to watch. Those "Rants" were brilliant right from the beginning—a big part of the success of the show.

RICK MERCER
I was a man possessed. In the early days, we didn't have any writers, and it was 24/7. That's the way the show was. If you wanted to get a piece on the show, you had to write it. So, I always wrote my "Streeter"—what I call the "Rant," now—and to this day, even on the *Mercer Report*, I write the "Rant" entirely myself.

So, that had to be written every week. And if it was a Rick and Thomey sketch—and there were an awful lot of those over the years—we would write them together, or sometimes we would each write them.

But the reality is, I was a lot younger and a lot hungrier than anyone else in the cast. Thomey, also, was launching his television career. But Cathy and Mary were established television personalities, with pedigrees and shows. The stakes were so much higher for me. I was like a man possessed.

BILL DONOVAN
I think what's not seen, which is a really hard part of the show, is that those people have to stay on top of things. They don't just wander into the studio and start shooting. They have to be reading and watching—God knows in

today's world, how can you keep on top of everything that's going on?

I used to walk by the Radio Room on the way to my office, and it didn't matter what time of the day or night, there would be somebody in there, very often Mercer, Thomey. They worked their buns off, and they made it look very easy. It's like a lot of other artists: making it look easy is really hard. It's a tremendous effort.

EDWARD KAY
Writer and Producer, Seasons 4–7, 1996–2000

I remember very distinctly there was something Rick was working on—I can't remember what it was—and I had this idea for a piece. He said, "No, no, I'm going to do this instead."

We all did this: we would overwrite—create extra material so we would have something in our back pocket, just in case. When I came in on the Friday morning, and we were going to tape Friday night, I said, "So how is the piece going?" and he said, "I don't know. It's not working right. It doesn't feel good. I worked all night on it."

He read it to me, and it was pretty good actually, but there were just certain things about it that he didn't like. So I said, "Just to put it out there, I do have that piece that I mentioned yesterday, if you're interested."

He took it and read it out loud to himself, and he just said, "That's fucking funny," and then he took what he had spent all night on and crumpled it in a ball and threw it in the recycle bin.

And I thought, "Now, that is a professional. There's no ego. He just wants the very best piece." And that really impressed me.

HENRY SARWER-FONER

I think the strength of that particular cast was in the solo pieces, even though they worked so well together and could, literally, finish each other's sentences on something like the Quinlan Quints. But what was unique about this show were the first signature solo character pieces. For Rick, obviously his "Rant," which was the very first thing I shot. Mary had Marg Delahunty and Dakey Dunn amongst others. Cathy—Joe Crow, Babe Bennett. Greg—Jerry Boyle.

I don't think, still to this day, there's any show where there are characters that give such a strong viewpoint. The new cast, I believe, does it as well. But the original cast members were brilliant at it, and I think it really resonated with the audience.

Originally, due to the limited budget, the performers were writing most of their own material. So these four very distinct voices emerged on the series, as these characters developed to showcase each of their strengths.

6

The Road

1993–2001

From the beginning, character-driven sketch comedy was an important part of the show. But very quickly, the show's producers began to realize that *22 Minutes* could generate valuable buzz by having cast members interact with celebrities and politicians—and that meant getting outside the comfort of the studio and into the real world.

GEOFF D'EON

We wanted a politician on our first episode. Before the show had even gone to air, I wrote a letter to the head of the Nova Scotia Liberal Party, Myra Freeman, asking her to use her influence to get [Prime Minister] Jean Chrétien on the inaugural episode. I wrote to [former prime minister] Kim Campbell's people, I wrote to Chrétien's people, but it didn't really happen initially.

GERALD LUNZ

They would go and do stuff because, as you know, it was cheaper than building sets. When you build sets and start doing sketches, they take a lot of time. This is quicker value. It's more smash-and-grab.

RICK MERCER

The first time that I went and interviewed [Reform Party leader] Preston Manning, he thought for sure that I was a local news guy. And I would never tell him otherwise. I mean, that's how I did "Talking to Americans," as well. People just assumed I was a news guy. I would wear a nice suit, I had the big camera, I had the producer who looked like he was the classic producer with me. Like, we looked every inch the local news team.

The first time with Preston Manning, I can remember when it starts to dawn on him that this is not a real newsperson. But, yet, he could see that it was the CBC camera, so we weren't, like, college kids. He was completely confused.

GEOFF D'EON

We were a Halifax-based show, and in the first season I don't think the budget was huge, so most of the celebrities we got, we got because they were coming to Halifax. I would work with the newsroom, and they would tell me who was coming, and I would look ahead and plan shoots. That's how we got Preston Manning and that's how we got [industrialist and media baron] Conrad Black.

Conrad Black was one of our earliest celebrity hits. Mary Walsh went to a Conrad Black book signing and knelt in front of him like she was kneeling in front of the Pope and said, "Mr. Black, you have so much money! Can I have some?" and he gave her a two-dollar bill.

She looked at it and said, "Just the two?"

People responded to that quickly and viscerally. They loved the fact that Mary had knelt in front of Conrad Black, so it became clear very quickly that the instinct to have celebrities on the show was a good instinct.

RICK MERCER

It didn't take long before they figured it out, of course. I mean, Preston Manning threatened to sue the show—the Reform Party threatened to sue the show—over something Mary said, which was very funny. I think she said, "Preston Manning's speeches are wonderful, but I hear they're even more edifying in the original German"—which is a great line! I don't think it's the type of thing you can sue over, but they certainly threatened to.

GERALD LUNZ

Michael's phone rang—lawyers from the Reform Party, about how they were going to come after him. And he was like, "Come ahead. Let's do this." And I learned this from Michael: if we are going to have a war, it's going to be on the front page. You can't buy this kind of publicity. And you are going to lose, because complainers lose.

Then within two weeks, Preston Manning was coming through town, and it was like, how can we get on the show? The mood had changed. That's how quickly it started to change, and they realized "No, this is good. This show has got a reach. If we don't come off like crazy people, this will be perfect."

GEOFF D'EON

Rick and I and Peter Sutherland, the cameraman—we went over to Dartmouth when Preston Manning was in town. I spoke to his aide, a guy called Rick Anderson, who has gone on to become a very famous pollster. I very quickly explained what we wanted Preston Manning to do, and he got it. He said, "Yeah, okay, we will do that." You could see the gears going in his head. "Why would we do this? Why would we go on a comedy show?"

The answer is because it will humanize my guy, Preston Manning. It will make him look like he's got a great sense of humour. So he said yes.

RICK MERCER

What developed is what I always described as the mutually parasitic relationship. Very quickly, the politicians decided that it was advantageous for them to be on the show, and very quickly, it was advantageous for us to have them on the show. So, quite often, what they learned—especially in Marg's case—was to stand there and take it, which is unbelievable. I mean, the abuse that Marg Delahunty would throw at some of them. But they knew in the long run it was an advantageous place for them to be seen.

GEOFF D'EON

So we had this little piece of tape with Rick standing next to Preston Manning, holding a microphone with a *22 Minutes* flag on it, and we gave Preston Manning a line. It was, "Under no circumstances will I appear on *This Hour Has 22 Minutes*." So we brought that back and we ran it in front of the studio audience—our focus group—and they loved it. They roared. They saw an actual politician doing something that was kind of fun.

It didn't take long for people in Ottawa to get that message. It didn't take long before the communications staffs of all these different ministers started to figure out, "Hey, if we go on *22 Minutes,* we are going around the news. We are reaching people without having to go through the prism of Peter Mansbridge."

So over the years, what started as a chase, with me on the phone trying to persuade people to go on—or alternatively simply going to Ottawa and ambushing people—transformed from that to having aides and communications people phoning me, or phoning *22 Minutes* to say, "The minister is going to be in Halifax next week, just in case you wanted to do anything."

We tended to not take people up on those kinds of offers. It was much more fun when we set the agenda than when they did. But I think the appearance of celebrities on *22 Minutes* was one of the many ingredients that sort of propelled it into the public consciousness.

• • •

GEOFF D'EON

Initially, not every attempt to get out of the studio resulted in good tape, but it was clear that getting the show outside the studio worked. At the end of the first season, or at the beginning of the second season, I suggested that we go to Ottawa. I used a metaphor that all Newfoundlanders would understand—

that Ottawa was the Grand Banks. If we were going to put politicians on the show, we should just plan trips to Ottawa.

And I was the guy to do that, because no one else in that unit had the skill set. They didn't know how a scrum worked, and they didn't have contacts in the parliamentary press gallery, but I did. I'm not bragging—I'm just saying I kind of knew that world. I knew how a scrum worked because I had done a hundred of them. And so I said, "I should be the field producer. I should take the unit to Ottawa." No argument from anyone.

It took a while for those relationships to mature. At first, nobody really knew who we were. We were sort of a sideshow carnival act, barking away at the periphery of news, but it didn't take very long before people who worked in newsrooms across the country started to watch *This Hour Has 22 Minutes*—some, I think, with a sense of envy, because *22 Minutes* was not beholden to the journalistic policy guidebook, and we could do and say things that they might have thought, but that they could not say.

We very quickly developed a fan base within the world of CBC news, which proved to be an incredible resource for the program. We could piggyback on satellite feeds—this was unheard of for a variety show. It was also unheard of for a variety show, as we did in the second season, to piggyback on the ability to get credentials to visit the White House or 10 Downing Street.

But while the field team had succeeded in capturing appearances by the likes of Conrad Black and Preston Manning, one really big fish still eluded them.

GEOFF D'EON

We eventually got the prime minister to appear on our show, which was a huge coup. I made a relationship with the people in Chrétien's office over a period of weeks, and eventually they agreed to do it. We didn't tell them what the script would be; that was part of the condition. The prime minister just had to agree to appear on the show. So they did their calculations and they thought, "Okay. Chances are they are not going to be vicious. Chances are it's going to be funny. It will be at our expense, but you know what? We will look big for having done it." So they agreed to do it. It was Marg Delahunty, me, and Peter Sutherland in Ottawa.

RICK MERCER

That was, obviously, the Holy Grail. Once we realized the value—how much attention we would get in getting these people—and then, once we realized we could get them, I mean, that was a huge deal. Obviously, the prime minister was the one that we all had our eye on.

GEOFF D'EON

We show up. We quickly explain what it is we are doing. The prime minister has no idea what is going to be said. I'm directing a bit. "Prime Minister, you will be sitting here. Marg is going to come through the door, the cameraman will be following her, and she will just do a commentary."

And he said, "Okay."

PETER SUTHERLAND

I remember we were in the prime minister's office and I was looking at the heavy window light coming in, which would make it impossible to shoot him against the heavy backlight. So I said, "Mr. Prime Minister, I'm going to have to turn your desk around." He said, "No problem; I'll help you."

I said, "You don't have to do that."

He said, "No, come on, let's go!"

So he turned his desk around with me. He was just that kind of guy.

GEOFF D'EON

I said, "Now everyone has to leave," so everybody left the room. So now I am sitting in the prime minister's office in the Centre Block, with just me and Peter and him, and my head is exploding. I'm going, "I can't believe that this is actually happening." The door opens. Mary comes in.

"Mr. Prime Minister, how are the balls of your feet?" Then she proceeds to go sit right on his desk. Like, way closer than anybody should sit next to anybody. She sat right on his desk, a foot from where he was sitting, and got right in his face and did this commentary. And he had one line that he wanted to get out, which he squeezed in: "Where is my RCMP?"

So the bit finished, and Mary had done a pretty good job, but I thought it needed to be done again. So, again, there was a surreal moment where I found myself giving stage directions to the prime minister about when he should use that line, and how I didn't think he should interrupt her. I mean, my head was exploding. And he took it! It was great! So Mary came in, and we did take two. She was dressed in a golfer's uniform and she teased the prime minister about some file he had screwed up on, and she said, "Ah, we'll call it a mulligan. But let's not do that again." It was kind of surreal.

He enjoyed it. He didn't really know *This Hour Has 22 Minutes* that well. Apparently, he didn't watch a lot of television, and when he did, he watched SRC—French television. He kind of knew that there was a show called *22 Minutes,* and he had been briefed. Apparently, they showed him a piece of tape of Marg Delahunty ambushing Garth Brooks which had just happened a couple of weeks before. So he knew Mary was this loudmouthed, barky character called Marg Delahunty, but he didn't really know what he was getting into. I thought that was a great credit to him.

And of course he looked good. The piece aired, and he looked great. We looked amazing! *22 Minutes* had the prime minister on that week, so it was a huge score for us, and it was good for him—at which point everybody understood that to appear on *This Hour Has 22 Minutes* was a badge of success. If you were an MP or a minister, and you worked on Parliament Hill and *22 Minutes* came after you, that was a good thing. There were bragging rights associated with that.

• • •

GEOFF D'EON

We did dozens of trips to Ottawa, and in some of them we did ambushes, some of them were pre-arranged appearances by politicians, some of them were songs that we would do. We did some music videos involving politicians. Rick used to like doing those.

PETER SUTHERLAND

We would land in Ottawa, and Geoff would be on one phone and Rick would be on the other, trying to get three caucuses together to sing a stupid song. A lot of them didn't want to do it, but they did it.

GEOFF D'EON

Rick was a big Trooper fan. Rick wanted to do a music video using "Raise a Little Hell," the focus of which was—vote. There is a lyric in the song that says, "If you don't like what you got, why don't you change it?" and so we had politicians lip-synching. We had the Chrétien cabinet lip-synching to "Raise a Little Hell," which culminated in Jean Chrétien sticking his head out the door for the button at the end, saying "Vote!"

RICK MERCER

I can tell you what the inspiration was for that. When I was a kid, [American music and dance TV show] *Solid Gold* was the big show, and near the end of *Solid Gold*, they went out into the street and people lip-synced a popular disco song. I always loved it. I knew it was cheesy, but I always thought, "That is the most popular part of this show, and no one will admit it." And I remember thinking, "That could be a whole show unto itself," because, when I was a kid, I only thought in terms of television. It was like—that could be a whole show. People lip-synching. Of course, the way the world evolved, it kind of became that way.

But, anyway, that was the impetus.

The "Raise a Little Hell" thing was one of my favourite pieces that I ever did. It was one of my first forays into—I won't say "using comedy for activism"—but the fact that it was, essentially, a public-service announcement encouraging young people to vote, and had everyone involved, was a big coup.

Geoff and I, shooting something like that, we were in heaven. To us, that was heaven.

Back in those days, of course, *22 Minutes* did not have permission for the vast majority of the things that they did. As a non-owner [of the show], it was never my concern, but it was only much later in my TV career that I learned you can't just put music on television! [*laughing*]

And, you can't just go—like, there was footage of Jean Chrétien riding a bicycle in Beijing, this famous piece of news footage, right? And he gets on this bicycle and rides away. And I realized that if you cut at a certain point, it looks like he almost takes a spill. So I said, "Can we get the footage of Elliott flying over the moon from *ET*?" You know, with ET in the basket. And, they would go, "We'll see if we can get the footage." They'd come back and go, "Yes, we can get the footage."

Well, that didn't mean, "Yes, we had a department that contacted the studio that owns that footage, and we acquired that footage."

That meant, "Yes, someone will go to the video store, rent the movie, and we will take it, put it in the machine, and copy it"—which you're not allowed to do—"and we will just put it on television." I mean, it's outrageous!

I think, retroactively, a lot of those things were straightened out. But certainly, there's no mechanism to take a scene from *ET* and cut it into a television show that's turning around in twenty-four hours.

But honestly, I didn't know any better.

• • •

RICK MERCER

I had to go to Ottawa, ostensibly for the budget. In those days, I'd go to Ottawa for any reason at all. I realized that this is what was going to make the show famous—not sketches, as much as sketches were great. That's not what was going to make the show famous.

So me going to Ottawa, that was really important. I was going for budget day, and I realized very quickly that budget day is, like, the most boring thing in the world you can cover. I mean, everyone's in lock-up; it's just terrible.

So I contacted Chrétien's office—they were sailing high in the polls at the time—and they said, "You hang around and we'll get you in the Rotunda [in the Centre Block on Parliament Hill] there, sometime between say ten and two o'clock."

I was like, "No, that's not good. Plus, it can't be in the Rotunda. I want to go to Harvey's." And he was like, "Are you mental? Do you want the prime minister to meet you at a fast food restaurant?"

See, I'd heard through the grapevine that Chrétien loved Harvey's. And I'd also heard, from an RCMP officer, that when Chrétien would leave late at night, he would go to the drive-through at Harvey's, and he'd get a cheeseburger and fries and all the business. He would eat it in the car, or he would eat it at home and then he'd throw the bag out the door, and the RCMP would get rid of the bag—just like anyone who's hiding their fast-food habit from their wife!

And apparently, [his wife] Aline came along one night, and she found him face and eyes into the Harvey's, and she put a stop to it. He couldn't go to Harvey's anymore, because he's in his sixties, then, I suppose, and she's like, "You can't be eating Harvey's all the time."

But I heard it was his favourite place. So I said, "I want to go to Harvey's." I pitched it left, right, and centre, and they said, "We'll get back to you. But, this is not happening—that's insane, right? Plus, it's essentially endorsing a restaurant chain. It's not going to happen."

Then they called back and said, "Okay, we'll do it!" And I thought I was a genius, because he likes Harvey's so much that he decided to do it so he'd get to eat Harvey's. And he'd have to say to his wife, "Well, I had to. It was my job."

PETER SUTHERLAND

We went in and checked out the place; we decided on a table and we waited about half an hour, and then all of a sudden we heard these sirens, a whole motorcade of cars with red cherries.

I looked at Geoff and Rick and I said, "Oh my God, we are so powerful! This show is so powerful. We've just summoned the prime minister of Canada. We have the power to make this happen." And it was really happening.

I just felt like, "Wow, this show really has a lot of clout." And we all giggled like little kids.

RICK MERCER

We were there, and the prime minister's motorcade shows up, way on the other end of town, on budget day!

But in hindsight, I realized what happened was—it was budget day. Paul Martin—I think it was the first time they'd balanced the books, and it was a big hullabaloo. But in some newspapers, all over the country, the day after budget day, there were pictures of me and Chrétien at the Harvey's.

And Paul Martin, the rock-star finance minister who'd dragged Canada's finances into the black, he was on page two. So, if you were completely mercenary, you would realize the prime minister's office said, "If we do this, we can move this photo and it will take some of the attention away from Paul Martin." And the history has taught us that there was, essentially, an all-out war going on between those two offices, so, it's entirely believable.

But imagine! We summoned the prime minister. To Harvey's.

I mean, it was amazing.

• • •

GEOFF D'EON

Celebrity appearances became a big part of the show. Greg Thomey, one of the funniest people I've ever worked with, came up with this idea called "Celebrity Headlock." I said, "What is it?" He said, "We just talk to famous people and get them to put me in a headlock." I said, "Really?" He said, "Yeah, it's going to be funny." So we started doing them. And my God, they were hilarious! They took fifteen seconds to do. Anybody famous we ever ran into, Thomey said, "Can we do this thing called 'Celebrity Headlock?'"

We had so much fun with this. My favourite was Colin Powell. We went to an official reception at the Library of Congress and all of the movers and shakers in George W. Bush's administration were there. They were all there in tuxedos. Women were in evening gowns. There was a small media contingent and we had accreditation for it. They had no idea who we were; we looked like a news crew. He went up to a whole bunch of people that night including Tom Brokaw, but my favourite was he went up to Colin Powell, the secretary of defense, and Colin Powell agreed to put Greg Thomey in a headlock.

One of the more surreal moments of my field-producing career. There were a lot of surreal moments. There were a lot of times where I almost couldn't believe what was happening. I was in this situation where people were doing outlandish things simply because we asked them to.

• • •

GEOFF D'EON

Mary had her own great idea, which was called "The Marg Delahunty Sleepover."

We would line up politicians in advance who would literally get into bed with one another and have a political discussion. Crazy, genius, funny idea. Those segments were successful. When you have [Member of Parliament] Myron Thompson from Wild Rose country—a cowboy, a crusty old redneck from Alberta—in bed with Svend Robinson, a gay NDP MP, that is a coup. And then you add [MP] Elsie Wayne, crazy New Brunswicker, and [NDP leader] Alexa McDonough, and you are literally putting politicians of different stripes in bed together.

That is a funny idea, and it was executed with very sparse resources. I would book a hotel that had a suite. I would tell the hotel in advance that I needed two king-sized beds brought in and jammed together to look like one giant bed. And, of course, the hotels were happy to do it.

Interestingly, Myron Thompson didn't take his cowboy boots off. Alexa McDonough had on pink slippers. People's feet were sticking out the end of the bed, and then we saw these cowboy boots.

These were great ideas—and my job was to help execute them.

• • •

GEOFF D'EON

There was a very interesting dynamic inside *This Hour Has 22 Minutes* between Rick and Mary. Very competitive. They each wanted to have the best segment on the show on a given week.

I remember when Mary's "Prime Minister" sketch played on the Friday night, and the audience went ape. They freaked out. The room exploded with applause. And the following week, on Monday, Rick came to see me. And he said, "So you got the prime minister for Mary. What are the chances of getting in the White House?" which was sort of thrilling and terrifying for me at the same time.

The competitive dynamic between Mary and Rick was real, and it had a profound influence on the quality of the show. It was like Lennon and McCartney. One of them would come in with "Eleanor Rigby," and the next week somebody would come in with "A Day in the Life." The competitiveness was real, and it resulted in some excellent, excellent television.

RICK MERCER

Once Walsh started doing Marg Delahunty, I knew that she had a lock on the ambush, and no one could touch her because she was just so good at it and it was so brilliant. Plus, because, she was Marg, I felt she had an advantage because Marg, being the saucy aunt, could say things that I, as a young white male, could never say.

There was also a respect issue. It's like, "You can't say that to the premier of that province." You know, someone might say that's disrespectful or rude to me, whereas with Marg, all bets are off, because everyone knows that lady. She's the one at the wedding who is going to say the thing that everyone is thinking, but no one can believe that she said it out loud, right?

And she's fearless. I mean, as a performer—and I know Mary would actually say that's not true, because, like all performers, she's actually suffering the nerves—but by all appearances, she is fearless. I mean, the outfits alone that she has worn in places like the Hall of Honour. It's the House of Parliament!

I defy anyone to walk in there and not feel intimidated by the surroundings, and the pomp and the circumstances that surround the House of Commons.

Walsh would go in there, and she'd just own it.

And then, in March 1997, Marg Delahunty transformed into Marg, Princess Warrior (a nod to the popular Xena: Warrior Princess television character made famous by Lucy Lawless), and all bets were off. Her first target was Ontario premier Mike Harris: "Mike, don't make me come back and smite you!"

GEOFF D'EON

It was an amazing moment, really. It was like Superman going into a phone booth, except this was Superwoman, and she would just drop the disguise and raise a sword and then it was game on, and what had been a routine, fairly boring scrum, became a full on attack on Mike Harris and the so-called "Common Sense Revolution."

She ripped him a new one, and it was the most interesting thing that happened in the Ontario provincial legislature that month, I can assure you. Even people who frowned on it and thought it was inappropriate, they had to admit it was pretty damn interesting.

There was nothing like this on television at the time. And not being a journalistic show, balance and fairness had nothing to do with it. It was saying things that we felt needed to be said. And what better person to excoriate Mike Harris than Marg Delahunty? Perfect.

PETER SUTHERLAND

I have a lot of respect for Mary. She's very brave and very brash.

GEOFF D'EON

It was so much fun. I had the best job of anyone I knew at CBC. When I first left the news department, people thought I was crazy. By about Season 5, people were saying, "How do I get your job?" Of course, by Season 5, we were travelling extensively.

We ambushed [Alberta premier] Ralph Klein, which was very controversial in Edmonton. We knew that if we asked for credentials in Edmonton we wouldn't get them, because Ralph Klein was one of our favourite targets. We picked on Ralph Klein relentlessly; he became a running gag.

So we snuck into the legislative building. In every city, we had allies in the newsrooms, and in Edmonton we had an ally who said, "If you want to get into the legislature for the scrum, just walk right through. You go through this door. There will be a security guard. Just walk in, say 'hi,' and keep going."

So we're in Edmonton, myself and Mary and Peter Sutherland. Mary is dressing as Marg, Princess Warrior, and strapping on the belt and the sword and the shoulder pads in the hotel room. It's like she is girding herself for battle, and she's running through the script. She's got pages and pages of script, and I'm saying, "It's all brilliant, but it's way too long. Cut it by seventy-five per cent. You've got four pages there, you need one."

And then she would throw on a huge overcoat, which completely covered up her wardrobe, although you could see her red boots, and then Pete Sutherland would drive and we'd park in the media section of the parking lot. We walked through the door, right past the security guard. I looked over. I said, "Good day," and he said, "Good day," and we walked in, and then we tried to be inconspicuous. Mary wouldn't take the coat off.

We had allies there. The CBC reporter would always give us a nod and a wink, and they would say, "The scrum is going to happen here." So we would be prepared. Mary would be running through the script in her head.

And Ralph Klein came out of his office to do the scrum. We joined in the scrum at the periphery, very subtly, quietly at first. Just on the edge. We waited. I always said to the guys, we are not going to just take over the scrum, we are going to wait for our moment. Let them deal with the story of the day.

So Ralph Klein dealt with the story of the day, and then I gave the signal to Mary. She threw off the coat. "Mr. Klein! Mr. Klein!" And she pulled out two toy pistols. They were obviously and clearly toy pistols. They were little plastic silver things with red caps on the end. And she gave him a tongue-lashing. It was very funny. People laughed, including Ralph Klein. He took it really well, and we got the hell out of there.

At breakfast the next morning, in the *Edmonton Journal*, there was a big picture of Mary Walsh right next to Ralph Klein with these two guns pointed in the air, and the headline was, "This Was Not Funny." And the angle they chose to pursue was how inappropriate it was that anybody, a comedian or anybody, would use guns of any kind in the provincial legislature. So we took a bit of a spanking over that.

But what I found funny was, the caption said, "This Was Not Funny." The photograph shows Ralph Klein laughing, Mary Walsh in full rant, and everyone in the picture roaring with laughter. So lighten up, Edmonton.

• • •

RICK MERCER

I felt that Mary Walsh had taken the ambush to a whole new level, and it was something that couldn't be touched. I could do it, but basically it was like, suddenly someone's doing your act down the street, and it's better. Mary was doing it in a way that just made the ambush her own, so I started looking for something else.

I loved those trips to Ottawa, and I thought—we'll go to the States.

GEOFF D'EON

So I said, "Sure, Rick, I'll do what I can." There was a guy called Henry Champ, a Canadian journalist. He had worked for years at NBC, he'd had a long storied career at NBC, and then he worked at CBC Newsworld in Halifax for years. So we kind of knew Henry Champ, this crusty old news guy. And Henry, by this time, was back in the Washington bureau, working for Newsworld.

So I called Henry Champ and I said, "Henry, how difficult is it to get credentials to get into the White House?" And he said, "Oh, I can help you with that. You've got to fax your names and your passports to this address, and you just ask for temporary credentials. And you can use my name as a reference if you need to." So we did.

A few weeks later, Rick and Peter and myself were on the southern portico of the White House, shouting at Bill Clinton as he walked to a helicopter. This was really heady stuff. The world was different then. It was pre-9/11.

RICK MERCER

Of course, the problem was, in the States, we had zero access—it was not like we could walk into the Capitol Building.

I went down with a bunch of different ideas over time, to try to make America work, and it worked for a little bit, just because, I guess, the audience would think, "That's cool—Rick's in Washington, and there's the White House and the press gallery room." That's all kind of exciting, but nothing really clicked until "Talking to Americans."

GEOFF D'EON

"Talking to Americans" came about by accident.

GERALD LUNZ

They were in Washington, Rick and Geoff and Sudsy [Peter Sutherland], the shooter, just a three-man band.

GEOFF D'EON

We went to Washington to try and get Bill Clinton at the White House, and we wanted to record a Rick Mercer "Streeter" with the Capitol Building behind us, which we did.

Our flight was at five o'clock in the evening to come back to Halifax, and it was about noon and we were done—we didn't have anything to do before we had to head to the airport. We had a couple of hours to kill.

GERALD LUNZ

They had done some stuff and then everything dried up, and they said, "What are we going to do? We've got to put something together here, we've got to come back with some minutes."

GEOFF D'EON

Rick and I and Peter Sutherland were sitting on a bench right by the Capitol Building and these tourists were walking by—busloads of tourists, mostly elderly Americans. We were watching them go by and Rick said, "Why don't I ask them a few questions?"

Sure. We weren't doing anything else. So Pete put the camera on his shoulder and we approached a group of American senior citizens who had just come off a bus and were walking toward the Capitol Building for their tour.

RICK MERCER

I just started talking to people on the street and I was telling them that—I think the first one was that the president of Canada was in town for the summit between the president of Canada and the president of the United States. And people were like, "Oh, yes! I heard that on the radio."

I was thinking, "Oh! They haven't heard it, but they want to be polite to us, so they're just going to pretend they've heard it." I said the story was a big story in Canada, because the question was whether it should be called the

Clinton/Benmergui Summit or the Benmergui/Clinton Summit, because our president was [Canadian radio and television personality] Ralph Benmergui. And they all weighed in on it, mostly saying that it should be the Benmergui/Clinton Summit. They were fine with that. But it was just so absurd.

GERALD LUNZ

It looked so authentic, it really did. Sudsy with the big camera on his shoulder and a sun-gun light. Geoff, the older producer, with the pad and everything. Rick in a box suit with a mic that had a flag on it that looked really pro. So he looked like media.

GEOFF D'EON

They walked away, and we went back and sat on the bench and looked at each other and said, "Geez, that worked."

GERALD LUNZ

If you talk to people and say, "What do you think of...?" do you know what is the first thing they think?

"I'm on TV. I am on TV." And people have opinions on shit they don't know anything about. But they are on TV.

Rick has such a straight face; he's like a little bold monkey. And it was just so funny.

GEOFF D'EON

Rick said, "Let's do some more." So over the next hour, we just stopped people, mostly older white people, because that was the tourist flow on Capitol Hill at the time, and we asked them a series of increasingly preposterous questions, all of which they answered with great seriousness and generosity.

After about an hour, we stopped, and I said to Rick, "I think we've got something here." And Rick said, "Yeah, there's something. I don't know what we can do with it, but there is something." Pete liked it, and Pete is always a good judge.

So we went back to Halifax, and I went into the edit suite, because part of my job was to edit the pieces that we had shot, and I sat with an editor, Greg Antworth, and I said, "I've just got a bunch of streeters with Americans answering daft questions and I want to try and package it somehow."

We started just rough-cutting it together, and we could tell within, like, fifteen minutes: there's something in here. This is pretty funny. We cut it fast-paced like we do. And then I said, "I think there's a piece here. We should give it a name."

There was a guy I used to watch every week on a show called *The McLaughlin Group* and he was an old, crusty American political commentator. And [*shrill*] this is how he spoke. So I thought of a name: "Talking to Americans." And I went in the booth and I said, "Taaaalllkiiiiing tooo Americaaans!" Then we found a piece of music; a big orchestral piece. By the end of that shift, we had this segment which had a name, it had music, and it had Rick asking ridiculous questions to a bunch of unsuspecting Americans who, because of their good-naturedness, and, frankly, their ignorance, answered the questions. They took them seriously.

I was pretty sure that we had something good. Didn't know for sure. Friday night, live audience—played it in front of the room. The room went crazy. People laughed and cheered and clapped. Rick and I looked at each other after the show and we said, "There is something here, man. This is good."

At the producer meeting after the show, Michael Donovan said, "Uh, yes, uh, that was very funny. Very amusing. We should do more of those."

So I said, "Fine—I'm in!"

RICK MERCER

We called it "Talking to Americans," and we put it on TV, and it was an overnight, instant success. I mean, the minute it played back, people went so crazy. I thought—unlike some things—this is a well that I will be able to go back to, time and time again.

GERALD LUNZ

It's a classic Canadian joke. We have been telling this joke since my old uncles. The Americans came up from Detroit in June with the skis on the car. It's that whole thing of "Who are we?" and "They don't know anything about us." So it was a field day. And that's how it started.

GEOFF D'EON

Then we started to organize specific "Talking to Americans" shoots. The formula was so simple: it was three guys—one who's obviously a cameraman, one who's obviously a news reporter in a suit, and the guy who is holding a reflector board. That must be the producer; he's got a clipboard and he has questions.

So we asked the writers to come up with some silly questions, and then we would get on a plane and we would fly to wherever. We went to New York; I think that was one of the very first ones we did. We went to Times Square and we asked people about whether the bombing of the West Edmonton Mall was appropriate, and people said yes. It didn't seem to matter how absurd the question was—as long as the questions were about Canada, people had no idea what we were talking about.

Every time we went away, we came back with a home run. They just all worked. And it got to the point where the writers would come up with questions, we would get on the plane, and then Rick and I would filter through the questions and say, "Not crazy enough; not absurd enough," and we would just go for the most outrageous ones and write some fresh ones.

EDWARD KAY

I wrote some questions for it. People would always ask me, "Did he have to go for hours and hours to find eight people that were that ignorant?" and the shocking thing is that it's the other way around. I'm not kidding. They had thirty or forty or fifty people who thought that there was a Peter Man's Bridge. Or "Congratulations, Canada on your first thousand miles of paved highway!" There were dozens of them, although I will say that I think a lot of the people are just very agreeable. Despite what is going on in the world right now, when you are actually in America, most Americans want to be agreeable. So if you say, "Congratulations, Canada, on your first thousand miles of paved highway," most of them won't call you on it.

GEOFF D'EON

Over the years, people have said to me, "Come on, you edited out the people who cottoned on." Seriously—people did not cotton on. Their ignorance about Canada is boundless. They just don't care. They just don't know. We are not a threat to them. We are less interesting than Mexico. We are this benign neighbour in the frozen North that they don't know anything about.

RICK MERCER

It was such a great gig. I mean, for starters, to be on the road with Pete Sutherland and Geoff D'Eon was always a pleasure. I honestly can't remember one cross word. I mean, maybe there might have been some grumpy comments here and there, but honestly, I can't think of one time. And being on the road is exhausting, so you want to be on the road with the right people.

All I can think of is the good times. We had tremendously good times. We all liked to eat, and we could go anywhere. I mean, literally, all we needed was a city with a landmark. A number of times we went to cities based on restaurant reviews. We were like, "This place has got great ribs! It's in Arkansas! Let's go there!" None of us had seen a ballgame in Wrigley Park. "Well, then, next week, let's go to Chicago!"

What a gift that was—three buddies who like each other, on the road. And it wasn't the hardest work. Once you got the right couple of questions, it was a little bit time-consuming. But certainly there's harder work out there than doing "Talking to Americans."

GEOFF D'EON

"Talking to Americans" became one of the most successful and popular segments in the show. They were dead easy to do. We would go to Chicago; we would set up on Michigan Avenue at noon, and we would be done by 1:30. We did a ninety-minute shoot, and we had more than we could use. We would ask the craziest questions we could think of, and then we would go to a baseball game at Wrigley Field. It was fish in a barrel.

I remember we were on the tarmac in Boston; we were flying back from somewhere else, and we were waiting for the Boston flight to take off. Rick turned to me and said, "We haven't done Boston. What's in Boston?"

I said, "Harvard," and his face lit up like a Christmas tree. Two weeks later, we were in the quadrangles at Harvard and we were asking people about the Saskatchewan seal hunt. We had a professor tell us that he thought the Saskatchewan seal hunt was immoral. We had a political science student congratulating Prime Minister Tim Horton on his double-double. It was the joke that just kept on giving. You couldn't really lose with a "Talking to Americans" segment.

RICK MERCER

Every week I ever shot "Talking to Americans," I'd think, "Oh, my God! If there was ever any way that any of these people could ever see this, I would die of embarrassment," because it was before YouTube.

I thought, "Luckily there will never, ever be a way for someone in Arkansas to watch Rick on the CBC. That will never happen in a million years."

GEOFF D'EON

One of the early places we went was Little Rock Arkansas, Bill Clinton's hometown. He was the president at the time. We stood in front of the Capitol building in Little Rock and we told people that their Capitol building was beautiful, and that the one in Canada was modelled on theirs, except ours was made of ice, and because of global warming, it was melting. And there was a big controversy in Canada about whether we should try and save it or let it melt, and the debate was huge in Canada—it was the number one news story in Canada right now. "People are talking about building a giant dome over the Parliament Building in Ottawa to stop it from melting." And what did people think? We called it the "National Igloo." And did people think Canada should preserve its National Igloo? Everybody believed us. Not one person batted an eyelid.

RICK MERCER

That one was a game-changer.

GEOFF D'EON

So that shoot went really well, and we asked people about the governor. "What kind of guy is the governor?" Mike Huckabee. "Oh, he's a smart man. Oh, yeah, he's a lawyer by training." One of the people who worked in the Capitol building came out—a woman, and we talked to her, and because we were from Canada, they were polite and wanted to help us out.

The first thing we would say was, "Excuse me, we're from Canada. Do you have a few minutes to talk to Canadians?" And they would go, "Well, yeah, sure," because Americans are polite. And she said to us, "Well, the governor is in, you know." And she pointed over to the side of the building where there was a black limousine. "The governor is in. Mike Huckabee. Yes, he's a great man. A Christian man." And off she went.

RICK MERCER

I remember saying to Geoff, "Do you think we'd get in trouble if we put a governor on 'Talking to Americans'"? And he said, "Do you think you can convince the governor that Canada's Parliament building is made out of ice?"

And I was like, "Those are fighting words! Now my powers to bullshit will be on maximum!"

GEOFF D'EON

Working with Rick is never boring, and sometimes it's a little frightening. So when Rick says, "We are going to go get the governor," I go, "Holy crap. Really?" And of course, he's absolutely right.

But you can't just walk into the governor's office. We can't ambush him. So we go into the Capitol building, and we ask the receptionist: "We'd like to see the governor." Next thing we know, one of the governor's communications people is with us. Very polite, very accommodating.

"You're all the way from Canada? What are you doing here?" And we fibbed. We said we were doing a travel piece about different parts of America and why Canadians should come and visit. There was a little dishonesty. But it was all for a good cause.

We say to the communications guy: "There's just been a major archaeological discovery in Canada. We have unearthed an ancient igloo. It's thousands of years old, in the far North, and we've figured out a way to preserve it. It's a huge story in Canada, the preservation of this National Igloo. And what we would like is for the governor to come on camera and say, 'Congratulations, Canada, on preserving your National Igloo.'"

He said, "Yeah, let me see what I can do." They bring us a cup of coffee and everyone is treating us really well, and he comes out and says, "Yeah, sure, the governor says come on up." So we go on up, and the next thing we know, the governor comes out the door and he says, "How can I help you boys?"

RICK MERCER

We just went in and talked our way all the way up! And we were terrified, too, because there was a chain gang outside putting Christmas decorations up. A chain gang, and we're inside!

This is just when Google was starting, and I was like, "If someone Googles us…" because we gave them our names. And if they'd Googled me, "Talking to Americans" probably would have been near the top, at that point.

GEOFF D'EON

So we explain that we would like him to say, "Congratulations, Canada, on saving your National Igloo."

"Happy to do it."

The camera pans down on him. "Hi, I'm Mike Huckabee, governor of Arkansas. Congratulations, Canada, on preserving your National Igloo."

We said, "Thank you very much," and we got the hell out of there, because all that communications guy had to do was place one phone call to anybody in Canada and say, "We have this crew down here asking about the National Igloo," and we would have been busted.

So of course, when the piece was cut, we had all these people talking about the National Igloo, and that our Parliament buildings are made of ice, but the button to the piece is the governor congratulating Canada on the preservation of the National Igloo. It's sleight-of-hand, but it is really, really funny.

And that busted open a whole new area of possibility in the Mary-Rick, Lennon-McCartney competition thing.

RICK MERCER

The first couple of times I went to the United States for "Talking to Americans," there were bean-counters at the show who were not into it at all, because it was expensive. And after two or three segments, it was never suggested that it was expensive—in fact, the only question was, "When are you going back?"

• • •

GEOFF D'EON

It was March 2000, and we wanted to get George W. Bush. He was an obvious target, because he had said, "You are not going to catch me out on the names of foreign leaders"—because he had already been caught out. He couldn't remember the name of the president of Pakistan.

So we went, "Okay, let's go get him." We got on an airplane and flew to Detroit. We had a long discussion about the name that we were going to use to trick him. We knew that we were going to give Jean Chrétien a false name, and ask George W. Bush about the support of this fictional Canadian prime minister. So, on the plane we were brainstorming names that sounded like they might be plausible, and I came up with Jean Poutine. Rick loved it and we said, "That's it!"

RICK MERCER

I give Geoff credit for "Jean Poutine," because there was no chance we were going to get me and George W. Bush. Even though we're talking years ago, this is still the man who is going to be the Republican nominee. Plus, we had talked to people who had been on the road with the candidate. He was in a bubble. He was taking fewer questions than anyone had ever taken. That was the big story—that this guy would not take questions. He would take very few a day, only by accredited people on the bus. We talked to people who'd been with him every day, for the duration, and he'd not taken any local questions. And they were, like, "Yeah, you can stand there, and you can yell, but it's not going to happen." So part of me wasn't prepared.

GEOFF D'EON

We went to this rally in a big arena in Canton Township, which is a suburb of Detroit. There were a few thousand people there. There was a media platform. He was going to make a speech, and there were going to be no questions. So I thought, "How are we going to get to him?"

There was only one way in from the secure area of this arena to the stage, so very quickly it became obvious—he's going to come out that door, and he's going to go on stage. He's going to make his speech, and he's probably going to leave the same way.

So we just hung back and waited. And sure enough, he came out that door, and he went up on stage, and he made about a twenty-minute election speech. We wriggled and pushed our way to the front of this little cordon, and we knew that he would be walking right past us. There were a few other reporters there and the security was all over, and there were communications people saying, "He's not taking questions. Don't bother asking."

We were one of maybe six or seven cameras in that little area. Then George W. Bush came off the stage, and he started signing autographs, and he was sort of working his way down that line. When he got to where the cameras were, he sort of picked up his pace, and Rick shouted out, "Question from Canada!"

RICK MERCER

Suddenly I was there, and it was like, "Question from Canada!"—entirely confident that he was not going to stop, because there were people yelling all around me. And he stopped, and he turned towards me. That pleasant, polite American—I guess he decided he couldn't keep walking when he heard that.

GEOFF D'EON

Very smart thing to do. Very few Canadian reporters would have been covering that campaign. And it intrigued Bush, you could just tell. He kind of turned, and in a way that only George W. Bush can do, he said, "What about it?"

Then Rick shouted out the question: "Prime Minister Jean Poutine says that you are the man to lead America into the twenty-first century. So what do you think of his endorsement?" He said it really fast, and he said it really loud, and for whatever reason, George W. Bush went for it hook, line, and sinker.

He said, "Well, I appreciate his strong endorsement, and he knows the importance of free trade, and I look forward to working with him," and off he went.

We looked at each other and we went, "Oh. My. God. This is goooold!" CNN and all the networks were there. We went back to our hotel, and that night all the CNN people and all the people from all the major news networks were post-morteming the day and filing their news reports. I was sitting there thinking, "We have got this little nugget which will mean nothing to them, but it means a whole lot to us."

So we didn't tell anybody, and we put that little piece together, and it caused a minor international incident.

RICK MERCER

The ramifications were huge, because that became an American news story. I was suddenly an American news story, and I realized how much bigger the United States is than Canada. When we became part of the news story in a presidential election, there was, like, ninety-five phone calls a morning! I could have just done media morning, noon, and night. Not for long—we were only, like, a twenty-four-hour story—but it was unbelievable.

GEOFF D'EON

It got picked up by all of the Canadian papers; the *Ottawa Citizen* ran a piece; the *Toronto Star* ran a piece; Canadian Press ran a piece. Every Canadian newspaper ran a piece about how Rick Mercer from *This Hour Has 22 Minutes* had tricked George W. Bush, and how George W. Bush apparently believed the prime minister of Canada's name was Jean Poutine.

RICK MERCER

It was very exciting. The fallout was that George Bush, his people, only knew the CBC as a news organization. So they felt that they had been ambushed by CBC News. And, allegedly—I've heard this from many people over the years—multiple times, George Bush's people refused to talk to the CBC, and cited "Talking to Americans" as the reason why. And each time, the producer of whatever show it was had to explain, "That's actually a comedy show."

GEOFF D'EON

Years later, George W. Bush visited Halifax as the president. It was a big deal; he went down to Pier 21; the streets were cordoned off, there were motorcades. He made a speech, which Newsworld carried live, and which I watched in my office at CBC. It was actually a pretty good speech; it was written by David Frum, a Canadian, so it was full of Canadian references. And he said things like, "It sure is nice to be here in Canada, where, when people wave at you, they use all the fingers on their hands."

Chrétien was there, and Bush said, "Mr. Prime Minister, I have one re-gret about my visit to Canada." And he paused and said, "I was really hoping to meet Jean Poutine."

My head exploded. I think I stood on my desk yelling, "Yes!" We had made a small mark in presidential history. It's a small mark, but it's a fun one. And it's indelible.

RICK MERCER

Yeah, that was cool! Not that I'm a big fan of George W. Bush's, but I thought, "Oh! He actually remembers that!" If I ever see him in an airport, I will be able to go over and say, "Hey, I'm the guy who yelled about Jean Poutine," and we might have something to talk about.

• • •

GEOFF D'EON

We had enough material for a special. I suggested it to Rick and Gerald first. I said, "Guys, seriously, this is such a popular segment and we have a bunch of stuff in the can; all we've got to do is go shoot another maybe ten or fifteen minutes of fresh stuff and we would have a really good special."

There was a bunch of negotiations with the network, and it took a while to put it together, but the network obviously wanted it, and ordered it up. I had to direct and produce the special, working with other producers from *22 Minutes* to put the resources together.

It wasn't difficult. We went to San Francisco and we had people sing Canada's national anthem, "O Canada, a great big empty land." Again, it was fish in a barrel. Anything we could think of worked.

The one time we got caught, we were in Florida. We were at a marina in Florida; I guess it was Miami. The question we were asking people was, "Canada doesn't have a navy because we don't have access to the ocean. So a lot of people in Canada are wondering if we should just pay the American

Navy to protect us? And maybe put some Canadian sailors on American ships?" Perfectly reasonable proposition.

It was going really well and we got five or six good answers, all of which were along the lines of, "Yeah, sure. You're our friends and neighbours." Then this one guy said, "Canada doesn't have access to the ocean?"

Rick said no, with a perfectly straight face. And the guy said, "Do the people in Halifax know that?" Busted. In all the months that we had been doing this, that was one of the first times we had ever been called. And it turned out the guy was Canadian. He was a snowbird.

• • •

GEOFF D'EON

So we gathered about fifteen minutes of fresh material and I edited it with Al MacLean at CBC Halifax. We finished it in February, and we sent it up to Toronto. It sat on a shelf for a month, and it aired on April Fool's Day in 2001. It had a prime-time slot; it was like eight o'clock on a Sunday night, so we knew it was going to do well.

We were kind of batting around numbers. How many people are going to watch? We were guessing 1.5 million. That is a big number. You get 1.5 million Canadians watching anything, that's huge. And by now, specialty channels had started to come online and audience fragmentation was starting, so it was hard to get a million. So we were thinking 1.5, 1.8, something like that, but we thought 1.8 would be unbelievable. The Stanley Cup hardly gets 1.8.

There was a little lag in the time the ratings came, a day and a half usually. I was sitting in my office at CBC talking to some people and Ginny Duzak, who was the line producer, stuck her head around the door and said, "2.7."

I didn't know what she was talking about. I said, "Sorry?"

She said, "2.7 million," and we went, "WHAAAT?" It was incredible. We did a happy dance. The network confirmed that was the highest-rated comedy special in the history of CBC television. They hadn't seen numbers like that before. Wayne and Shuster didn't get those kind of numbers when there were only two channels.

It still holds today. It's still the highest-rated comedy special in Canadian television history. And then they repeated it, and on the repeat it got, like, 1.7. And then they repeated it again, and it got, like, 1.3. And then they repeated it again. They started beating this thing like a dead horse. And every time they aired it, it got more than a million viewers. It was astonishing.

RICK MERCER

None of us had heard of a number like that. We were confident we were going to break a million—but 2.7 was like, "Yeah! Those are Stanley Cup numbers!" That's without a Canadian team in the series, but still—that's a big, big number.

It had so many people talking that my father called me. My father and I are very close, and he's perhaps the most supportive person in my life. But he never, ever watched me live. He always found it too stressful to watch any of his kids do anything live. And we never talked about the show. We'd talk about politics, but we never talked about the show.

He called me up and said, "I saw the show, that *Talking to Americans* thing you did." I said, "Yeah," and he said, "Boy, a number of people have mentioned it to me, that they watched it. They liked it very much."

I said, "Dad, it's unbelievable. Like, everyone's talking about this thing." And he said, "Promise me one thing. Promise me you'll never, ever do that ever again" [*laughing*].

He was just mortified. He just thought it was shocking. But he's one of the most decent people that I know, so if it passes most people's smell test, it can offend his decency. But, yeah, he was appalled. Then we never spoke of it ever again.

GERALD LUNZ

Rick's father is always such a great supporter of Rick's and our work, and the only thing he ever said was, "I find that's kind of cheap, Rick. I think you're fooling people."

It was the only time he ever said anything negative, and that kind of clinched it. I figured, "Oh, we are done."

GEOFF D'EON

We entered it into the Gemini Awards, in the category of Best Comedy or Variety Special. I had really high hopes for it.

It got nominated, and then 9/11 happened. Rick and Gerald, who were the producers—there were two producers: Salter Street Films, and their own company, Island Edge, that they had set up to do [CBC dramatic series] *Made in Canada*—they felt that it would be inappropriate to attend the Geminis a matter of weeks later, and potentially accept an award that was mocking Americans after this devastating thing had happened. So they withdrew it from competition.

GERALD LUNZ

That's when we said, "Okay, our neighbours are really getting the shit kicked out of them."

It's so Canadian, eh? "Oh, geez, neighbours, sorry." That's why we withdrew it from the Geminis. It was a historical move. I'm sure Geoff was pissed off, but that was mostly Rick and I.

RICK MERCER

Certainly some people thought it was the wrong choice, but I kind of thought, "If I was on the air right now, I would not go down and do a 'Talking to Americans' in New York City. And I wouldn't go and do a 'Talking to Americans' in Florida right now." That's just the way I felt.

So I thought, "I'm not going to go off to this awards show and celebrate it right now." I mean, I'm proud of the show. I was proud of the show then. Sometimes awards can mean an awful lot when it comes to whether your show is renewed, or whether you're looking for an audience. But it wasn't that kind of scenario. It just felt like it wasn't the time. It just felt like it was a time to be, you know, unconditionally supportive and nothing else.

GEOFF D'EON

I was of two minds about it. I thought that it might be a mistake to withdraw it—that there was an element of political correctness in withdrawing it. But it was their call; it was their decision to make, and I respect the decision they made. It was made for the right reasons.

Rick never wanted to repeat the trick. Very shortly after that, Rick left *22 Minutes* to pursue other things, and he did not want to repeat the trick. He felt that it was a good joke, and we had taken the joke as far as it could go.

GERALD LUNZ

We walked away from it because it was the biggest thing. We had told the joke. We could tell the joke again, and I'm sure it would be really fun and people would laugh along, but then after Show 6, it would be, "Okay, we get it." It would be defining. And Rick didn't want to be defined that early in his career.

RICK MERCER

Michael [Donovan] wanted to revive it desperately, but people who produce television, they're not in the business of caring about the overall impact. I was moving on. I could have done another special, and I could still do another special. I mean, literally, every single time there's a change in leadership at the CBC, whoever's top dog will call me up and say, "Listen! Have you ever considered…?" and I know exactly what they're going to say: "Have you ever considered doing a *Talking to Americans?*"

I always say, "Yeah, I'm not going to do that anymore." because I've done it, right? I told the joke, I told it to best of my ability. Times have changed. When we started, it was pre-YouTube. People honestly—it didn't even cross their minds that it may be a prank show, or a fake news show. It was pre-*Daily Show*. I don't even know if it would work now.

It certainly was a younger man's game. I have no interest, and I wanted to move on.

Michael certainly tried to bring it back. Michael tried to continue doing it at *22 Minutes* without me—and, yeah, I put a stop to that.

GEOFF D'EON

Years later, there was a guy running CBC Television who demanded of Michael Donovan that he reintroduce *Talking to Americans*.… It was kind of levied on the show as a fiat from on high. This was like a papal decree: "You *will* go do *Talking to Americans*."

And against everyone's better judgment, it happened. Gavin Crawford was sent to Boston, but it wasn't the same. Rick found out about it, and was affronted because he felt that it was his intellectual property—he had invented that segment. He appealed to the top managers at CBC, who relented. So I don't think that piece ever saw the light of day.

GEORGE ANTHONY

There was a lot of interest on both sides for spinning out *Talking to Americans* as a series, and the only people who didn't want to do it were Rick and Gerald. Gerald said, "It's one joke! Come on." And Rick just thought it was funny that the network was all gung-ho for a series.

And Michael, of course—he would say yes to a series and then ask later which one you were talking about.

But nonetheless, the numbers were so astonishing. It was one joke, but it was a brilliant joke. Other people have tried it. It just falls flat, because it had that wonderful moment where the chemistry was just there. And that was Rick.

GEOFF D'EON

That was pretty much the end of it. I always argue that the joke wasn't solely at the expense of Americans. We weren't merely mocking the relative ignorance of Americans about Canada. I mean, we were, but in a way, the joke was kind of on us, because it revealed, if you really thought about it, how insignificant Canada is when you are considering global superpowers. We, in the public consciousness of the Americans, are about the equivalent of Belgium. That says something about who we are, in a way.

So, yeah, that joke makes fun of Americans—of course it does. We all take huge pleasure in that, but it says something about Canada, too—about how quiet and unassuming we are. We don't make a lot of enemies, and when you don't make enemies, you don't achieve notoriety. And when you don't achieve notoriety, you tend to be, relatively speaking, invisible to Americans.

I don't really blame Americans for not knowing much about Canada. I wish that they knew more about world affairs in general, and I wish that they knew more about their most important trading partner and closest neighbour, but they don't. They just don't. And the fact that they don't was a gift to us, who were trying to make people laugh.

To this day, people tell me that, of all the things *22 Minutes* did, *Talking to Americans* was one of their favourite things. I know kids who are thirty who remember their teachers showing them *Talking to Americans* in the classroom. Because it was funny, and it spoke to the value of education and why you should really know things about the world that you live in.

I think *Talking to Americans* wrote an indelible small page in Canadian comedy history.

7

A Tight Ship

1993–1999

JACK KELLUM

In the beginning, the cast used to write an awful lot of the material for the show, but as the years went on, as the show became more successful, we had to spread our wings a little more, and we started to have to bring in writers from everywhere, basically.

GERALD LUNZ

Just look at the credits of any show that rolls by. The late-night shows? It's like, "Holy fuck there are sixteen writers!" We had four! Four!

GEOFF D'EON

A lot of good writers passed through that writing room. They didn't all stick.

That was one of the challenges. There are a lot of very talented comedic writers in the country, and a lot of them came through the doors at *22 Minutes*.

JACK KELLUM

There were writers from Newfoundland, but there were writers from Alberta and Toronto and all across the country. They didn't necessarily stay all that long.

One of the difficulties of shooting the show in Halifax was that you had to make a long-term commitment for at least half a year, and if you lived in Toronto and you were married or had a partner, that was very difficult. It was a long time to be away. So there was a big turnover in the writers' room.

GERALD LUNZ

Ed [Macdonald] and the other writers really came in when we needed them, because we had been running on vapour at that point. It was so hard to push that thing up the hill.

ED MACDONALD

I came in Season 2. I had met Cathy the year before at the wrap party for Season 1, and we hit it off. That's why I got hired, basically—Cathy, I think, got me hired. I knew that there was a revolving door of writers; everybody did. I knew about ten people who had been through for like a week or two. So that's what I was expecting: I will come for two weeks, get fired, and leave. I had no intention of doing it, but I was a huge *CODCO* fan.

GERALD LUNZ

Eddie was great, because he was a Cape Bretoner. That's quite close to being a Newfoundlander—that attitude toward the rest of the world: the Islander versus the mainlander and those fuckers that control everything from away. So that was good.

ED MACDONALD

I just got a phone call out of the blue one day from Michael Donovan. They kind of knew who I was because of my live shows and stuff, but he just said, "I want to bring you in, but not this week because it's a nest of vipers down there."

And I said, "That sounds fun." But I really didn't think about it as a job or anything I would want to do, because I do not care about politics, or the news, or anything like that. I find it all kind of one-note and pointless because it's just the same story over and over again.

So he said, "Not this week, but next week." I came in and it was super weird. We were sitting in the Radio Room in the CBC Radio building on South Park Street, and it was very quiet. There seemed to be some tension in the air. But maybe that's every writers' room, I guess. I don't remember much about it, except that all I wanted to do was meet Cathy and Mary because there are whole sketches of "House of Budgell" that I think I could recite. I loved *CODCO*; it's one of my favourite shows of all time, so I just wanted to make my brother jealous. Literally, that was all I had in mind. My goal was to make the phone call and say, "Ha-ha! I met Cathy and Mary."

PAUL BELLINI

I believe I started around the first week of November 1994, which was pretty much two months into the second season. My agent had said, "Michael Donovan wants to meet you," and I was aware of *22 Minutes,* because I had watched the first season. It was on in a shitty time slot, too—like 11:30 on a Friday night. And I remember thinking, "Oh, all my favourite *CODCO* people are back." *CODCO* was a show that Scott Thompson and I worshipped.

So when I heard Michael Donovan wanted to meet me, and it was in some little coffee shop in Yorkville, I was very excited. First of all, because it was a job, and I didn't have one, having finished *The Kids in the Hall*. I was feeling a little abandoned because everyone sort of went to the States and I was the only one who didn't have an offer from *Saturday Night Live* or anything. So I got an offer on *22*, and I thought, "Wow, you're going to have to go and live in Halifax."

I didn't mind at the time. I was about, thirty-five, maybe? I was single, and I have a lot of friends in Halifax.

GERALD LUNZ

Paul Bellini—what a sweet man. He is the sweetest guy ever. And the fastest typer. He can type a hundred and forty words a minute! You put him in a room with a bunch of comics and this guy is just whizbang. Very, very interesting and very lovely man.

PAUL BELLINI

I went for a two-week trial period, because that's what they would do. They would bring everyone in for two weeks. We met in that Radio Room on Sackville Street. I liked the vibe of the room right away. I liked the oddness of the room with that ramp that sort of came into it and just the way the space was laid out. It was very unconventional. And everyone's sitting around the big table—immediate access to the cast—and I thought, "Oh, this is really exciting!" And at the time, the only writers on the show were Alan Resnick and Ed Macdonald and myself.

ED MACDONALD

[Producer] Jenipher Ritchie would call and say, "Come back next week," and I was like, "Okay," and I'd come back, but it was still a contributing-writer contract. And then about five or six weeks in, I finally went, "You know what? I don't think I want to do this." And then I got a contract.

That was my lesson in how to do TV. Be a whiny baby because the whiniest baby gets everything.

Writing for *22 Minutes* meant mastering two very different types of material: sketches and "copy jokes," which were short takes on events in the news, presented newscaster-style by cast members at the anchor desk.

GERALD LUNZ

Ed had been writing for [his sister, comedian] Bette MacDonald [*who, it should perhaps be noted, spells her last name differently than her brother*], so he was just a gem. He was exactly what the show needed at that time when the writing was in a lull, because he always knew how to write for women— funny women. He had it in his bones from writing with his sister.

And the more we were on the road, the more that took time away from writing. If we had put Mary out to do Marg Delahunty someplace, then the sketch writing would be lagging. So Ed was great.

ED MACDONALD

Cathy and Mary were not at all what I expected. I had never met anyone like them. Their relationship is really interesting, because they're like sisters in a way, but they are complete opposites. It's an interesting dynamic. I wrote a lot with Cathy. I wrote a lot of the Babe Bennetts and stuff like that. Cathy was more in my wheelhouse, because we both love sketches and we both love sketch characters, so I kind of get what she does.

PAUL BELLINI

Gerald and Rick made it clear that a lot of people had tried, but didn't fit in, 'cause they had been trying other writers at the time. So I understood that the stakes were fairly high, but I liked them right away and I got the idea of writing a copy gag right away.

I loved Gerald Lunz because he was kind of like the voice of everything. He would explain everything to me; he made it very clear what he wanted for the show and what I should do.

And I wrote this—I thought it was a stupid joke. Pierre Berton had just published a book called *Winter* that was mostly pictures of snow, so I wrote that his next book was going to be called *Dump* and there would be pictures of a dump. And for some reason, Rick Mercer loved this joke and it made it into the show and, all of a sudden I was like the big hero and everyone was going, "Oh, that's a really great joke."

I remember thinking, "Is it?" It didn't seem that great to me. But I also wasn't producing anything better, so I thought, "Okay, just take the praise; maybe it'll stick, right?"

ED MACDONALD

I wrote character monologues mainly, and desk jokes. I wrote a lot of copy jokes. That was the most tedious part. I remember a lot of Thursday nights writing a lot of copy jokes for the taping the next day. Yeah, there are still *Seinfelds* that are new to me because of years of working every Thursday night.

I have a copy joke that I always liked. It was when a lot of the Beatles reissues were coming out. It was about how if you played "Helter Skelter" backwards, you would hear Paul McCartney saying, "Buy more Beatles stuff; Ringo needs a hip."

PAUL BELLINI

There's one joke that never made it to air, and it was, probably, I think, the funniest thing. It was Mercer. He came up with this joke and he asked what I thought of it: I laughed out loud. I still, to this day, think it's hilarious.

Two companies are merging, Bombardier and Fokker, and the new company name was going to be Bomb-Fokker. And I remember I laughed so hard—but I think that they were very squeamish about having such an overt gay joke, even if it's a great pun, on the show. I'm pretty sure it didn't make it to air, but I think that is one of the funniest puns I've ever heard.

EDWARD KAY

I was hired in Season 4. I had been a freelance journalist in Toronto; I was a regular writer for the *Globe and Mail Report on Business* and something called *Eye Weekly*, which was a *Toronto Star* entertainment weekly magazine, and I wrote for *Canadian Geographic* and *Reader's Digest*.

I knew Henry Sarwer-Foner, who was the director at the time; we grew up together in Ottawa and we used to write together on different things. So he brought me in in Season 4, because they had a lot of really great stand-up comedians writing, but they didn't have anybody that really had a lot of political or business background.

I was brought in to do what were called "the leads." They would take the four big stories of the week and do a satirical take on them. Very much in the style of a news lead. So you would have Mary, Rick, Greg, and Cathy throw to stuff that was partially real footage and partially inserts that we shot.

PAUL BELLINI

It was great! I thought, "I really like this job." I wanted it to stick. And then, in the spring, they announced the Gemini nominations, and I got nominated for both shows at once. All of a sudden, here I was, nominated in the writing category for both *Kids in the Hall* and *22 Minutes*, and I thought, "Wow, I'm really happening!"

But then you realize, "Oh, it's Canada." But it was a very exciting period, those first few months.

EDWARD KAY

I remember my very first day at *22 Minutes*. I came in mid-week, and I was brought in as the guy that would do the video stuff.

Gerald set me up with a television and a bunch of videotape and he said, "They had a freak snowstorm out in Calgary. Why don't you write something about that?" And it just so happened that, on the same day, Ralph Klein had announced cutbacks in education in Alberta, and I had footage of that. It was a real gift. This was literally my first hour on the show.

I also had footage of these kids on a playground throwing snowballs—just stock that the CBC in Edmonton had shot. One of the kids throws a snowball and hits another kid right in the crotch. It was like a laugh-out-loud thing, but it wasn't part of an actual story on CBC.

So I had this footage of Ralph Klein wearing outdoor clothing, and I think we actually had him making a snowball. And I managed to pull it altogether: Ralph Klein made the announcement, and to drive home the point, he said, "Well, kids, from now on it's going to be kind of like this." Then we have Ralph Klein throw the snowball, and then we cut to this kid getting it in the crotch.

It only took about twenty-five minutes to put it together, and Gerald walked back in, and went, "So how is that Calgary snowstorm piece going?" And I thought, "Are you fucking kidding me? You actually expect me to have something after twenty-five minutes?" But he did. Because that was the lead time of that show.

PAUL BELLINI

The big challenge for me was that I'd never bothered to read a newspaper or watch the news. And, all of a sudden, here I was writing satire. *The Kids in the Hall* was mostly characters and sketch situations. We never did impersonations, or any commercial parodies, or any parodies of any type. It was always suburban and white-collar situations with absurd characters.

So here we're writing news jokes about corporations and existing individuals and a lot of politics. I'd listen to Rick Mercer and I'd go, "Wow, he knows a lot about politics. I'd better read."

EDWARD KAY

I got involved because I was a person with a news background who was funny, and once I got to the point where I was able to comfortably produce the first few minutes of the show every week, then I started writing other things. I used to love writing Cathy Jones's Babe Bennetts. And Joe Crow. They were a lot of fun. I did a lot of those.

PAUL BELLINI

With *Kids in the Hall*, I was on a show that was very much a band of brothers, in that it was the five guys, and they eventually created a circle of about a dozen writers.

It was very much like being in the mob. There's a certain *omertà*—the things you don't say. And I realized that it's simply—you have to protect the integrity of the group. Comedians have very frail egos and quick tempers, and if you're going to work with these people, you have to be your best at it, right? It's not about you, it's always about the show. The show has to be number one.

So, I went from that situation into a very similar one, and I guess I was ready for it. I felt completely comfortable.

EDWARD KAY

Some pretty big names came through as people trying out for the writers' room. Shaun Majumder was one of those people who had a knack for it. He started off as a writer and ended up being on the desk and in the cast.

But there were other people who would come out and they would come in all excited—they got the big tryout on *This Hour Has 22 Minutes,* and by the time forty-five minutes was up, they were just crumpled. If they didn't succeed, they got two shots at it; you got a two-week tryout, and if you didn't get anything on by the end of the second week, they would put you on the plane back to wherever you came from. It was harsh. There wasn't any room for anybody that couldn't cut it.

So people would come in, and it was a great opportunity, but there was also—you are failing in public; you're failing in front of your peers. So that was probably the biggest fear that everybody had.

GEOFF D'EON

They didn't all stick, and it's not because they're not funny writers. It's because the particular format of *22 Minutes* requires a particular writing skill. Some of the writers that came through could do anything. They could write a news parody, but they could also write sketches. Some of them could only do sketches. And some of them refused to do anything but sketches.

PAUL BELLINI

What I understood immediately was that there was a certain pressure to produce that I'd never been under before. I remember Ed Macdonald saying, "You've gotta write about forty of these copy jokes every week just to get by," and I thought, "Holy shit!"

So, you know, you're writing copy gags to save your soul, just churning them out, and a lot of times at a Wednesday read, they'd fall flat, or they'd get a bad read, or no one would understand them, or they just weren't appropriate for the show, or, you know, they were too dirty or dicey, or whatever.

EDWARD KAY

I think the key was getting the voices of the cast, because they each have their individual voices. I think a lot of stand-up comedians write for their own voice, and when you are doing a show like that, Mary, Cathy, Greg, and Rick have extremely distinct voices. Even though you might be writing about the news, you can't write the exact same wording for each of them; there might be different phrasing or timing.

I actually came from a print background, so I wasn't really sure that I would survive, but I just had fun. I really made a point of picking topics that I knew they would love.

There were certain things that I knew a particular cast member was passionate about, so I would choose that topic and I would go back and watch a bunch of their pieces from earlier. I would analyze it and make a note of what phrases they typically used—so I would try to make it as much like the way they actually spoke as I could.

I analyzed the Babe Bennett sketches the most, because they had a very particular voice. At the time I was working on the show, I started getting into *noir* literature, so I started reading Raymond Chandler, and I had this epiphany one day when I was reading it—that basically, it's a dialect of 1930s and early 1940s, hard-boiled stuff that Babe uses.

So just as a habit, whenever I was reading Raymond Chandler or Dashiell Hammett, and I came across one of these oddball phrases, I wrote it down—so I made my own lexicography of Babe Bennett.

I would write the sketch in plain English, and then I would get out my lexicography and I would look for every word that could be replaced. When

I was writing the one about marriage, for example, instead of "walking down the aisle," it became "sashaying down the aisle." And instead of "with that man," it became "with your big palooka."

I spent a lot of time working on this lexicon. I developed it over months, and it was probably one of the most useful things I ever did, because it was like a generator. You could just write something in plain English and then look for every word that you could replace with a Babe Bennett word, and it sounded like her.

PAUL BELLINI

I tended to gravitate towards Rick, because I thought he was a great wit and I understood what he was doing. I didn't always get the references.

I also liked writing for Thomey, because he was kind of crazy. He kind of reminded me of Kevin McDonald from *Kids in the Hall*, in that his approach to comedy was very unhinged, very personal.

I liked Mary Walsh. She scared me, obviously, but that fear is part of what you admire in her. I remember with Mary, she would write torrents and then cut it down, which is something Scott Thompson used to do—write an eleven-minute monologue and you'd have to chop it down to ninety seconds. So I understood that.

Cathy was the one I had probably the most difficult time writing for. We used to write a ton of copy gags for Cathy, and sometimes you'd have to explain them to her because she wasn't always aware of what was happening, necessarily, in the news. But it was hard to write character pieces for Cathy; she was fussy about them. I remember Ed Macdonald used to do a good job with those—like Babe Bennett and Joe Crow and those early signature characters of hers. I didn't have the same success, necessarily. I liked her personally, but I didn't really understand her approach to creating.

EDWARD KAY

I was actually the first writer to use the internet on the show. It sounds unbelievable now, but yeah.

We would try not to have all Halifax news, obviously, because it's a national show, so on Monday or Tuesday mornings, I would read the *Calgary Herald* and the *Vancouver Sun* and the *Victoria Province*. There were always two really good newsstands in Halifax that carried those papers, but the thing is, they were flown in at a discounted rate. So if a flight was coming direct from Vancouver and they had a lot of cargo, the first thing they got rid of was the newspapers, because they're heavy and they got almost nothing to ship them.

I would go in, and they just wouldn't have the papers. My girlfriend at the time was a lawyer, and I remember her showing me this thing called "the internet." It was actually through some university somewhere that had their own search engine. It was really, really primitive, doing a search, but I figured out how to do it, and I used to get just the headlines and the first paragraph from papers like the *Vancouver Sun* and the *Calgary Herald* and the *Winnipeg Free Press*, so I would know two days before everyone else what was going on out there, and I would have stories ready when they hadn't been heard of yet in Halifax.

That would've been in 1997. I started using it more and more; by 1998, I was using it a lot. But, really, for my first two years on the show, that was something I don't think anybody else was doing.

PAUL BELLINI

One thing I absolutely loved: it was different from *Kids*. On *Kids*, we would have these seven-week periods where we would write, and then two weeks of production where we would shoot all the location stuff, and then we'd have two weeks in studio where all of the material was prepared, and we'd do our shows live in Toronto at the Mutual Street studio that no longer exists. And then we'd take those seven weeks, again, to just be hippies and, you know, write whatever we wanted.

22 was a weekly schedule, so, all of a sudden, the first challenge was writing that fast and that much—starting on Monday morning with a blank page, having a giant script by Wednesday night, throwing out half the stuff, and then putting the stuff into production Thursday and Friday.

Friday night we were shooting in front of the audience and it was, like,

"Holy cow! Four days. We did enough to create a whole show, and a show that worked," and then, all of a sudden, it was on TV the following Monday night. We'd already started the next episode before the broadcast.

So, it was really intimidating at first, because of the speed, but I realized, "Oh, this is great," because it does not allow you to reflect on failure or success. You have to move forward.

ED MACDONALD

It was interesting. It was not fun. There were sort of fun moments, usually on show nights sitting in the trailers. We had these two portable trailers in the parking lot. We were like the poor relation to the building. I swear to God, the writers' trailer, for a whole winter, did not have heat, and that is not even a joke. We would wear our coats at our desks and write hilarious jokes about the government.

Paul Bellini was right: it was essential to keep moving forward. Putting out a half-hour show each week that was both topical *and* funny meant working at a relentless pace. And it meant that the weekly workflow had to follow a consistent pattern—a pattern that is still in use on the show today.

HENRY SARWER-FONER

Every week we'd start with nothing, and by the end of the week, the show was on the air.

GERALD LUNZ

We created a template. I still use the same template for the *Rick Mercer Report* in terms of how a week works. We meet on Monday mornings. We make a broad thing of—what are we going to do? What can we do? What's happening in the world? Who's got an idea? So you can look at the board and say—that, that, and that.

HENRY SARWER-FONER
Monday was primarily a writing day, so I could sort of catch my breath.

ED MACDONALD
Monday we had the ideas meeting. That was sort of dominated by the cast. We would make the list of ideas, Gerald would write them all on a board, and we would just start writing.

GERALD LUNZ
Then there was a meeting Tuesday for production sketches and stuff that we were kind of working towards.

ED MACDONALD
Tuesday evening would be when we were shooting something, so we had to have at least one or two things done for that.

HENRY SARWER-FONER
Wednesday I would shoot Rick's "Rant" in the late afternoon, and then we'd have a read-through of all the material.

GERALD LUNZ
It's called the "humilatorium." I invented that word. The humilatorium—that's when all your writing gets read out loud to everybody.

EDWARD KAY
Everybody would have Monday, Tuesday, and Wednesday mornings to write their material, and then it would be photocopied and put it into this book that the cast would read in front of the art department and the crew. It was

ostensibly sort of a heads-up so the art department could hear what pieces were in the works, so if they had any concerns about production issues—if it was something that was too big of a build, or they wanted to use existing props—then they would have a heads-up about what might be coming down the pike.

But the other purpose of the humilatorium, or the Wednesday read, was if something died, it just didn't get done. So it was an early method of sifting out the chaff.

ED MACDONALD

I never understood what everyone was so wound up about at that meeting; I could never get my head around why everyone was so nervous. There was, like, a real tension at the humilatorium. It just never occurred to me that they were actually competing for airtime, they were competing to get their own material in the show. And when my shit wouldn't go on, I'd be like, "Oh, well, I guess they'll fire me." And then I would come back the next week, and I would get something on, and I then wouldn't get fired, so I didn't really think about it beyond that.

GERALD LUNZ

Everybody reads their own stuff. It's so uncomfortable sometimes, if you don't get a laugh. That would end up being the funniest part. Walsh would be screaming at Geoff sometimes, "Okay, laugh! Why can't you laugh?"

But you've got to do it. How else are you going to do it? If you've got the balls to put it on paper and you want to put it on TV, you've got to, at one point, say, "This is what I think it is."

ED MACDONALD

Gerry is intense; he is just wound up. He has a ton of energy. But he loved that show—I've never seen anyone so into it. It was almost like, "Are you putting me on? Really?" Because I am not that into *anything*.

It was a mania. He loved that show and he had enormous drive to make it a hit. He was just bound and determined. And the nice thing about it is that he understood that it started with the writing. Most of them don't. Most of them think anybody can write. Gerry knew that a joke is gold, and not everybody can do it, and you have to protect them.

GERALD LUNZ

Even some of that half-baked stuff, you can put your faith behind it. You can put your dollar on it. We would go upstairs and say, "These are the things we can do. This is what we can literally afford to do in the time."

ED MACDONALD

It is hard to balance. There's four big personalities who just have a lot of material and it's really hard to balance a show. There would always be the week when Thomey or Cathy were not in it nearly enough.

GEOFF D'EON

The challenge was that there was not a lot of time for debate, so we did a lot of flying by the seat of our pants. We did a lot of instinctive decision-making. It was just fortunate that the people who were working on the show—the showrunner, the talent, the camera operators—it was just a talented bunch of people with really good instincts. That was an asset.

But you really didn't have a lot of time for debate. An idea was either good, or not as good as the other one, so we just did the very best ideas we could.

HENRY SARWER-FONER

The producers and I would choose what we were going to produce that week, and, then, that evening, I'd meet with the art department—Stephen Osler and Tom Anthes, who were both fantastic. They would design the sets and I would scout locations. Then, later that night, I'd have to come up with the blocking [*a plan for the performers' actions and associated camera angles*] and the vision for the pieces, and an efficient shooting strategy.

ED MACDONALD

Michael had final say, but he wasn't in a vacuum. There were other producers throwing in their two cents. And I'm sure there was pressure from the cast at some point.

ALAN MACGILLIVRAY

Michael was the executive producer; he had ultimate say. He deferred to other people sometimes—he deferred, sometimes, creatively to Gerald. When stuff seems to be working, he will just step back a little bit and let it work. But there wasn't any shyness in the room. People stated their opinions and fought for what they wanted, and he very wisely let that happen, and would ultimately make the final decision. He respected the creativity of the people in that room.

GERALD LUNZ

The final decisions were up to me, Geoff, Michael, and Jack. But basically Geoff and I were pretty well running the game. Michael at this point was going to Los Angeles, New York; he was dealing with the people who own the *New York Times*. Michael was always way ahead of the game, right? So he was always busy.

It really came down to me. Michael, of course, could say yes or no to anything. It's your buck, dude. But I'll fight you every inch of the way—which was my job: to be the voice of the talent.

ED MACDONALD

Good luck making Michael Donovan laugh. You could never read Michael most of the time. I mean, he would crack up over the same sorts of things that would crack up the room, but he would never really show his hand.

ALAN MACGILLIVRAY

Michael has his own unique sense of humour, but he watches very carefully around him to see what other people are finding funny, and he analyzes that.

HENRY SARWER-FONER

On Thursday—literally, the next day, we'd shoot the pieces, so the sets were built overnight. We'd shoot at least four in one day, and then I'd start editing them that night. And after that, I'd start blocking the live show for the next day, because I'd have some version of a script.

ED MACDONALD

Thursday was a full-on shoot day. We would tape all the stuff for playback on Friday night.

Thursday would be when Mercer was all like, "I don't like any of my jokes." And then he would throw them all out and we would have to start all over with his desk copy. There was always that—punch-ups and replacements. Some politician would die and we would have to change something. But we never really got caught out in a big way.

HENRY SARWER-FONER

Friday, I'd continue editing the pre-recorded stuff and start rehearsing the live sketches and the news desk. Then we'd shoot it all in front of a live audience that evening, and roll back all the pre-recorded bits.

ED MACDONALD

I remember everybody getting the flu once, and there was just me and Mercer at the read. Then everybody came in sick for the show on Friday night. That's how you know they are theatre folk, right? They still showed up.

HENRY SARWER-FONER

After the show, the producers and I would do a cull for time and line up the show.

Saturday, I'd edit the complete show, fine-tuning the pieces as I go, and bringing the show to its final running time.

Sunday, around noon, Michael Donovan would come in and screen the show, and later that night, I'd approve the sound mix, and off it went!

And then the next day, it would start all over again.

GEOFF D'EON

We taped the show on Friday night, edited it over the weekend, and by the time it was on the air on Monday, we had already started working on the next week's show.

GERALD LUNZ

We created a pattern and it worked. And then it becomes this machine that churns it out, and churns it out, and churns it out.

HENRY SARWER-FONER

We'd do twenty-two episodes, plus New Year's Eve specials, and I was the only director. Now, I think they have two, but, yeah. It was a lot. Thank God for the ignorance of youth!

BILL BRIOUX

The first trip I made to visit them, around 1995, it was really amazing to see. I was there for a week, so I could see them start with the newspaper clippings and end with a taping, and see the whole process. It was fascinating to see them pull that show together.

GERALD LUNZ

We were all working collectively and it was so fun. Once it took off and started becoming a hit, the infighting pretty well stopped, because by that point people said, "It's going in this direction, and this is the right direction."

You know, everyone has their cranky moments. We were living on top of each other, which as adults is not as much fun as when you are in college. So there was a lot of conflict, but nothing more than any other human group in a collective would have.

ED MACDONALD

The challenge was just the bulk of material. You had to write a lot to get a little bit. That twenty-two minutes was really more like fifty minutes of material. Ordinarily, a show like that would have ten or twelve or twenty writers. We were three. So we were under the gun a lot.

I remember a reading—this would be like a Thursday morning before we go to shoot, and I was kind of in a pissy mood because I was tired. I look over at Cathy's chair and she's upside down and her feet are sticking straight up out of the chair. And she says, "I'm having trouble accessing my adult side today." I laughed so hard, the two of us got asked to leave the meeting. We had to stand out in the hall.

There was another reading where Thomey read "Jerry Boyle's Christmas Adventure." It was just about Jerry Boyle's night out on the town on Christmas Eve, and I remember it stopping the reading. There were tears. People were pounding on the table. [Script supervisor] Helen [Pelham] couldn't time it, because it was just too insane. I remember laughing so hard I almost lost my mind; that was one of the funniest things ever.

But by the time it got on the air, it wasn't the same version, really, and I don't think it worked as well. That's the thing about TV: there's so many hands and there are so many edits that it's nobody's show. It's everybody's show.

GEOFF D'EON

Successive generations of writers have gone through that show. I know stand-up comedians who have done a stint on *22 Minutes* as a writer, and they have all been incredibly energized by it. Working on that show is a kick in the pants. You either take to it and you thrive, or you realize it's not for you and you leave.

ED MACDONALD

I didn't realize how much money you could make in TV—then I realized, "Oh, that's why people do TV. Because you can make good money." So I hung in purely for that reason.

Around the time I was leaving, I kind of felt like I wanted to do other things. I was writing this thing at night, so I was working all day, eating, and then I would start working on this other thing, and finish that about three or four in the morning, then sleep for a few hours and then go back over and do it all again. That was just getting to be too much, so I quit. Everybody told me I was insane and that my career was over.

PAUL BELLINI

I left in Season 5, because I wanted to write a novel with Scott Thompson, which we did—we wrote a novel about [Thompson's character], Buddy Cole, called *Buddy Babylon*. I made enough money on that book deal that I could take the year off. And then I went back to Halifax to do a season of Bette MacDonald's show as a story editor.

EDWARD KAY

I really loved the show, but it was incredibly high pressure. At the time, I was the longest surviving writer. People either had nervous breakdowns or got fired, and I had four really good years. They offered me a fifth year, but I had been given my own show as showrunner and head writer. It was a show called *The Itch* with Jason Jones, who later went on to do *The Daily Show*....

So I really left to do that; it's one of those really difficult decisions you have to make, because I really loved everybody on the show.

• • •

The core team was getting restless as well. Just four seasons in, Rick and Gerald were already developing other projects—including a dramatic series called *Made in Canada*, which they shot when *22 Minutes* was on hiatus, using many of the show's crew members and support staff. Then, in 1998, Gerald Lunz left *22 Minutes*.

GERALD LUNZ

I did five years. I did the first five and then…Rick and I came up with this idea called *Made in Canada*. Which is a mockery—bite the hand that feeds you!—of the Canadian [television] industry at the time, which was so full of itself, and all the corny stuff we were up to, and all the crazy people.

We did a pilot and it went really well. They wanted more. They said, "Great—we will take something like thirteen." And I said, "I can't do both." I was co-exec with Michael Donovan, just on paper, because he wasn't really involved with the project; he was working with Michael Moore on *Bowling for Columbine* at the time.

I was running this thing with Rick and Mark Farrell; Mark was a writer on *22,* and eventually the showrunner. I went to do that, and Rick stayed with both shows for three more years. So I did five, Rick did eight. And then the network offered us this opportunity to do the *Rick Mercer Report*.

RICK MERCER

Gerald probably had to leave. I would say that Gerald is the best creative producer and showrunner the country has ever seen—but, of course, he's also my partner. We live together, and we lived together back then. So Gerald probably had to leave, because there was no doubt about it: the show was very successful, and segments of the show that I was involved in were very successful. You don't have to be much of a conspiracy theorist to think, "Well, the reason these segments are getting on is because of his relationship." I was in a relationship with management.

So he had to go. He fell on a sword to leave, because he didn't want to leave. He's absolutely one of the creators of the show, and super proud of it, and he worked super hard to make that show work. Like everyone else, he wanted a show that was absolutely successful, and that's what he got.

But he had to go in order for me to stay, basically.

Gerald's departure left a void that would prove challenging to fill.

JACK KELLUM

I feel somewhat responsible for this, so I have to be careful. Gerald was a good player. He was fair. He didn't necessarily favour anybody. In that position as showrunner, you can favour one performer over another, and Gerald did not do that. He was pretty straightforward—right down the middle. He didn't favour Rick, for example.

But when we lost Gerald, we were in a bit of a conundrum. I had been working with the *Bette MacDonald Show* at the same time, and had run into Paul Bellini. I got to know Paul pretty well, and he was showing me some aspects of his own background. He spent quite a number of days on *The Kids in the Hall*. So Paul immediately jumped to mind as a potential for Gerald's replacement.

PAUL BELLINI

I was offered Gerald's job, because Gerald was going to produce *Made in Canada*. I think Jack Kellum might have made the recommendation. So, all of a sudden, I was invited back as a producer for Season 6, which was a very big deal, and it was a job that—even though I did my best to imitate Gerald—was really hard, because I realized what the story editor on a show like *22* does is speak on behalf of everyone else, to everyone else.

So, you're often telling a writer why they won't get stuff in the show, or you're often telling a cast member why this certain monologue or something won't be produced. So you have to hold in all your own emotions for the greater good.

RICK MERCER

Paul Bellini is a guy who has show business in his blood. He's great, but I don't think he was the guy for that job.

But I don't know if anyone could have been the guy for that job. I mean, Gerald had a lot of history. Gerald worked with Mary Walsh in Sheshatshiu in Labrador. Gerald brought Cathy Jones's one-woman show, *Wedding in Texas*, across the country. Gerald knew Greg Thomey. This is a guy who had relationships with every single one of us, and we all go way back.

I mean, we are all each other's pallbearers—or at least in the front row of the church. So, I don't know who could have taken that job on, quite frankly.

GEOFF D'EON

It didn't really work. Discipline kind of fell apart. Super nice guy, talented writer, didn't know how to crack a whip, and discipline lapsed substantially— to the extent that people stopped coming to the read-throughs. There was a brief period of time where the Friday read-through, on the show-taping day, would start at twelve o'clock, and people started to arrive later and later. It was not uncommon to be sitting there at 12:15 waiting for some of the cast members. Not all of them. And then I remembered there was one meeting where basically only one of the cast had shown up and it was 12:25. And Michael just said, "The hell with it, we are not doing a read-through."

So that was kind of a shame.

RICK MERCER

Plus, you know, we had rules. We had the two-minute rule—keep it under two minutes. We stuck with that for a couple of years, and then things started getting longer and longer. Gerald always tried to hold to that ideal, but, you know, that's a real fight. I would have that fight with him every week, but so would Mary, and so would Cathy. No one else could go in there and have that fight. Plus, you know, Gerald had been there from day one, and you know what it's like. Someone who clearly wasn't there from day one—it's suddenly like, "What are you telling me anything for? We built this show! This is our house!"

Plus, we were four Newfoundlanders, and Gerald is not a Newfoundlander, but he lived in Newfoundland for years beforehand. So, now you've got a guy who's like, flying in.

That said, Bellini's a sweet, sweet man. He's a giant in the industry. He's a tremendous talent. But he was an odd choice.

PAUL BELLINI

It was very hard, because the thing with Gerald's role was that he had nurtured it for the better part of that decade. He'd worked on *CODCO*; he had a personal relationship with Mary; he understood Cathy's temperament; he knew Greg as a kid; he was with Rick.

I mean, essentially, he had an incredible relationship with the four of them that I just couldn't replicate. I was an outsider, I was younger, I didn't have the authority or the history that he had. So, I didn't…I couldn't do it.

JACK KELLUM

I think that was probably the closest the show ever came to sinking, because Paul didn't have the smarts that Gerald had to run it. All the producers have to take responsibility for that decision, because we were all responsible for hiring him.

PAUL BELLINI

I remember, a couple of times, bursting out crying on the drive home, because I was just so full of anxiety over the production. It was a difficult year, because Rick was still on the show; Gerald had gone off to lay the ground-work for *Made in Canada*. Rick was still a cast member, but he didn't have Gerald around.

I remember, at one point, he wrote a very elaborate Christmas sketch. The other producers said, "Well, we can't really produce this, because it would take a day and a half; it would eat up all of our production time." It was a Scrooge thing, with big sets and a lot of characters. And I had to tell Rick that we weren't going to make his baby. And, you know—it was a difficult thing, because how do you say no to Rick? He's the star of the show.

Rick was writing a huge amount of the show at the time—not just his own stuff, but he was generating material for everybody. And Rick was the reason we'd won all those Geminis—let's be honest, right? Well, better not say that, because I don't want to step on toes, but he was riding a crest of popularity at the time with the "Streeters" and everything. And I had to say no to him for this one thing, and I remember how difficult it was. Then I realized, "I don't have the strength to do Gerald's job." It's really hard.

RICK MERCER

If he didn't work out, it wasn't because of anything he did. It would have been the behaviour of the four cast members that he inherited. I don't think anyone would have pulled that off.

PAUL BELLINI

Yeah, it was like trying to drive a coach where the horses are out of control, you know? You can't even keep it on the road [*laughing*].

GERALD LUNZ

Oh my God, he got eaten alive. He's too sweet. He's too nice. Cathy ate him up; she was so mad at me for leaving.

PAUL BELLINI

Then came the strike. The union went on strike after our thirteenth week of a twenty-two-week show. All of a sudden, everybody's suspended without pay, and everyone's freaking out, and it kind of destroyed—first of all, it destroyed the flow, because not only did we lose the season, we came back and did, like, a two-hour special at the very end of the strike. I think the strike had lifted by the end of the spring. So we came back and did a two-hour special just to mop up and use all of the material that we had produced and never shown.

And it was really sad, because it kind of blew a hole in my efforts to get to the next level as a producer. And that was it. I actually didn't go back to the show after that. It wasn't even offered, actually.

JACK KELLUM

He was just there one year; he wasn't asked to come back.

• • •

JACK KELLUM

In the meantime, Mark Farrell started raising his head. He was a writer. He's a perfect example of the impact of stand-up comics on the show. Mark was a stand-up comic. I met him through the *Comedy Fest*. He became a writer on *22*, and then applied to be the showrunner of *22* and was successful in his application. I think, maybe, we were a little more careful this time around, but Mark was hired, and he was there until I left.

GEOFF D'EON

So Bellini didn't last too long, and then Mark Farrell came on as the show-runner. Mark had been a writer on the show and he was a very effective showrunner—a good disciplinarian who ran a tight ship. And I believe it was then that the writing pool got a lot bigger. I think today there are something like eight writers, ten writers? In my time on *22 Minutes* we never had a writers' room that big.

JACK KELLUM

Mark had very strong likes and dislikes. He had to run the show and keep it on time, on schedule, and on budget. By Farrell's time, Thomey was getting—I don't want to say it, but I have to say it—more and more difficult. He wasn't learning his lines, he was partying an awful lot, and so in not knowing his lines, he used to hold up the system. That was really frustrating for Mark.

And Cathy was also starting to hold things up by not knowing her lines and causing great aggravation to Mark. It caused aggravation to everyone, because everyone had to wait. We would talk to them, but it just seemed to do no good. So Mark was very much in favour of getting rid of both Thomey and Cathy at one point. By the time I had left, Thomey was gone. But Cathy, of course, is still there, and that's cool. Mary pops up now and then too, which I think is really great. A healthy part of the evolution of the show.

BILL BRIOUX

Mark already had a reputation in Canadian television that was pretty strong. He had a good resume.

When I was there, he had a keyboard in his office, and I remember that's how he would unwind—he would sit and play music for a while, just to chill out.

Mark always seemed very laid-back, but I think he worked hard on that show, and sweated the details. He was kind of a taskmaster. I watched him assemble the jokes and come up with the desk bits, and they threw more out than they kept. It was a process that was very demanding.

• • •

GEOFF D'EON

The idea that the show could be moved to Toronto was always in the air, fuelled by a certain amount of paranoia. Rumours would circulate on a regular basis that the CBC wanted to have *22 Minutes* produced out of its spanking-new broadcast centre, which had huge studios with not much going on in them. They had *Rita and Friends,* and they had built this huge broadcast facility with gigantic sound stages and not much was happening. So those rumours would circulate every year.

The greatest bastion against that ever happening was Michael Donovan. Michael Donovan always was extremely proud of the fact that he and his brother had started a film company in Halifax, Salter Street Films. They were proud that they had made a go of it. Michael was now proud that he had a huge hit on his hands that was coming out of Halifax.

Michael never showed any interest at all in moving the show to Toronto. In fact, I heard Michael argue on more than one occasion that the show could not be done in Toronto. Not for technological reasons, but for editorial reasons. The reason this show works, the reason this show has the editorial point of view that it has, vis-à-vis the rest of the country, is because it is out on the edge. We are doing this from Nova Scotia. If we were trying to do this show in Toronto, the thinking was that we would slowly but surely—by osmosis and invisibly—be sucked into a Central Canadian mindset. And the humour would be affected by that in no uncertain terms.

JOHN DOYLE

I do think that being based in Halifax is both an advantage and a disadvantage for the show. One of the advantages is that it's away from the media and political capitals, and they can have a perspective on events which you're not going to get if you're in Toronto or Ottawa or Vancouver.

It also means that the humour is informed by a Maritime sensibility, which is really the dominant form in Canada. I think one of the impacts that television, particularly CBC, has had on the Canadian culture, is that it has made Maritime humour the dominant form of humour in Canada.

FRED MATTOCKS

Well, I'm a bit of an East Coast chauvinist, and I believe the fact that the show comes from Eastern Canada and has very strong Newfoundland roots, but also very strong Maritime cultural roots, is a big part of its success.

It doesn't take itself too seriously, it doesn't take itself for granted, it doesn't take success for granted, it works hard, it knows that the world can be a cruel place, and it does its best—and it has, consistently, over the years.

There aren't many production teams in the business that can claim to have that kind of longevity, and I really think the root of it is cultural.

PHYLLIS PLATT

There is something about that great Newfoundland spirit that was very important to the show. Being outsiders. Growing up as outsiders. Knowing what it felt like to be outsiders was, I think, quite important. I don't think you could have done that show out of Ontario.

JACK KELLUM

Rick Mercer is done in Toronto. I'm sure that *22* could have been done in Toronto, but the politics of the time would not have allowed—unless they got into fisticuffs with Bill Donovan—they would not have allowed *22 Minutes* to have been done in Toronto. And I suppose over the years, now that Donovan is gone, they have had plenty of opportunities to pull it out, but I think they realize the success of it is due in no small part to the fact that it's done in Halifax.

BILL DONOVAN

It has been my belief, and I believe it's been proven, that it is the regional voice in a national context that works well in this country. I'm not saying you can't produce programs successfully in Toronto. Of course you can. But somehow you have to be able to capture that regional perspective, that regional voice. And I think we have proved it with *22* in spades.

FRED MATTOCKS

I'm not sure that *22 Minutes* could have, or would have, survived in any other place. But I think a better way to look at it is: *22 Minutes* is one of the best manifestations of a creative community that is powerful and thoughtful and aware and committed.

One of the things that East Coast people often forget is how much we value talent, and how much we value the expression of talent. And it's not that other Canadians don't; you can find great collections of talent across the country, and great celebrations of talent across the country.

But I actually believe that on the East Coast, it's in the water. It's more visceral; it's more connected. It's just more a part of life.

8

Passing the Torch

2000–2007

Rick's eight-year run on the show would soon come to an end, but he still had a few watershed moments to come.

In 2000, Canadian Alliance leader Stockwell Day proposed—as an election tactic—that his government would hold national referendums on any issues that earned the support of 3 per cent of the electorate, or about 350,000 Canadians.

RICK MERCER

I really had a problem with this. I'm not against referendums, but I felt that this was nothing but a back door to stopping same-sex marriage, and to putting the death penalty and abortion in the ballot box. So I had a real bug up my ass about this.

GEOFF D'EON

Once the internet came along, we were always looking for ways to harness it to kind of promote *22 Minutes* as a brand. We didn't really know what we were doing. There was no dedicated person with an online strategy; we just sort of made it up as we went along—unlike now, where they have a very rigorous, well-thought-out and highly functional online strategy. This was back in the early days of the internet.

So Rick came to me one day and said, "I want to get Stockwell Day on this referendum thing." I said, "Good for you, what's the idea?" He said, "I want to get people to sign a petition that Stockwell Day would have to change his name to Doris Day."

"Hilarious," I said. "Great idea."

RICK MERCER

It was so early in the internet world that *22 Minutes* didn't have a website. We didn't own the name ThisHourHas22Minutes.com. It didn't exist. So, that's how early we're talking about.

GERALD LUNZ

There are a couple of highlights of Rick's career and Doris Day was one of them. Rick was the youngest of the crowd, and he was more tuned into what was happening with the internet and what you could do. It was crazy. You had to have a server in India to set this up.

RICK MERCER

I was thinking about the petition, and one of my points was: any idiot can get that many signatures on a petition. And then I read this article talking about how hard it is to get 350,000 signatures. It was practically impossible, but in the not-so-distant future, it could be done in twenty-four hours with the internet.

So I came up with the idea, with [writer] Luce Casimiri, and we wrote it up and contacted Salter Street. Salter Street was the production company. It had nothing to do with us. No one who worked at Salter was ever at *22 Minutes*. Michael would come to the meetings, but other than that—it's not like we used their resources.

But I knew that Salter was kind of starting to put their toe in the water when it came to digital. So I went to them and I said, "How do we do this?" Literally, there was no website. I said, "I want to put this petition online," and they agreed to get the website.

GEOFF D'EON

Rick wrote a studio piece in which he laid out his argument. It was brilliantly written.

RICK MERCER

I went on television and I said, "We will kick off the first referendum. If 3 per cent of the people sign this petition, it will force Stockwell Day to change his name to Doris."

The producers told me they almost didn't put the piece in the show, because it wasn't that funny. There was me, standing near a monitor and talking about policy. I mean, the truth is, there weren't that many jokes in it. There was only, you know, something that could unite the entire country—French, English, Black, white, straight, gay…especially gay [*laughing*].

Other than that, there weren't a lot of jokes. It was me explaining the policy, and then explaining how to go to the internet and sign this petition, and they almost didn't put it in, because it didn't get a lot of laughs. But the truth is, the company had invested a bit of time and, I'm guessing, a little bit of money. They went out and created the website, so they put it in.

And I know the producers had a bet. They all put, like, five or ten bucks in an envelope and guessed how many signatures I would get, and I think the producer that won guessed, like, fifteen thousand. Of course, that won, because it was the highest number.

GEOFF D'EON

The response was astronomical. Within, like, forty-eight hours, he had hundreds of thousands of names, and Stockwell Day was kind of a laughingstock. The idea was revealed to be as stupid as it really was, and Stockwell Day had to back down.

Rick had made a very trenchant and effective piece of satire which caught traction, and which actually effected social change. That's the best you can hope for if you're doing a satirical news show—that you can do a piece that engages hundreds of thousands of people, and something changes as a result of it.

RICK MERCER

I mean, it became such a phenomenon. It was unbelievable. At one point, forty-two people a second were signing the petition.

GERALD LUNZ

How it ended was with way over one million people saying, "Yes, I think you should change your name to Doris," and then they changed their campaign song to "Que Sera, Sera." It pretty much killed Stockwell Day. It was quite famous. But it was the first use of that technology from the ground up.

FRED MATTOCKS

That was amazing, you know. That was another industry-changing moment. It was absolute brilliance, and it was the internet phenomenon of the day.

HENRY SARWER-FONER

That was a shot in the arm, the whole Doris Day thing. I mean, it just got people talking, and it actually worked. It was a whole other way to satirize what was going on in the world.

RICK MERCER

I was told afterwards, by Conservatives who would know, that Stockwell Day and the Reform Party had been celebrating every week up until that moment, because what they called "soft support" in Ontario was growing exponentially at a very healthy rate, and they felt they were in a position to make massive gains in Ontario.

They said that, within seventy-two hours of the Stockwell Day petition, all "soft support" completely evaporated.

So I have had conversations with people who held *22 Minutes* personally responsible for them not achieving their goal in that election, which was awesome!

It was also the first time—and this is something that I would probably avoid now, but it was pretty heady—it was the first time that we became part of the news cycle. We were there to make fun of the news, but suddenly, we were making the news, and that was pretty exciting.

GEOFF D'EON

So flash forward to Christmas 2000. Rick wanted to do something with the military. He didn't know what it was, he just wanted to give the troops some kind of boost. At the time, Canadian peacekeepers were active in the Balkans.

I encouraged him; I gave him the name of a guy I knew in naval affairs, and I said, "Call this guy." Rick took it upon himself, and he started to make phone calls, looking for the right idea. How could he harness the internet and do something for the troops?

I'll never forget it. He came into my office with his eyes as big as pie plates and looked at me and said, "How do you feel about going to Bosnia?"

I said, "Bosnia—yeah. Why?" And he said, "The Army just invited us to go to Bosnia. They've got a regiment down there." And I said, "Absolutely! We should do this."

RICK MERCER

That was one of the most personally satisfying pieces I have ever done.

I grew up around a number of people in the Canadian Forces. Not a lot, but they were on my street. And when we did that, it was a bit of a different time. The military had come out of a hard time, plus they had just gone through a lot of years of cuts.

I've always gone overseas and entertained troops—that's something that continued. It was a relationship that basically grew out of Bosnia. At the time, it was considered kind of outrageous. People were like, "What are you going there for?" Bosnia was a bit of a forgotten mission. In that piece, when I pointed out how many Canadian peacekeepers were overseas for Christmas, it kind of came as a shock to people. We'd just totally forgotten that we were doing that.

So it was a very exciting trip for us, just because it was so far-fetched that we would go to Bosnia.

GEOFF D'EON

We left Halifax on a Saturday afternoon. We flew to Frankfurt. We were in Frankfurt at 6 on Sunday morning. We flew into Zagreb at 1:30 on that Sunday. We were picked up by the Canadian military and we were driven into Bosnia to this camp—myself and Rick and Patrick Doyle, our cameraman.

We started shooting on the Monday. Anything we wanted. They just said, "What do you need?" We had this idea that we were going to get the military to do a music video with us based on Trooper's "We're Here For A Good Time," so we wanted to visit a whole bunch of different places. I had a little cassette player with the song, and I would just hit the cassette and the soldiers would mime along to different lines.

We wanted to go to some of the far camps, because they were stationed in several different places in Bosnia at the time. And they lined up some helicopters for us—Griffon helicopters. It was the Princess Patricia's Canadian Light Infantry, and they had access to these Griffon helicopters. But they tend not to fly in singles; they tend to fly in pairs for safety and security reasons. So they gave us a pair of Griffon helicopters.

So, we take off in these Griffon helicopters, and I ask the pilot, "Can we leave the door open so we can shoot?"

"Oh, yeah, just clip in so you're safe." We take off from the camp, and we've got the door open, and there's a helicopter flying parallel to us. We have these headsets on, and you just press a button and you can talk to the pilots, because the rotor noise is really deafening. So I get on with the pilot and I say, "Can you have the other helicopter fly closer to us, parallel so we can get a shot?"

"Yeah, no problem." Next thing you know, the helicopter is right beside us. Patrick Doyle is getting these great pictures of the helicopters flying over these villages. I got on the headset and I said, "Can you have him peel away, do a really dramatic bank to the left?"

"Yeah, no problem." Anything we ask them to do, they are doing for us. And I'll never forget this: Rick looks at me and he shouts over the noise of the rotors, "I feel like we're in a Jerry Bruckheimer movie!"

RICK MERCER

From a pure TV production point of view, that was exhilarating, and it's something that I continued to do for the rest of my television career. I've often shot with the military, and I won't say I do it for the toys, but the toys certainly make for some good TV every now and then.

GEOFF D'EON

We fly over these villages, which look really picturesque from the air until you descend below two thousand feet, and you can see these villages are, in fact, all burned out. Shells have gone through the roofs, and they're all burned out. You quickly get the sense that you are in a war zone.

So, we were shooting from the air, and Rick wanted to get them to spell out some kind of message by using personnel, so we settled on "Hi, Mom!"

From a helicopter flying over the parade square, we watched them rehearse it on the ground. They put parachute tape on the ground, and then they had about fifty guys in precision form the word "Hi" and then as we fly over on cue, they all scramble so there's no word, and then it solidifies into the word "Mom." It's a beautiful thing.

RICK MERCER

And everyone lip-synced again, and we did the "Hi, Mom!" from the helicopter, which, to this day, is one of the absolute highlights of my television career.

GEOFF D'EON

For two days they fly us around, they drive us around, we meet literally hundreds of Canadian soldiers. And Rick has arranged for Clearwater to send in a shipment of lobsters—like, two hundred pounds of lobsters, which arrived from Clearwater at the mess that night.

RICK MERCER

Yeah, we convinced Clearwater Lobster to give us a shitload of free lobster, and we somehow got that shipped to Bosnia. Because we thought—we gotta bring something!

GEOFF D'EON

So we do that shoot, we fly back. It takes us all day Wednesday to get home. We edit on Wednesday night. Keith Bradley and I put that piece together. We put it in front of the audience on Friday and it was on the air the following Monday. The turnaround! And it's, like, a four-minute music video.

There was not a dry eye in the house. When we showed that video, when those soldiers scrambled into the words "Hi, Mom!" people were weeping in the audience. People stood and cheered. It was the thing that I did that I was most proud of, ever, at the time. I had never been more proud of a piece.

It's just a testimony to how a good idea, simply executed, could be put together so fast by *22 Minutes*, because that was the metabolism of the show. You wouldn't have shot a piece like that and put it together later in the month. The show always moved at this breakneck pace. It was insane to go to Bosnia and shoot a piece and have it ready by Friday. It was an insane thing to agree to, but we did, because the people we were working with were really good. Everybody was really good at their job.

RICK MERCER

I remember when we played it back to the studio audience for the first time. Quite often, because the show moved so fast, we would not have even seen the pieces ourselves, when they were finally edited. And, certainly, we wouldn't have seen each other's.

I remember when that played and the "Hi, Mom!" happened, and the audience erupted, and I was really proud of the piece. But we would come out of a piece, and then we would roll right into a desk joke. And I remember Greg Thomey looked at me, and he was weeping, because he's a big sook! God love him! He's such a sweet man. He was weeping—tears were pouring down his face, and now he's about to do a thing and he says, "You son of a bitch!"

GEOFF D'EON

The piece started with Rick doing a prologue saying, "Canadian soldiers are here, and they want you to send them a message on this website."

He said, "We've used the internet for evil. Today, we are going to use it for good. Don't worry, we will use it for evil again later, but for now, we just want you to send these soldiers a message."

RICK MERCER

The idea of the piece was that people could go to this website and send the soldiers a message at Christmas. That type of thing's done all the time now, but at the time, the Forces didn't have any mechanism in place to do that. Again, it was very early use of the internet. There was a place, apparently, where you could send a card to soldiers if you wanted to. But no one was doing that.

GEOFF D'EON

They were inundated. They had thousands and thousands and thousands of cards and letters. Schools, communities, people from all over Canada. It was another reminder for me that this show has clout. Just like with the Stockwell

Day thing, this show has real power. It can motivate people to do things.

What a gift! This show has more power than *The National*. That wasn't hubris. I had calls from people I knew at *The National* saying, "Unbelievable! Unbelievable piece."

About two years later, I went to the War Museum in Ottawa, and there was this corner devoted to peacekeepers. On a loop, constantly playing on the TV screen was *We're Here For A Good Time*, and I watched it, and tears just streamed down my face. It's such an emotional piece. Even today, it's like— wow, it's got the goods. When you see them spelling out "Hi" and it turns into "Mom," I cry. I can't help it, I cry.

But I guess the point is the power of the show to motivate people, which became really obvious at a certain point, and this and the Stockwell Day idea were both ideas that were turned around in a week. This is not people slaving over concepts with huge camera crews and craft trailers. This is really small numbers of people executing really good ideas.

RICK MERCER

If I had to make a list of things that I was most proud of over my eight years at *22 Minutes*, that would be very high on the list.

It was also among the last pieces Mercer would ever do for the show. In July 2001, he announced that he would not be returning for the show's ninth season.

RICK MERCER

I actually left twice. I'd left the year before, but the CBC, ummm, actively encouraged me to stick around. At the time, I was doing *Made in Canada*, so it was suggested that it would be in the best interest of that show if I stayed on *22 Minutes*. So I did. Yeah, that's the way these things work.

JACK KELLUM

It definitely threw us out of kilter when Rick left.

Everyone could see that Rick was headed for bigger and better things, and I still think that he is headed for bigger and better things than the *Rick Mercer Report*.... I mean, he's funny. No one can dispute the success of the *Rick Mercer Report*. But I think that he has more to give, if he doesn't kill himself jumping off the CN Tower.

RICK MERCER

There was no animus reason. I mean, there were times that I was frustrated. I was certainly frustrated over the name issue. But then, once *Talking to Americans* happened, we pretty much lanced that boil, and I'm sure if I'd stuck around, I would have started using my name.

Basically, from the very beginning, from the very first week of the show, I realized I had a real interest in the production side of television—embracing your budget, or figuring out what you can and cannot do, and the scheduling, and all of that whole business.

I would equate me leaving to do my own show to the way someone who works in a kitchen in a restaurant decides they want to own their own restaurant. It's a completely different set of skills, but it's something that I like. I wouldn't even say it was about creative control. I mean, obviously, I have 100 per cent creative control on *The Mercer Report*. But on *22 Minutes*, I pretty much had creative freedom to do whatever I wanted to do anyway, within the confines of the show.

So it's not like there was anyone saying, "No, you can't do that." I just wanted to own my own show, because television, at the end of the day, is a producer's medium. And it's the producer who calls the shots, and the producer who decides. In all the years at *22 Minutes*, when we pitched trips, I always wanted to go to Iqaluit. I never got the green light to go to Iqaluit, because it was kind of like, "What do you want to go to Iqaluit for?"

Well, when the *Mercer Report* started, that's the first place I went. It was my own personal thing. It was always something I wanted to bring to the show, and it just didn't happen. I mean—it's complicated getting to Iqaluit.

You can get stuck there, and there's all sorts of things that can happen. But I wanted that to be a big part of what I wanted to start doing in my own career.

BILL BRIOUX

When he left, that was a big defection. It was sort of akin to Chevy Chase leaving *Saturday Night Live*.

HENRY SARWER-FONER

He was big part of the show, for sure. Mary and Rick were the ones with political acumen. That was primarily his focus—the topical stuff. So it was, "How are we going to replace him?"

RICK MERCER

I never considered, for one second, that the show wouldn't survive without me. And, had I actually considered that as a possibility, I probably would have stayed. If I thought for a second that it meant the show was stopping, I wouldn't have left. I would have driven it right to the grave.

You know what my father said? It was big news in Newfoundland—there was a big headline: "Mercer Leaves *22 Minutes*" or something.

And Dad said, "Well, if Winston Churchill's replaceable, you sure as hell are!"

GEORGE ANTHONY

We looked at four other people to substitute for Rick. Michael was on his way to Toronto for the auditions; he was on an Air Canada flight from Halifax to Toronto, and he ended up sitting next to [actor and *Whose Line Is It Anyway?* star] Colin Mochrie. They got to chatting, and Michael said, "There's going to be five. I've asked Colin Mochrie to come."

I said, "I don't know…" So we saw the four, who were very good. And then Colin came in, and Colin became the next Rick.

COLIN MOCHRIE
Cast Member, 2001–2003

I was doing a guest spot on *Made in Canada*, and Mark Farrell was the show-runner on that show, as well as on *22 Minutes*.

Rick had announced he was leaving. At lunch, I was with [actor] Peter Keleghan and we were talking; at that time I was doing *Whose Line* and some touring. I was really busy, and Peter said, kind of jokingly, "You should try out for *22 Minutes* since you have weekends free." And I laughed. I think Mark Farrell was walking by at that time; I don't know if he actually over-heard. I like to think, in my version of the story, he overheard and that's where he got the idea to audition me.

JACK KELLUM

I always felt that one of the magic elements of *This Hour Has 22 Minutes* was the fact that the cast were Newfoundlanders. Newfoundlanders see the coun-try differently than [other] Canadians. Absolutely. I used to get into argu-ments with the showrunner, Mark Farrell. To Mark, the Newfoundland thing didn't make any difference to him. It was his belief that the cast could come from anywhere. And it was both my and Michael's belief that the uniqueness of the show was, in part, due to the fact that everything was being looked at through Newfoundland eyes.

So with Mark in there, we started to bring in non-Newfoundland charac-ters. And I see now that they have gone back to all Newfoundland characters. Maybe it was just my strong belief that the Newfoundland aspect gave the show its difference. Obviously that is debatable.

GEORGE ANTHONY

I think, at the beginning, perhaps there were some questions about the choice, but it was Colin Mochrie, so that made it easier. Having a sensibility that wasn't a Newfoundland sensibility could have been seen as a liability or as an asset. I certainly saw it as an asset.

The cast of 22 Minutes *poses for a photograph after winning Best Comedy Series at the Gemini Awards in Toronto in 2008. They are, from left to right: Nathan Fielder, Cathy Jones, Mark Critch, Geri Hall, Gavin Crawford, and Shaun Majumder. (Nathan Denette/CP PHOTO)*

Geri Hall's ambush interview with then-Ontario premier Dalton McGuinty fell flat. She did not know that the premier had been fielding sensitive questions about Stelco layoffs. (Maria Babbage/CP PHOTO)

Former CBC creative head George Anthony played a key role in bringing hits such as This Hour Has 22 Minutes *to Canadians. (Dimo Safari)*

*Rick Mercer leads Brian Tobin, then federal industry minister, in the singing of
"Raise a Little Hell" in Ottawa. (Jonathan Hayward/CP PHOTO)*

Peter Sutherland has been shooting video for This Hour Has 22 Minutes *since the first episode. (Peter Sutherland)*

Edward Kay was a journalist who became a writer and producer on 22 Minutes. *(Mika Kay)*

Susan Kent, Shaun Majumder, Cathy Jones, and Mark Critch are shown at the Canadian Screen Awards in Toronto in 2017. (CP PHOTO)

Jennifer Whalen became head writer on 22 Minutes *after three seasons in the show's writing room. (Ali J. Eisener)*

Rick Mercer was one of the original cast members and creators of 22 Minutes.
(Jon Sturge/Mercer Report)

*Bill Donovan was the regional director for CBC Maritimes from 1985 to 1997; he
helped pave the way for co-productions like* 22 Minutes. *(Grace Adams)*

Geri Hall had been best known as a commercial actor before she became a cast member on 22 Minutes. *(Pierre Gautreau)*

Whose Line Is It Anyway? *star Colin Mochrie joined the cast of* 22 Minutes *when Rick Mercer left the show in 2001. (Helen Tansey)*

Geoff D'Eon brought his expertise as a former executive producer in news to his work in the field with 22 Minutes. He oversaw many of the show's famous road pieces. (Geoff D'Eon)

Field producer Mark Mullane orchestrated numerous political ambushes, including Mary Walsh's ambush of former Republican vice-presidential candidate Sarah Palin. (Mark Mullane)

COLIN MOCHRIE

They asked if I was interested, and I said sure, because at that point I was younger and I was always into things that really scared me. And I figured, "Well, it can't really get much scarier than trying to take the place of someone who is established as a major part of *22 Minutes*."

I don't really remember the audition well, except that I had to make up some pieces, and then they threw something at me and I had to improvise, which I felt all right about, because that was really the only thing I had to hang my hat on. And then they informed me I got it a couple of days later.

GEORGE ANTHONY

I was really happy about that. I thought it was a stroke of luck, and a stroke of genius for Michael, because my concern had been that no matter who we put in there, the first review was going to be, "He's no Rick Mercer." I couldn't figure out a way around it; when you are dealing with new talent, it was just a hard thing. So obviously we had to replace him, but Colin was the perfect choice because he was a great buffer to get over that moment. And then when Colin left, it was easy to start expanding the franchise and the cast, because the seal had already been broken.

COLIN MOCHRIE

Once I got the job, I thought, "This is great!" And then it sort of dawned on me what that entailed. I was taking the place of Rick. They always said, "Don't think of it that way," but I still thought of it. I really had no experience in writing any kind of political satire, and it was happening right after 9/11, which was a difficult time to write comedy. So I felt there was a lot of pressure on me, mostly put on me by myself, because of the times. It was not the best of times.

I knew my point of view was probably different from everybody else's on the show, so I thought that would be my strength—or weakness—depending on how it went, just to bring what I saw as funny. My humour tends, I think, to be a little more surreal and goofy. So I hoped that would be a nice balance to the hard-hitting stuff that was also going on.

I did a "Mansbridge One-on-One," where Peter Mansbridge went to people's houses and knocked on the doors and gave them news updates. That was a lot of fun. Then one time I was at CBC in Toronto, and someone punched me in the arm—and I turned and it was Mansbridge. He went, "Just watch it."

PETER MANSBRIDGE

Well, actually, I do a better Colin Mochrie than Colin Mochrie does of me! [*laughing*] We argue about who actually has the brand that's being copied.

I don't have a problem with their brand of entertainment. I think it's important that people like me, or people in other positions in the public eye, are made fun of. I think that that's totally fair game, and it's an opportunity for us to look human. Of course, we end up trying to be funny, too, and we're not. But I think it's good for the system, and it's good for us to be taken down a peg or two.

The cast wasn't the only thing in flux. Salter Street Films had gone public in 1998, and in 2001 Alliance Atlantis Communications acquired the company for a reported $80 million. Michael Donovan continued to produce *This Hour Has 22 Minutes* for the show's new owners; he also persuaded Jack Kellum to leave the CBC and join Alliance Atlantis as an executive producer on the show.

In 2004, Alliance Atlantis shut down Salter Street, but Donovan and business partner Charles Bishop soon launched The Halifax Film Company—and took back production of *22 Minutes*.

JACK KELLUM

Alliance Atlantis had bought the company, but one of the reasons that they bought it was because of the show. It was starting to become a valuable property. I know that they paid an awful lot of money for it, and I know that three years later, Michael bought it back for not so much money, because Alliance got into huge trouble. They had debts being called all over, so they were desperate for money.

So they sold it off, and then Michael created Halifax Film and then DHX. It was a good investment on his part.

But back in the studio in 2001, Colin Mochrie was struggling to find his place on the show. During an unplanned absence, he unintentionally gave one of the show's future stars an opportunity to move—at first, temporarily, and later, permanently—from the writers' room to the news desk.

COLIN MOCHRIE

I was going between Toronto and Halifax, and we were shooting *Whose Line*, so it was LA, too. It was a lot of air miles. I would be in Halifax from Wednesday to Saturday, and then go and do other stuff. There was one point when I was actually suffering from exhaustion, and I had to miss a taping, and I think it was Mark Critch who filled in, because he was on the writers' desk. So I like to think I was part of launching his career.

GEOFF D'EON

He must've made a very favourable impression, because we all know what happened with Mark Critch. He became the engine of *22 Minutes*. He is a prolific writer—very fast. He could ad lib probably for ten minutes on that desk, if needed.

Mochrie left the show after sticking it out for two seasons.

GERALD LUNZ

I don't think it was the right fit for Colin. Colin is a very brilliant comedic actor and personality; it was just that it was steering away from the drive that this was about the news. But it's great that Critch—I know Mark very well—that he could bring that same voice back in. He seems to understand the core show, the body politic.

GEOFF D'EON

Critch was a great fit for *22 Minutes*, just like a hand in a glove. He was interested in the news. He could write copy stories, he could write news gags, he could write characters—he was just an all-around talented, funny guy.

BILL BRIOUX

Critch is the star of the show now, and has been for a while. He's very important. He drives it. He's the face of it. I'm a big fan of Shaun and the rest of the cast—I think they're all great—but I don't think there's any doubt that Mark has been the guy for at least the last five years. He stands the tallest.

DANNY WILLIAMS
Premier of Newfoundland and Labrador, 2003–2010

I don't recall how many times I've been on the show, but I've made many different appearances, under many different circumstances, and Mark has probably been involved in over 90 per cent of them.

It's amazing the kind of chemistry that happens. It's just like—it's easy. He just makes you feel so at ease and comfortable. And I've got to be honest—we would just roll in and roll out, usually in one take.

He is such a natural; he can bring that out. If you get nervous, or are easily embarrassed—I'm sure some people have probably tightened up, over the years—you've got to trust him, first of all. Sure, there is satire and there's humour, and he will try and say things that could generally embarrass you, but there's no nastiness in it. I think that is the real trademark. He's not trying to totally embarrass you.

BILL BRIOUX
He just brings a lot of energy to it. He throws himself into those parts and he has more of an edge. He's very good on his feet. He's glib.

That was Mary Walsh for many years, and I think Mark is cut from the same cloth. He's got a brazen way of entering into those things, but he's also got a good nose for the funny.

That brazenness got Critch into some trouble early on.

In November 2004, Critch and the *22 Minutes* team travelled to Ottawa to record a segment with Liberal MP Carolyn Parrish, an outspoken critic of president George W. Bush's administration. In the process of taping the piece, Parrish was asked to step on a doll that represented Bush. The stunt went to air in a "promo" for that week's upcoming episode—but when it was brought to the attention of prime minister Paul Martin, he reprimanded Parrish and removed her from the Liberal caucus.

As Critch later explained to John Doyle in the *Globe and Mail*: "We were going to do an ambush of her, but then she agreed to play along with us. It was supposed to be a funny bit about her doing a kiss-and-make-up with George Bush. It was satire, yes. And then we asked her to do this promo where she'd stomp on the Bush doll, and that was something that somebody around here happened to have…. Suddenly, all of the big, big news outlets from the States are calling here. It was insane. Parrish got fired. But all the people who were upset about it hadn't even seen the whole piece. It was all over by the time the piece aired a few days later."

And Critch wasn't the only new cast member courting controversy in the field. Shaun Majumder had recently joined the cast, and was becoming known for his character of Raj Binder, a naïve reporter with a thick accent and a serious perspiration problem.

Majumder's gaffe came during a trip to Edmonton in 2003 to cover the NHL Heritage Classic hockey game between the Edmonton Oilers and the Montreal Canadiens. After the game, as the players posed for the official commemorative photo, Majumder—as "Raj"—snuck alongside the players, and wound up in the final photo.

Organizers of the event said it was out of line—one spokesperson called the move "idiotic"—and Majumder later apologized. But as Geoff D'Eon told The Canadian Press: "It wouldn't be the first time people from *22 Minutes* have been somewhere where people said they shouldn't."

BILL BRIOUX

Shaun is just flat-out funny. When he started doing his sweaty Raj Binder, that character really connected, and people across Canada saw that guy and laughed. That was a breakout character, and there hadn't been one for a while for the show.

He is just very good. You can throw Shaun in almost any situation and he can pull it off. He can do all the elements—the desk, the ambush, the characters. He's very versatile.

JOHN DOYLE

When I went to the taping of an episode, it was Majumder who created the whole dynamic at the taping. He was really good at keeping the room going. It's very much a stop/start process where they're doing stuff in the studio, there's stuff they have in the can, the audience has to wait while they redo something, or somebody needs more makeup. Majumder was brilliant at handling the audience and keeping them laughing, and going out into the audience and charming some of the older ladies who were there. He had material prepared, just to keep that going, which I thought—there's great skill in that.

And he was interested in doing it, and it wasn't just about sitting at the desk and waiting for the floor director to tell them to have a go at telling that joke. He was interested in keeping the room hot with affection for the show and with laughter.

I think that's very much his personality when he does live comedy. When he's on stage, there's almost no pause button with him.

GEOFF D'EON

Shaun loves a live audience, and in the course of a *22 Minutes* taping, there's lots of opportunity between takes for the cast to interact with the audience. It's a small studio, so everyone has a great seat. Anyone who goes to a *22 Minutes* taping has very close proximity with the mechanics of how a television show is made, which people seem to enjoy, and also with the cast themselves. Sometimes they're literally sitting twelve feet from Shaun Majumder doing a character, or Cathy Jones doing a character. Shaun has an easy facility to make an audience laugh. He is incredibly charming in person, and he loves it. Like most performers, they feed off of love. Love is the fuel, and Shaun always gets a lot of love from the audience.

But Majumder hasn't had a constant presence on the show. He's often absent from the cast, as he pursues "serious" acting gigs elsewhere.

STEPHEN REYNOLDS
Director, 2004–2012
Shaun was kind of a rising star in the rest of the country, and he spent February and March in Los Angeles, during what's referred to as audition season or pilot season. He didn't want to commit to the show for the season.

JOHN DOYLE

At one point, I went out [and] did a longish feature on *22 Minutes*. I went to the offices and talked to pretty much everyone individually, and then I went to a taping of the show.

With both Gavin and Majumder, the first thing they wanted to emphasize was how many other things they had going. Both of them were talking about development deals they had with an American network; something they had written was going to be a pilot, or somebody was looking to cast them in something. They were going to LA regularly.

I was amused by it, because their first impulse was essentially to say, "I'm so much bigger than this," you know? "I'm so connected to, like, real show-biz—not this little show here in Halifax."

BILL BRIOUX

Yeah, he's been in and out of the show, but I think his presence is so strong that it sort of blends together. You don't realize that he's been stepping off the show several times in the last eight or nine years. He goes down and makes a show for ABC and he's gone for a few months, but his contributions are pretty strong.

In January 2004, Rick Mercer and Gerald Lunz launched *Rick Mercer's Monday Report*, which would eventually become the *Rick Mercer Report*, on CBC. That show would have an impact on *22 Minutes* in many ways—including a newfound rivalry over ratings—but, more immediately, because it lured away the only director *22 Minutes* had ever known: Henry Sarwer-Foner.

HENRY SARWER-FONER

I kind of left halfway through a season, around Christmastime. I gave everybody lots of warning, and then they decided to have [*Trailer Park Boys* director] Mike Clattenburg job-shadow me for a couple of months.

Clattenburg directed just seven episodes in Season 12 before leaving to shoot *Trailer Park Boys: The Movie*. Attention then turned to Halifax director Stephen Reynolds, who had directed numerous episodes of Salter Street's *Made in Canada* series, and who had also been a producer on *CODCO*.

STEPHEN REYNOLDS

Jenipher [Ritchie] is the line producer, and she reaches out to me. She says, "We think Mike is not going to continue with the show. Geoff D'Eon doesn't know you, but could you do a little trial?" I guess it was probably a month.

The show was a very efficient machine, and you'd need to do a couple of shows to get a sense of what it was. I don't think I got beyond the first week when Jenipher approached and said, "We'd like you to finish the year. We don't know anything beyond that, but let's get started."

JACK KELLUM

It was difficult for us to fill Henry's shoes, but we did. Stephen Reynolds was very good, but things had already been set. Henry had already set it into a style. Other than changing the set periodically, every five years or so, Stephen really couldn't make drastic changes to the on-air look of it—nor do I think it was reasonable to do so.

STEPHEN REYNOLDS

My first season was 2004/2005, and my perception at the time was that there was a rebirth happening, that there was a kickoff going, that there was something new about the show. There was a refresh happening—demanded—and I was going to be part of that.

By now, Mary Walsh was spending less and less time on the set because of her other commitments, which included two CBC series—*Open Book*, and

Hatching, Matching and Dispatching. With Shaun, Mark, and Cathy rounding out the cast, another young comedian and performer, originally from Alberta, began to draw the attention of *22 Minutes* producers.

GAVIN CRAWFORD

Cast Member, 2003–2011

I think I was on their radar a little bit because of *The Gavin Crawford Show*. Way back in the early 2000s, I remember I was up for a Gemini for that show; it was in the same category as all the cast members from *This Hour Has 22 Minutes,* and I was really jazzed. I felt very humbled just to be in the same category as those guys.

Then they asked me, I think the next year, if I wanted to come and try out for *22.* It was right after Rick left, and I said no.

I said, "I don't think that's for me. I don't do the same thing as Rick does, and I don't think I would be a good Rick replacement." I didn't want to be that guy that stepped into *22* right after Rick left and everyone was like, "Oooh, that's terrible!"

So, luckily, they got Colin Mochrie to do that instead. Colin is kind of unflappable, and so good that it wouldn't matter. So that was perfect.

I thought that was it. I remember Michael being surprised, and he asked me to come and have a meeting with him. He was like, "Why is he saying no?" I've had the tendency to surprise him, it seems, over the years.

I just said, "Well, we are doing another season of *The Gavin Crawford Show*, and I just don't think it's the right place for me right now," and I sort of thought that was that.

• • •

GAVIN CRAWFORD

A couple of years later, they called me and said, "Do you want to come in? Mary is taking a break for two weeks, so would you come in for two weeks?"

So I came in to do two weeks for Mary, thinking, "I don't know if I'm going to be at all good at this, but I will give it a shot, because it's only two weeks." It was kind of a nice luxury, knowing that you're just done after two weeks and it doesn't really matter how good or bad you do. It's just a finite contract so you just go, do your best, and don't worry about anything other than just trying to do your best.

I did that, and it went fairly well, and then Mary kept coming back for two weeks and then she would go away for two weeks again. They would always call me, like, two days before, and they would be like, "Hi, do you want to come back for another two weeks?" And I would do the show for two weeks, and at the end they would say, "Great—thanks for coming. We'll maybe see you when we see you."

Then Mary would come back, and then they would call me again, and that sort of happened through the whole first year. I think I went in about eight times. It was like every other two weeks for the season, which is nerve-racking and super fun.

I never actually worked with Mary on *22 Minutes*, because she was always out when I was in. I was super excited to work with Cathy, because she does characters like I do. It was the character stuff that always drew me to watch *22 Minutes*—that was always the stuff I liked the best.

So I did that whole year, just coming in and out, which was actually probably the best year that you can have at *22* because you are never fully hired. You don't care about the politics. You're just doing your thing, and you know you're fired at the end of every two weeks, so you don't worry about it.

STEPHEN REYNOLDS

Gavin is a true force, and has an incredible talent base. He is the ultimate chameleon. He can do an incredible number of impersonations. He has an incredibly elastic voice and face and could fit in a number of places.

GAVIN CRAWFORD

Performing in front of a studio audience was new for me. For a performer, it's more fun to tape the sketch live—it just is.

You can make the sketch look better if you pre-shoot it, but when you're shooting a sketch during the week, you are there with the crew, but the crew can't laugh because the mics are on. Even if they think it's funny, they can't laugh. So you're trying to do funny things and you're stuck in this quiet room. It's very weird, especially if you are used to doing theatre, or any kind of thing where you get instant feedback. It's a totally different energy.

I always enjoyed taping the sketches live in front of the audience, because you get that actual feedback, and you can play. Usually, we taped them through twice, so you can kind of goof around a bit on the second take—which is maybe not great for the producers, but it was very much more fun for us, and sometimes you just end up with some really hilarious stuff.

JENNIFER WHALEN
Writer, 2003–2007; Head Writer, 2007–2009
I think Gavin coming into the show was a big change, because of his incredible gift—he is able to, basically, do anything—I think it opened up the doors for the writers in a lot ways. Whatever you throw at him, he can do.

STEPHEN REYNOLDS
Gavin became principally charged with critiquing contemporary culture. So, not quite politics. He could talk about TV shows or commercials or the entertainment industry, but I know he was pushed towards that politicizing of culture—to find the funny inside why daytime talk shows had a stranglehold on much of society, and how could we talk about that?

GAVIN CRAWFORD
People think a sketch show is always a super fun joke-fest all the time, which it is, onscreen, but it is an intense thing to do. It's very hard to put out that amount of material every week. You have a number of writers and actors, and everyone is trying to do their very best, everyone is trying to get their voices heard, and then you have another layer of people on top of that who

are making the decisions about what ideas get through. And sometimes you agree with them, and sometimes you don't, so it's a difficult thing to do. In every environment that I've done that kind of thing in, it's always an intense kind of process.

So to go in and not be a permanent resident was nice, because it just took all that pressure off. You didn't have to worry about anything. You had kind of no say in anything at all, but in a weird way that's almost a better place than thinking you have any say when, really, you probably don't.

Gavin didn't have a chance to luxuriate in that impermanence for long. In 2004, Mary Walsh officially left the show to pursue her many other film, television, and writing projects, although she retained a standing invitation to return for a few episodes each season.

GAVIN CRAWFORD

They called me and said, "Do you want to come in for the full season?" And I said yes, because I had kind of gotten over most of the things that I was afraid of in that first season.

I knew from watching the show that either Mary, or Rick, or whoever it was would go out and ambush politicians. I am very shy in real life, and I like to obey the rules. If there was a "Keep off the Grass" sign, and my friends ran onto the grass, I'd be like, "But there's a sign!" That kind of stuff makes me nervous, and the way they do it is, they just literally say, "Oh, Brian Mulroney is going to be at the Delta in Halifax on Tuesday. Let's go down and get him!"

The writers will drum up a few things, but they can't really do too much. Because, first of all, they will write things that you could never say to a person's face. Or you don't know the context. So they arm you with as much stuff as they can, but you're really kind of out there on your own.

Then you just have to jump out and corner the politician and turn the camera on. And because they are politicians, when you turn a camera on, they generally don't freak out. They generally try to be polite and go along.

STEPHEN REYNOLDS

I know, at the base of it, he'd be pushed by the producers, pushed by the rest of the writing team, to be more daring, or be more edgy. He would find himself slightly fearful of how it might impact negatively on somebody.

GAVIN CRAWFORD

The first one I had to do was the opening of Parliament. They needed to send somebody up to the opening of Parliament. They used to do that in the days before Harper formed the government and they locked it down, and comedians couldn't go there anymore. But we used to have full access.

So they were like, "We want you to go and cover the opening of Parliament" and I was like, "I've never been in Parliament before."

I had this sort of German fashion-designer character I used to do, and I thought, why don't I just go as him? Then I'll just pretend I'm critiquing their fashions like it's a red carpet opening. So we did that, and it was fine. It was a little bit terrifying, but I had a fair amount of prep for it, and they were like, "Don't worry about it—no pressure. Get who you can get, and we'll see what you come up with."

• • •

GAVIN CRAWFORD

The next time, I think was actually Brian Mulroney, and it was one of those things where he was doing a speech in Halifax that afternoon, and they told me in the morning, "Oh, we need somebody to go down and talk to Brian Mulroney."

I was like, "Do we have an appointment?" and they were like, "We don't make appointments, we just go!" and I was like, "I don't think I can do that." The fashion-designer character made no sense, and I didn't want to just go and be myself, because I didn't think I knew enough about politics. Certainly not about Brian Mulroney's politics, because I was very young and not really paying much attention to what was going on during the Mulroney administration.

So I just said, "Look, I have this teenage character that I used to do on *The Gavin Crawford Show* that's a zitty kid with braces and a crappy wig like he has a bad bowl cut." And it was one of the more popular characters from that show.

I said to Farrell, "Can I just go as Mark Jackson? Then I'll just do the tilt like I don't know who Brian Mulroney is, but I'm really a super big fan of Ben Mulroney." It gave me something to improvise with, which was what I needed. And also, Mark Jackson is super awkward, so if I was nervous to jump up and start asking questions, I didn't have to project any level of confidence. Because I didn't have any. I could use my own non-confidence and just ramp it up—lack of confidence squared—and then I figured I would be able to do it. And it worked really well.

A lot of times, politicians just thought they were talking to some awkward kid. I mean, we had a *22 Minutes* mic flag, but they must've thought, "Oh, they hired this kid to do interviews" or something, so it would disarm them very nicely because they wouldn't want to be rude to a kid. And I could also kind of come from a place of innocence, so I could ask quite pointed questions, but from that place of not really understanding how politics works.

• • •

GAVIN CRAWFORD

Mark Jackson became my most famous character on *22 Minutes*. It was a fun character for me to do. I had done it for a number of years on *The Gavin Crawford Show* and I had really kind of honed it. He has a whole backstory you never see on the show.

You can see it in bits and pieces in sketches: he has a gay dad who left his mother for his dental assistant, and the mother is really bitter about it; his mother was always quite hard with Mark, and he's always trying really hard, but his mother always treats him like he's a failure. I wanted to make a modern kind of Charlie Brown-type character, except not aware of how depressing his life is—just sort of unflaggingly positive, no matter how badly everything is going.

It's a fun place to make jokes from. It's a fun mindset to be in, to see how much torture you can put this poor character through and have him still looking on the bright side.

I think maybe the year after that, or two years after that, there was an election cycle, and that's when I really had to do a lot of Mark Jacksons. I had to do Stephen Harper and Jack Layton.

That was a hard year, because you work all week writing sketches, and then every weekend you're flying to Ottawa or somewhere else to try and track down one politician or another. So thank God for Mark Jackson, because I would have died of horror and embarrassment if I hadn't been able to do that.

Even still, it's like, "Oh Gilles Duceppe is speaking in Montréal. Fly in to Montréal tomorrow and then—here's a café; change in the bathroom. Draw these zits on your face, run to the thing."

I'm sure it was torture to work with me, because I would be so nervous. From the time they told me that I had to do it, until the time it was over, I would just be gut-wrenchingly nervous, so I'm sure it wasn't relaxing to be on the road with me. I don't think I was terrible, but to the producers, this was fun. I was always green, like I was about to go on a roller coaster.

PETER SUTHERLAND

He was always worried, for sure. I remember chasing one of the prime ministers; I had my headset on, and I could hear him saying, "What am I going to ask him?"

But it's frightening! It's tough to go in front all the media and put yourself out there.

GAVIN CRAWFORD

Oh God! One time, they were like, "Let's send Mark Jackson to do the Much-

Music VJ audition." And I was like—really? Because you actually have to do it. It was in a mall in front of everyone, and for some reason I thought it would be funny if he just wet his pants—went up and tried to do the best audition, and slowly wet his pants as it was happening. So we rigged up this balloon and a water bottle, and we didn't tell the host what was going to happen.

I don't even know—she must've known that I was from *22*, but I can't remember, because usually what they try to do is don't tell anybody anything about what's happening. So they just put me on the list, then you're kind of going up cold into this kind of pranking environment.

I had to make up a VJ audition, and I remember just being like, "Oh, this is my nightmare, here in this mall, with nobody knowing that I'm not real." When they know it's a sketch, it feels different than when everybody thinks this is just me. It ended up being a very funny bit, but I was nervous.

PETER SUTHERLAND

Gavin is amazing. He is a brilliant character actor. He got onstage and pretended to pee his pants for MuchMusic.

GAVIN CRAWFORD

I guess it's fun to do in the moment, but I'm so in the moment that I often don't remember what was happening, because I just have to start doing it. And one of the things that's frustrating sometimes is, you basically hand the tape off to the field producer and they take it away and you don't see it again until it's the night of the show. They can cut it any way they want it, and sometimes it can be frustrating because you can be like, "But you left out this thing or that thing."

I used to be frustrated sometimes at the beginning, because they would cut out the responses. They would sort of do flash cuts, so it would be a funny question from me, but they wouldn't show their response, really—they'd just show their face before their response. And I would be like, "You've got to leave some of them talking. Otherwise it's just a flash cut of me being like dumb question, dumb question, dumb question." And you think: why did I bother going all that way to get them, when it's just me standing beside them, saying things?

It's always a bit of a power struggle. You're essentially kind of improvising a piece, and then you have to hand it over to someone else, and just sort of trust that they will make it the best thing it can be.

• • •

GAVIN CRAWFORD

I actually killed Mark Jackson. Well, I didn't kill him; I retired him. We had him grow up and move to LA to become a model. It's on YouTube somewhere. It was a sad kind of bittersweet sketch with me and Cathy.

I will still do him sometimes in stand-up, when it's far away and you can't see that I'm not anywhere near being able to pull off being a sixteen-year-old anymore.

One of Gavin's many strengths—and one that he could exploit in the studio, where he was much more comfortable—was his ability to do impersonations.

GAVIN CRAWFORD

I was very excited at first when I got to do Chantal Hébert. That took a long time, because I kept pitching it and pitching it, and the powers that be were like "No, people don't know who Chantal Hébert is." And I used to make the argument that if they are watching *22 Minutes*, they are watching *The National*. It's not like the CBC audience comes just for *22*.

I said, "It's twenty minutes in the studio in front of a green screen. Can we just try it? And if the audience doesn't laugh, then I will shut up about it." Sometimes you have to go that far to the mat—you have to be a little bit tenacious about certain things.

So they agreed to do that, and we shot it and we showed it in front of the audience, and of course the audience knew who Chantal Hébert was—and because we have kind of similar-looking jaws, it just worked—and people really liked it. So that was really fun.

But then what happens is that every week, they want to do a Chantal Hébert sketch. And you are like, "But it doesn't make any sense in this context." It's such a fine line between a sketch that has a point of view and just the cartoony impressions. I am certainly guilty of doing both at different stages, but the goal is to have the point of view behind it, because that's what makes the sketch really kind of resonate.

The point of the first "At Issue" panel we did was that everybody on that panel was supposed to be having a debate, but they all just constantly agreed with each other. If you watch an American panel, they are all screaming at each other, but if you watch a Canadian panel, they are like, "I think my arch-enemy, the Conservative, has a very solid point." So that was kind of the undercurrent of what we wanted to do with the "At Issue" sketches.

STEPHEN REYNOLDS

Gavin did an amazing Rufus Wainwright impersonation. Those pieces were generally always funny, but they played to a very niche market. And it needed to work in concert with something that was in the news, or something that was big and broad.

GAVIN CRAWFORD

Getting Rufus Wainwright on the first time was fun for me, because that was a bit of a push. And to be fair, in my circles, Rufus Wainwright was very famous and very popular, but in larger circles—not so much. But enough people were familiar enough that I could eventually get it on. And it worked.

STEPHEN REYNOLDS

We found ourselves often not choosing to do those sketches, and if it wasn't Mark Farrell or somebody else, it was me who was the reason we weren't doing those sketches. So, some vitriol would come at me as a result.

One of the last sketches he did was another Rufus song that was ultimately really funny and really biting, and I put a little extra effort into the execution of it. It's a beautiful-looking piece, and it's an incredibly well-played piece on his part, and it really sang.

When he finished, we had a hug and a great heart-to-heart and he said, "Even though I hated the decisions that you made often, Steve, you always made me look good. Especially in this last piece. You might have despised the way I treated you, but you always made the sketch look great and play wonderfully."

I'm exaggerating a little. I think he said, "Steve, you're okay." But in my mind, it was all those other things.

Greg Thomey left the show in 2005; some reports suggested that he had been "let go," but his reasons for leaving were not disclosed. He would return again as a writer and occasional performer in 2012, but his departure opened up another vacancy in the cast.

STEPHEN REYNOLDS

So Shaun was a part-timer, Gavin Crawford had replaced Rick, and Mark Critch was essentially moving into the centre with Mary gone, even though Gavin and Mark were the replacements. There was a need for another voice—another female voice—and that became Geri Hall.

GERI HALL
Cast Member, 2006–2011

The first season I did *22 Minutes* [in 2004], they brought me in just for a two-week trial. At the end of that period, they said, "Do you want to stay another week?" and I said, "Oh my gosh, I'd love to." And then I think I had to skip a week—somebody else was coming in for a trial—and then they asked me if I wanted to come out for the final show of the season. So that first season, I just did a few episodes.

At the time, they didn't tell me much. I just knew that I was coming out as a guest. But the longer I was out there, I sort of realized: they are checking on chemistry, they are seeing what you have to offer, they're keeping an eye on you to see, "Is this someone who could fit in with us, or is this just like a fun little temporary guest who can liven up the desk while someone is on vacation?"

STEPHEN REYNOLDS

There were two or three other women comedians who were invited as part of the process, and they all did tremendously, but it felt like Geri had a distinctive voice—which she physically does—but she had an interesting range, and a particular point of view that was lacking in the company at the time.

GERI HALL

It felt to me like it went well. I came home thinking everyone seemed to be happy. Fingers crossed—let's see. And my agent heard a rumour: yes, indeed, they were trying a few women this year, and they are looking for somebody.

I think the reasoning was, if I'm not mistaken, at that time Shaun was starting to book a lot of work in the States. They were very supportive of his career there, and whenever he booked something, he had to go, and go quickly. So I think they were looking for that extra cast member so that initially, when Shaun wasn't around, they would have someone they could rely on.

So the next season started up, and lo and behold, nobody calls from *22 Minutes*. And I thought, "Well, maybe they're just starting the season off with a core group. Maybe someone will need a weekend off." And nothing happened.

I called my agency at the time and I said, "Hey, it really felt like it went well. What's going on?" and they said, "We haven't heard anything, sorry. If they want you, they will call you." So that whole season went by, and I would turn the show on—when I could stand the heartbreak of it all—and see various women being tried out, and I thought, "Oh, they're back to looking, so I guess it didn't go as well as I felt it did."

So I switched agents, for different reasons, and when I sat down with my new agent, Lorne Perlmutar, at our first meeting, he said, "Tell me about your career. What's your goal? What do you want?" so I started listing what my goals were.

I said I wanted to do more dramatic work. I said I wanted to try to break out of this and more into that, and I gave him sort of the wish list. And I said, "And you know, I really want to try get back on *22 Minutes*. I want to figure out how we can do that, because something in my gut says that it was working, and I just don't know why I didn't get called again. So I just want to find a way to get back in their minds."

And he said, "Well, do you want me to make some phone calls? I know Mark Farrell, the showrunner. I can make some calls for you." And I said, "You know what? I think I've got a fun idea, and it's a little bit crazy, but I'd rather do it this way."

So I sat down—I was someone with nothing to lose at this point—and wrote a "fan letter" to *22 Minutes*. It went something like: "Dear Mark Farrell and *22 Minutes* producers: I was on a plane the other day and caught a rerun of *22 Minutes*. Lo and behold, there was this quirky saucebox of a red-haired actress who was so hilarious in the opening scenes. Then she was in a sketch and—my lord!—she disappeared into her character. I barely knew it was her! And the next thing was a double-ender, and she really made me think about politics. She made me laugh, but she made me think, too."

The letter was this silly, silly thing that just got more and more implausible, and by the end of it, I said, "If you have half a brain, please get her back on the show, because I feel like I won't watch it again unless you do. Sincerely, Geri Hall, care of Diamondfield Entertainment, available anytime you guys need me." Phone number, mailing address, all that stuff.

I showed it to my agent, and he said, "This is ridiculous." I said, "I know, but it feels right, for some reason." And he said, "Really? You are going to do this?" and I said, "I'm doing it."

We emailed it, and I don't think two weeks went by before Mark Farrell called me and said, "Hey, I got your letter. Pretty funny. Do you want to come out and do some more episodes?"

And I said yes.

• • •

GERI HALL

So I went back out, I think for another two weeks. I had booked a pilot that was shooting in Vancouver, so I let *22* know in advance that I could work up until a certain date, but I would have to fly to BC to do that pilot, and I could come back to them if they still wanted me.

Mark Farrell had to fly to Toronto that same day, so we ended up sitting on the plane together, and because of one of those amazing Halifax storms, we ended up stuck on the tarmac together, sitting side-by-side, just talking about anything.

He said, "I'm glad you came back. We didn't think you were interested."

My jaw dropped. I said, "What do you mean?" and he said, "Well, we called your agent at the very beginning of the following season and said that we wanted to have you back, and they said that you had two days as a principal on this other show shooting in Québec, and because of that, you wouldn't be able to come out and do the show."

They never told me that *22* called, and it was for, literally, a two-line part—like, a little comedic pop-in in this series in Québec. So if I hadn't written that crazy and very undignified letter, *22* would have just thought that I was giving them the brush-off, or that I didn't understand what an opportunity I was passing up. It was quite shocking. My jaw hit the floor of that plane and I said, "Well, thank you so much for responding to the letter, despite what looked like a brush-off from me. I'm thrilled to be back here."

So after the pilot, I went back to *22*, and at that point, at the end of every two- or four-week period, they would say, "How about another two weeks? This time do you think you could stay for four?" So two weeks turned to eight weeks, turned to ten weeks, and then I was a regular on the show.

It really was a roller coaster. And you know actors—we are not really known for our confidence and self-esteem. We are good at faking it, most of us, but that year of wondering—"Why didn't they like me? I tried my hardest."

You get so used to rejection as an actor. Of course, initially I was disappointed, but I just thought, "Well, it wasn't my part to have." And then you go on with things and focus on the next thing. You get rejected way more than you get chosen, and you grieve for some losses more than others as an actor.

But yeah, I'm glad, obviously, that it turned out the way it did.

• • •

Season 15 featured a new character: "Special Correspondent" Nathan Fielder, who played "Nathan on Your Side"—an awkward consumer reporter whose role was ostensibly to investigate questions from viewers.

Fielder's deadpan style failed to resonate with the *22 Minutes* audience, and he lasted just two seasons, leaving in 2009. Michael Donovan remarked to a reporter that, while "many fans of the show [didn't] get Fielder's style, [there were] plenty who thoroughly enjoy his awkward, sometimes painful interviews." Fielder himself emerged unscathed; he later spun this persona off into a series on Comedy Central called *Nathan for You.*

Fielder wasn't the only so-called "special correspondent" ever featured on the show. Over the years, dozens of actors, comedians, musicians, and even athletes—from actors Alan Thicke and Jonathan Torrens, to NHL hockey player P. K. Subban, to musician Joel Plaskett—would be granted guest spots, or offered trial runs, on the cast.

It was all part of keeping the show fresh—as was showrunner Mark Farrell's practice of continually testing out new writers.

GERI HALL

I'm going to guess that the writing room, over the time I was there, averaged between eight and ten people. Sometimes it was bigger, sometimes it was smaller. And not unlike the cast, there would be a core group of writers, just like there was a core cast, but then they would always bring fresh voices into that room. So a lot of stand-ups would get a call to say, "Hey, you've got two weeks on *22 Minutes*. Come on into the room and see what you can offer." And some of those people were offered longer stays and permanent jobs, and then, for some people, it maybe wasn't the right fit, or the pace of the show was wrong, or they were going on to other work. So that constant flow of the potential for new talent, it sort of happened both onscreen and behind the scenes there.

JENNIFER WHALEN

How I got hired was, I had a project in development with Disney; they had green-lit my show and they were going to make a pilot of it. That was sort of early fall 2003, I think. So I knew I had a job in January, but I didn't have anything until January. I was like, "What am I going to do? It's not really long enough to get a job." Jen Robertson was working there, and Jen said, "Well, I'm doing *22 Minutes*. Why don't you come down? They're trying new writers all the time, and it would be a short-term job. It might solve all your problems."

I said, "Okay, I'll do that." I sat down and studied the show, and wrote a package and gave it to her, and she made sure that it got on the right desk. I think Peter McBain was a writer at the time and, and he was very helpful and sent me some samples of what a sketch looked like. So I knew the format and sort of the ballpark.

I went and did a two-week trial, and then they asked me to stay. I think I stayed up until maybe just before Christmas, and then didn't come back because of my pilot. And, then, of course, as things do, I sort of went into development hell with that. So that summer I just happened to be at the Rivoli on a night where Mark Farrell, who was showrunner at that time, was looking at stand-ups—he was looking for writers—and he ran into me and was like, "Oh, yeah." Then a couple weeks later, I got the call to say, "Would you come and be a full-time writer for us?"

TIM MCAULIFFE
Writer, 2006–2009; Showrunner, 2010–2011
Mark Farrell hired me based on a small sample, I guess. I just basically submitted a package. What they do is, they give you a two-week trial, and then, in that two weeks, they have to figure out if you're worthy of hanging out, and if you're catching on.

JENNIFER WHALEN
I didn't have very high expectations, because I kind of knew through the comedy community that it was a difficult gig—difficult in terms of, you know, it was competitive. The pace of putting on a weekly show was very different than other TV shows, which generally take months and months and months to write. But this is like—it's gotta be done by the end of the week. So I knew that going in.

GAVIN CRAWFORD
They would try people out, and that's always a hard thing for a new writer. It's like, "Yes, we want your voice," but really they want your voice tailored to the voice of the show, and it's hard for some people to come in and be like, "How do I crack this?"

JENNIFER WHALEN
I totally agree with Gavin. It's finding a way to make what you personally think is funny fit into the mould of the show. That's kind of the challenge and the game of it. "How can I do what I really like, but make it within the ballpark of what the show does?"

TIM MCAULIFFE
I love that. To me, that's very exciting, the idea of writing for a specific voice. I don't really feel like I have my own voice a lot of the time, so I do enjoy the idea of writing for other people.

Mark Critch is one of my best buddies—he married my wife and I. He is just a great dude, so I love writing for Mark. And then Gavin is so funny; I love writing for Gavin.

I'd watched the show growing up. It's weird; that show has been around for so long that I really watched it growing up. I knew the style of comedy, and I loved Cathy and all those people. So I kind of knew the tone going in.

GERI HALL

I can't fathom what a new writer goes through, because as an actor, I get to sort of do what I do. But when writers come in, they have to try and write something that's right for the cast, so my heart always went out to them. Even on the most challenging days we had as actors, I think it paled in comparison to what people went through in the writers' room.

GAVIN CRAWFORD

I wrote for myself and for others as well. I would write stuff for Shaun and I to do together. And I would write stuff for Cathy to do. I would sometimes write stuff for the women to do together because they would sometimes be… how do I put this delicately? Sometimes the women would get short shrift in terms of what was written for them to do, at least when I was there. So sometimes I would try and write stuff for the women to do.

JENNIFER WHALEN

I loved to write for Cathy, because she can do anything. She's so gifted that it was really fun to sort of knock it out. The other thing about Cathy is she will make anything her own.

I remember in particular, there was this one scene. I think there was supposed to be two males—I think they were hydro workers or something. And Cathy's like, "I want to play one of the guys; I'm going to do it in drag." And in the read, she just did it, and it was so funny that everyone was like, "Yeah, of course, you have to do that!" because she really knew how to make things her own.

GAVIN CRAWFORD

The writing process changes all the time. When I first got there [in 2003], not a lot of the actors would write. Greg wrote stuff, but it was always really bizarre. Sometimes it would get on and sometimes it wouldn't, but Greg is so funny. I just loved to hear whatever sketches Greg had written for the week, because sometimes they were so bizarre, but so hilarious.

JENNIFER WHALEN

I remember this sketch that Greg Thomey wrote. I still think about it. It was like an infomercial for, like, a clear Plexiglas box that you could put over your head when you were in public. So, you're riding the bus or you're in a bank lineup—so people just know not to talk to you. I still think about that sometimes. I'm like, "I actually would like that!"

JOHN DOYLE

I was surprised at how few writers were working on the show. I think there were four when I was there, which seemed to me to be a low number, and only one of them was a woman—Jennifer Whalen.

I talked to Jennifer and—like many people in that circumstance—she was not going to dish the dirt to me about anything that was going on behind the scenes. She said she had a perfectly good experience working on the show with only male writers, and it kind of worked in her favour, because the kind of material she was able to write was not something that other writers could do. That gave her a certain cachet, and it meant that the other writers were not hostile to her, because they knew that she had unique material to bring to it.

JENNIFER WHALEN

I did my first season in which I was just really learning the job, and that was difficult because you're away from home, you're away from your friends and your family. I was the only woman in the room at that point and I was just trying to make my way and negotiate that.

So after the first season, I felt like, "Okay, I think people respect me. They think I'm funny now." Also, I had written sketch, but I'd never really written an actual set-up-punchline joke before. So that was a big learning curve for me. It's something that I eventually mastered, but—boy, did it take a lot.

And then in the second season, I was like, "Well, okay. I should come back, because it was a tough job to learn and I've learned it, and now I think I can do it." So I did that, and then, the third season, I was like, "Okay—this will be fun." And then, once I was done the third season, they asked me to be head writer, and I was like, "Well, of course I have to do that!"

Being head writer means that you are helping to manage a room full of writers, to make sure that the showrunner gets the materials they need to manage the personalities.

With the news cycle, sometimes you have hard weeks when there is not a lot of good news. Political scandal is great for us. Missing children, murdered police officers—those are terrible news stories for us...so in those weeks, it's trying to figure out different ways in, and different angles that we can take as a room, to try and find something funny for the show, because it's sort of a beast that must be fed. There is a certain amount of material you just have to generate, whether or not the news is giving you the raw material for that.

GERI HALL

What I found the most intimidating about it—I was never worried about the potential of offending with satire, or of saying something that people might disagree with. It was more that I felt like, "Oh my gosh, I've got to get up to speed on the state of this country and the issues, so that in this tiny little window of opportunity that is about a day and a half when the whole show gets written, I've got enough of a satirical eye, and I can look at the newspaper—which is so full of awful things—and still see the opportunities for comedy and for levity."

So that stuff was intimidating, for sure. There are people on that show, in the writing room and some of the cast members, who are just prolific and gifted satirists. That stuff is their life, and for me I had to learn that stuff. I think some of them were born to it.

Gerald's tradition of the weekly "humilatorium" continued, although it had evolved with the addition of more writers. By 2008, the show's airdate had shifted many times, from Mondays at 9 P.M., to Fridays at 8 P.M., to where it had settled at this point—with the show taping on Monday nights, and airing on Tuesdays at 8:30.

GAVIN CRAWFORD

When I was there, the writers had to write probably five sketches a week, and you have about two days to write those sketches, from ideas meeting to handing them in. And then of those sketches, they compile a book, and if you're lucky, three of your sketches will get into that book. If you're unlucky, none of them will. So before you even get to the first read-through, a good 40 per cent of everyone's work is tossed out the window without ever even being read aloud. So that's hard for people.

And sometimes, of course, you'll write three sketches that you think are brilliant and then one that you just dash off to fill your quota, and then the next morning that will be the one that's in the book, and you are like, "But I spent literally two minutes on this."

JENNIFER WHALEN

We'd generally start the week with an ideas meeting. Everybody comes in, and we all pitch ideas, and it's mostly just to make sure that everybody isn't writing the same jokes; that there's a variety of news things that are being covered. That's kind of like an hour or two. There's a lot of joking around, there's a lot of drinking coffee, waking up, stories about what you did the night before, that kind of thing.

Then people go off to their separate quarters and write, and then the next day, by about noon, one o'clock, you have to have all of your sketches in. I think it was five sketches that you had to have in. You may see writers humming to themselves happily if they're like, "I have great things." And then you'll see the nervous writer gulping coffee because they're like, "Oh, God! I have three sketches—I need two more, and I have no ideas."

Depending on each writer's personal struggle, you may see different things in different cubicles and then you hand everything in. And then you'd wait, because Mark, the showrunner, would read them and decide what got in the book.

So that was kind of the first hurdle of the week—if you wrote five sketches, how many of your sketches did you get in the book? If you got all five, that's fantastic. If you got four, that's great. Three…? But it was entirely possible, if you were a new writer, to get nothing in the book, and that just kind of meant what you wrote wasn't quite in the ballpark for them. That was just a horrible feeling if that happened to you.

So after the sketches were picked for the book, then later that afternoon, around four o'clock, we'd have a read-through with the actors. You'd sit at a table with all the actors and they would read all of the sketches, and from there you would find out what lived and died.

GAVIN CRAWFORD

It's tense, and it's difficult for the writers, because they have to hear their stuff out loud, and they have to be sitting there. They want it to go well, and they want people to laugh at it. Plus you get the politics of, are certain friends of this person just laughing because they're friends with that person? Are they going to laugh at my sketch because we are not as good friends? Is the actor going to mess my sketch up? If they do, was it on purpose?

JENNIFER WHALEN

I was continually amazed and impressed with Gavin's generosity towards the writers. I mean, you know, the most junior person would come in with not even a fully formed idea, and he would sit down, and he would work with them until they had something. And he never dismissed somebody's idea or was like, "Echhh." He always was just like, "Yes!" and jumped in with both feet. And, you know, in the read, he gave everybody's sketch his all. I just thought that was, professionally, one of the most generous things I've ever seen in my life.

GAVIN CRAWFORD

I sort of made a point to try my best when I was there to just read every sketch the best that I could, because I think that's the best way to go about it. But sometimes it can be difficult when you are reading through the book and you think, "This is a terrible sketch."

I would sometimes read a sketch and be like, "Oh, this is so *Benny Hill.*" But you've got to give it your all, and you know they are going to pick it, just because you know the machine. And you're like, "Oh, this is an interesting sketch that goes off in kind of a new direction" and you know this is going to be such a hard sell, even though it's a really great sketch, because you know the kind of stuff that they like to make.

JENNIFER WHALEN

So, say you had a great week and you got, you know, your five sketches in the book and you're feeling good, then, after the read-through, the showrunner and the head writer and some of the producers go away and decide what's gonna get made. The writers sit and bite their nails and perhaps have a drink. And then you come back down and it's usually around five or six o'clock and you would find out what was getting made and what was not getting made.

So you might have started off being, "I am on top of the world." But there's five sketches in the book, and none of them are getting made, so then you feel terrible. And then the person who got one sketch in the book—that sketch sung at the read-through and everybody loved it. It was going to be the hit of the week. They're getting it made, so they feel good. So, you had to sort of be careful about how you celebrated that, because although you might be personally having a great week, the person next to you might be having a terrible week. So you sort of had to be either quietly pleased or quietly angry.

GAVIN CRAWFORD

Sometimes you can push something through, and sometimes it's as arbitrary as, "We already have that set," because it's a fast work environment. Everyone has so much to do that sometimes they will just be like "Oh, great. One of those sketches. We have the set for that. We can just pull it out of storage. We don't have to build a new costume. Got some new jokes. Great—let's go."

And sometimes as a performer, that can be frustrating, because you're like, "But I've done that eight times this season." But the reality of working in that fast environment—sometimes that's just the way it goes.

GEOFF D'EON

There was a team of producers whose job it was to help assign the material that was to be shot that week—or to have an opinion. The showrunner was paramount. The showrunner was the de facto executive producer, so Mark Farrell was the showrunner, but he was also an executive producer. So he had the loudest voice in the room, for legitimate reasons.

TIM MCAULIFFE

After the read, you just basically have a couple of drinks, and then they come back and tell you if it's going to be on the show, and then over the next two days they film it. They build the sets overnight on Wednesday night, and then they film them. It's pretty amazing. I love the immediacy of the whole thing. The idea of being able to write something and then have it shot so quickly is so cool.

JENNIFER WHALEN

Then, after that, it becomes more about the joke writing—the copy jokes. For the rest of the week, it would be like, we'd get to work and have to write—I forget how many now: ten or twenty—by noon. So you'd just sit and look at the newspaper and write jokes.

Then we would read them out, and either the showrunner or the head writer would decide which jokes were in the ballpark of moving forward. Those ones would go into one pile, and then you'd have this pile of dead jokes. That would continue in the week, and the pile of dead jokes would just grow. People would start mining the dead-joke pile just to see if—is there a set-up that I can use? That's also when, if there's a funny story about a blue lobster, you'll get thirty blue-lobster jokes. Kind of a pain.

GAVIN CRAWFORD

The copy jokes are a whole other thing the poor writers have to go through. Luckily, the actors don't, because they just have to churn out so many. I remember seeing the writers who were doing copy jokes come down for lunch, and their eyes were like, "I've just spent an hour doing a hundred jokes."

We would have a read-through of copy jokes, and I think we sort of got to pick the ones we liked, or the ones that we could see reading in our voice. So a lot of them would get chucked out, and we would get a pile of them, and then we'd go up and we'd read them, and then more of them would get chucked out.

There would be forty jokes maybe? And we would read through them all, and go around and pick. Shaun would be like "I'll have this one," Geri would pick this one, and "I'll take this one," and it would go around and around until everyone had five copy jokes that they were reading on the show.

JENNIFER WHALEN

Either you came in and you were really comfortable writing sketch, or you came in and you were really comfortable writing jokes, but you had to do both. So, in my case, that means I had to learn to write jokes, and in the case of someone like the legendary Irwin Barker, who was an amazing stand-up, he had to learn to write sketch. [*Barker died of cancer in 2010.*] But I think he would say he struggled a bit with sketch because it's just—it's a different way of thinking.

That's also why they needed to try writers all the time, because it was hard to find people who could do everything.

GAVIN CRAWFORD

It's a life-eating venture to be working on that show, especially since they moved the taping to Monday. It's a hard process, because you never really have a break. You do the taping, and then you immediately need to start thinking about what will be your next sketches for next week. And as soon as the sketches are done being written and picked, then the writers are into copy jokes, and the actors are into actually shooting the sketches.

JENNIFER WHALEN

Then after the joke-writing happens, there was a night—it used to be a night, and then it became a day—where we would write the leads, and that was usually towards the end of the week. Those are the pieces that are based off footage. So, we have a researcher who transcribes all the news, and then you would go through the transcripts and see if you could find anything that you thought might be a joke, and then you go and look at the footage and write an intro and an extro for it, and just try and craft that into a joke. And that was kind of the week.

And then you would have a live taping. It changed. We used to tape on Friday when I first started; at the end of it, we taped it on a Monday night. So you would come in on Monday, do the catch-up stuff, all the cleanup stuff for the show. You'd tape the show Monday night. Generally, there'd be a party after the show, so you'd have a few drinks.

TIM MCAULIFFE

And then, on the night of the show, they play a lot of stuff. They will play probably twice the amount to the audience, to see what gets laughs, and then all the writers and actors go in the back room and they just chat and hang out after the taping. The producers decide what is going to get made and they put a list out; once the list comes out, you know what's on the show, and that's always kind of an exciting time.

GAVIN CRAWFORD

I still don't know who made the decisions. Everyone tells you someone else. I know from [my partner] Kyle Tingley being head writer for a while, it's usually kind of by consensus. I think Michael Donovan can push something through that he likes, even if nobody else likes it. Mark Farrell probably had that power too. Mostly it's—I would suspect—if there's four people in the room, it's probably a majority of those four people. But then that's entirely the taste of those four people. It's maddeningly arbitrary sometimes.

JENNIFER WHALEN

And then Tuesday morning you would come in, hungover, and start it all over again.

TIM MCAULIFFE

The reality is, it's not that bad. It really isn't that bad. It shoots on Monday, so on Tuesday you sort of go in and pitch new ideas, and then by Wednesday at noon and we read them. So it's really fast. It's like *SNL* in that way, where you just basically figure out what you want to do that week, and you pitch it.

JENNIFER WHALEN

It made me a better writer, because the things that I thought—"Oh, my gosh! I've got a great sketch this week! I really cracked the political angle of this thing!—the read would start, and everybody was way ahead of you. Nobody cared. And the really embarrassing sketch that you're like—"Oh, my God.

There's five minutes left and I owe one more sketch. And I have this idea, it's kind of dumb, but I need one more"—that would be the thing that hits. So it really taught me not to be precious, and just let the audience decide what was good and what wasn't.

GERI HALL

If I could only thank one entity in that show for what they did, it's the writing room. When I think of the pressure that those people were under....

The actors, we have that sort of shiny job where we get to sit there on show night and say funny things and people clap and cheer for us, and a few days later, we hear the ratings were good. We get to constantly enjoy the gravy from all their sweat. Mmm, sweat gravy!

I used to fantasize about a show where the writers just came out and did their own desk jokes instead of me getting to do them. If I was showrunner, there would have been one writers' episode a year.

GAVIN CRAWFORD

In a way, it sort of is a machine that doesn't change, or if it does change, it changes incredibly slowly. You are kind of a cog in a big machine at 22, especially by the time I got there. It's a machine that runs along, and to try and change that machine's direction—which everybody kind of wants to do, especially if you are young, and a new writer, and you want to make it a little more current, or little more edgy—but it's amazing how quickly that goes by the wayside. You do what you can, but it's in very small increments.

TIM MCAULIFFE

So many friends of mine have gone through there. Sometimes it's just for two weeks and sometimes it's for years. Shaun Majumder lives very close to me in LA now, and we hang out a lot. The idea of being able to have that experience and chat about it is so cool—it's an amazing opportunity for Canadian comedy writers to basically get out there and create something.

So now in LA, we basically have a group of people who get together and talk about writing on the show, and we are still friends. It's pretty cool.

9
Making the News
2008–2017

Geri Hall had survived her first season, but it was clear that her particular strength—as a commercial actor, now doing commercial parodies—wasn't going to be enough to make a significant mark on the show. Out of necessity, she invented a new character—one that would draw considerable attention.

GERI HALL

Year one, I think that was when I had the most fun. When the show wrapped that year—every year we would find out pretty late in the summer whether or not they were calling us back. But I started thinking, "If they want me for another season, what would I love to do?" I was racking my brain; I'm not a Gavin or a Cathy. What do I, as a performer, offer them? And I thought, "Well I'm a good improviser. I should probably try doing one of these road pieces." I'm quick on my feet and I have done that kind of stuff.

So fast forward to the very end of that summer. My contract was renewed and I was heading back, and my husband and I decided we were just going to go to a beach for the weekend. We were driving up to the beach, having our last bit of time together before we separated, and I said, "We can do this road trip, as long as you are okay with me combing through newspapers—because it's been a whole summer, I still haven't had any sort of lightning bolt of something I am dying to do, so I'm not coming back from this trip without an idea."

He said, "Of course."

As you may remember, the federal election was coming up. Every story in the newspaper was about—"Who is going to win this? Who are the contenders?" And I was reading and thinking, "Oh, what could I do with that?"

At the time, we had a dear friend who was single, and she was really struggling all that summer with—how do you find nice guys? How do you find them at our age? How do you trust people? How do you know to take that leap of faith for a first date? So we were talking about her, and then I thought, "I've got to get back to work." I opened the newspaper, seeing Stephen Harper.

And this light went off. I was like, "Oh my God, it's right in front of us. What are we, as a nation, about to do? We are about to go on a speed date with a bunch of party leaders. And then we are going to decide who we get in bed with for the next four years." And all of a sudden, I knew.

So I started thinking, "What would her name be?" The day after that weekend, I had to pack up and get on the plane, and the very first meeting on the day after I landed was an ideas meeting. Mark Farrell, the showrunner, said, "Hey guys, how has your summer been? What's on peoples' minds? Who's got ideas?" And all the prolific writers were shouting out tons of amazing ideas.

He looked at me and said, "Geri, you got anything?" and I actually felt nervous, because I had never pitched a character there. I had pitched sketch ideas, but I had never pitched a character. And I said, "Okay, walk with me on this. Speed dating with these leaders, we are going to get in bed with them for the next four years. What if I go on some of these ambushes, road trips, planned or unplanned, as this character who basically uses the language of romance and dating and love to discuss politics, and to try to decide which man is Mr. Right, or in the case of Elizabeth May, maybe Ms. Right?"

And Mark went, "Okay." He smiled and chuckled. But my initial impression—I had to keep a brave face—was that he didn't like it.

Her first test came soon enough.

GERI HALL

So, I had been sent on a road piece to Tatamagouche, NS, parodying [the CBC reality series] *The Week The Women Went.* I was coming back from that road trip at 10 P.M. when Mark Farrell phoned and said, "Listen. We just found out that Stephen Harper is going to be at a hotel tomorrow morning for a business meeting of some kind. Our show has had a really hard time getting to him. It's really hard to get anywhere near him since he became prime minister. It is so unlikely, but do you want to go and try to do this character?"

My heart was pounding out of my chest, because it was one thing to pitch it; it's a whole other thing to have to wake up at six in the morning and put the makeup on, but I said, "Yes, let's do it."

He said, "All right, I'm sending Jen Whalen up to your room. You can explain the character some more and she will help you come up with a bunch of jokes. Just go and have fun. Don't kick yourself if it doesn't turn out, because that's just the way it is with Stephen Harper."

So I got back to my room and Jen came up. I explained the character, and she said, "Oh, she's sort of like a single female voter." And I said, "Exactly!" So we sat and talked. Jen seemed to love the idea. We riffed on what some of the joke angles were, and what things we could talk about.

She went back to the writers and said, "Geri is going to do this road piece." And this is essentially how all road pieces work—you are either assigned one, or you pitch one, and the writing room is alerted. The writers immediately go into work mode, and come up with as many jokes as they can by deadline, on that topic, in that character's voice.

Within a few hours, the writers had sent me, I think, four pages of potential jokes. And since it's you going out there, you just swoop through them, and if you like a joke, you circle it and you memorize it, so you've got it in your back pocket if an opportunity comes up.

But it's not TV—it's the real world, so you start a conversation with these people, and you've got those jokes in your mind, but there's also stuff that's just completely improvised, because you don't know where a conversation or a situation is going to take you. You are armed with as much comic weaponry as possible.

After a very sleepless night, I woke up, went to *22 Minutes* to find some basic costume pieces, and we hopped in a car. It was me and a fellow named Mark Mullane, who was going to be the field producer, and Peter Sutherland, the legend, who is so amazing. He was the camera operator and warrior-in-kind.

MARK MULLANE
Field Producer, 2008–2012
That was my first shoot, actually.

The assignment was pretty clear: Harper has a press conference down at the Sheraton. Go down—Geri was going to be in her Single Female Voter character—and just see if she can get some questions in.

GERI HALL
We got in the car, and my heart was pounding out of my chest. Pete just explained to me, "Okay, this is how these go. We'll go in; we've got our press passes"—because as a part of *22*, you do get a CBC pass. He said, "We will go sign in, we'll sit with the rest of the media. I will set my camera up at the back of the room with all the other cameras. How this usually works is, you just go sit with the other reporters. What *22* always does is—we are respectful. We wait until last-question alert. So you let the press conference happen the way it is, but when they yell, 'Okay, last question!' that's your signal. If you're going to do something, you've got to stand up and ask your question, and do whatever you've got to do."

MARK MULLANE

That was when *22 Minutes* did a lot of field stuff, and there always seemed to be some sort of wig involved, you know—in the early days, obviously, with Mary and Cathy. So the wig trend continued.

Geri had this wig on, and she was playing a character called Single Female Voter and the whole idea was just for her to say, "What do you have to offer me?"

GERI HALL

I went and sat down, and this, honestly, was one of the craziest, most surreal days of my life. I'm sitting there, thinking about the jokes, thinking about the piece, thinking about the character, thinking, "Oh my gosh, I want this to go well, because I want *22* to like this, and I want to keep doing this character. I hope we get one joke in."

Knowing the way Stephen Harper is in press conferences, I thought, "I will be lucky if I get one jokey question out, because he is just going to leave the room." So I had to sit there for this thirty-minute press conference. Thirty minutes, when you are new to this sort of environment, felt like ten years. My heart was beating like a rabbit's.

MARK MULLANE

So we went there and, just like any other press conference, we set up our camera, and Geri waited patiently during the breakfast Harper was speaking at. It was a business conference breakfast. And then, as he was going to do the press conference, she went, sat down, took her place, and you could just tell she got eyeballed right away because she was wearing a wig. But also because, you know, she was still new to the show, and she was a reporter not generally known to Harper's cronies.

GERI HALL

At first, there was no one sitting beside me, but then I saw some whispering off to the side, and a woman who was one of Stephen Harper's people came and sat down beside me as the press conference was happening. Stephen Harper was answering questions in French and English, and she leaned over and started whispering in my ear, "You don't belong here. You need to get out."

MARK MULLANE

They knew something was going on, for sure. Geri was a little bit more inconspicuous than Mary, in her costume—I mean, I've done a lot of shoots with Mary, too, where I don't know how on earth we even got in the door. Even when Mary had the trench coat on, she still had the crazy makeup on, and the big glasses and the whole bit.

GERI HALL

I thought, "Oh my God." I turned my body away from her, because I knew—my actor's instinct was—if you engage with this, or you get out of character, you are not going to have the confidence to do this. So I angled my body away from her, and she just kept leaning over and very quietly saying, "You are not the real press; you don't belong at a press conference; you and your friends should go home." And I would turn my body a little farther away.

MARK MULLANE

There was also a female security person with Harper's crew and she definitely had her eyes on Geri the entire time.

GERI HALL

So I ignored her, and after a hundred years of adrenaline, they said, "Last question." So I stood up and said, "Um, excuse me, Mr. Harper, I just want to ask you a question." And before I got those words out, Halifax police, and, I think, the RCMP too—we weren't sure who was who at that point—they descended on me. They put my hands behind my back, and they started pulling me out of the room.

MARK MULLANE

When Geri stood up to give her question, she wasn't even allowed, basically, to say anything. As soon as she stood up, it was pretty much over. Everyone gave each other the signal, and then they just grabbed her and escorted her off.

GERI HALL

My actor's brain—everything at this point—went into slow motion. I thought, "You have two choices. You either stop and cave, and this is all just a waste, or you stay in character and you at least get one thing in on your way out the door." So I just started yelling as loud as I could, "Mr. Harper, please, I just want to fall in love with you! I just need to know if you are the right one for me! Please—I just want to fall in love with my leader!"

MARK MULLANE

Geri, much to her credit, stayed in character the entire time—did not break character one bit. She took it to the next level, and I'm back there, as the producer, thinking, "This is great! This is pretty much exactly what we would want." This is, like, classic *22 Minutes* style.

GERI HALL

And by the time I did that, the doors closed. They had me now in the concrete hallway beside this press-conference space, and they put handcuffs on me. They pushed me up against a wall—face up against a wall. "Who are you? Where are you from? What are you doing?" And I stayed in character, and I said, "I'm from *22 Minutes*. I just want to talk to my leader."

MARK MULLANE

So she gets dragged off, and it's like—"Pete, let's go!" Pete grabs the camera off the tripod and we chase after her, down the hallways of the Sheraton. She's still in character, and she's still miked up. And I remember her saying something like, "I just want to ask him some questions. I just want to make him love me."

GERI HALL

Thank God for Pete Sutherland. Pete followed me. I was wearing my sound pack, so he could hear everything. Pete popped those double doors open, so he got that angle that everybody ended up seeing on the news, and I said, "I just want to talk to my leader!" and one of the officers said, "Well, this isn't how you do it."

I said, "We are from *22 Minutes*. This is exactly how we do it!" and as soon as I got that out, I thought, "We've got a piece. We are okay now."

Because, of course, the backdrop politically—one of the big things that was happening that year was that Stephen Harper was making press events much less accessible than we were used to, as Canadians. There were so many people telling us that journalists would have to submit their questions in advance, and many sources told us Harper and his people would decide which questions they would answer, and which ones they would not. That was not anything that any of us was used to in this country. So, in that moment, I thought, "My God, this really highlights that thing that we've been talking about—that somebody harmless from *22 Minutes* just tried to get up and do a silly little joke, and I am in handcuffs now."

So I thought, "Well, we've got a piece." It's certainly not the piece that I wanted.

The bit that I was going to do—Stephen Harper had recently put out some promotional pictures where he was sitting with his kittens and wearing an angora sweater. And as the Single Female Voter character, I thought, "Are you trying to show your feminine side?" I was going to ask him about that, and poke a little bit of lighthearted fun at it.

As a newbie to these sorts of road pieces, I also thought, "My God, he's the prime minister of Canada; he's an incredibly intelligent man. There's a really good chance that I'm going to crack my little joke about his sweaters, and he's going to come back at me with something that I'm probably not even qualified to answer. So I thought, "Please, just let that one cute joke work." And then I was in handcuffs.

STEPHEN REYNOLDS

No doubt her heart was racing. You're in a moment and, "Oh, my God! What am I going to do? I guess I'm going to just leap and do this," or, you know, "Wait! I'm locked up!" And she stayed in character for the whole thing. "This is not really happening to Geri Hall, this is happening to my character."

GERI HALL

So cut to that back room. I am up against a wall. I can feel the handcuffs starting to rub the skin off little bit—they're not comfy. And they kept saying, "Who are you? Where are you from?" And I said, now that the piece was over, "My name is Geri Hall, I'm from *22 Minutes*, we were just here to do a little lighthearted piece in the run-up to the election."

They said, "Where is your ID?" and I said "I am wearing a mic pack; my ID is in my purse in the car." It's all kind of a blur, because it was shocking. But the thing that was going through my head was, "My God, this is going to be on the news. My husband is going to see this, and he is going to wonder what the hell is going on," because all of those news cameras in the other room would have seen all of that. I thought, "Oh my God, my mom saw it!"

I later saw what happened immediately after. Stephen Harper said, "Oh, sorry, was she from *This Hour*? I don't know—I don't watch that show." But someone in his gang of supporters had sent a woman to sit beside me for twenty-five minutes, telling me I wasn't the real press. If they didn't know we were *22 Minutes*, who did they think we were? *TMZ*? So while I was being questioned by the authorities, literally a couple of feet behind me, I saw what turned out to be a group of Stephen Harper's people, who were starting to talk. You know—"This is a problem; we need to make this go away; we need to fix this."

MARK MULLANE

After all that commotion sort of died down, I remember talking to the police, and, then [Stephen Harper's director of communications] Dimitri Soudas came down and said, "You know, that was not cool at all, what you guys did, but we understand it's all in good fun." Blah, blah, blah. He knew he was doing damage control at this point. He said, "The prime minister would love to see you up in his suite."

So we said, "Great! That's what we want. Sure, let's do it!"

GERI HALL

The woman who had been doing most of the talking walked over to me and said, "I'm sorry, are you Geri? Oh, Honey, I'm so sorry! We had no idea who you were! We had no idea you were with *22 Minutes*. Can you guys take those handcuffs off her? Honey, we've got a surprise for you."

I said, "What's that?"

And she said [*in a baby voice*], "Somebody wants to talk to you!"

It was so transparent. The Canadian actor in me would say, "Hey, maybe they didn't recognize my face," but they knew who we were, or they wouldn't have asked us to leave.

MARK MULLANE

We go up to the suite. We get off the elevator and we're just getting everybody's angry stares at us as we walk towards the room. We're led into the room, and Harper's there.

GERI HALL

So they brought me up. They asked me to take my mic pack off so that I could speak with Mr. Harper first.

We had a little chit-chat and he said, you know—"Post-9/11 world; we've got to be careful; we are more secure at these things, and I'd be happy to do a little piece with you. What were you thinking?"

Dimitri Soudas, Harper's director of communications, came up to me and said, "Listen, we are going to give you two questions, no more. You need to tell us what the questions are." So I got that first-hand experience of giving questions to Mr. Harper before he refuses to answer them [*laughing*], and I said, "I'm just going to do this little thing about what just happened, and then I will maybe make a joke about the GST—that you are dangling this GST cut in front of potential voters—and then we will call it a day."

So I went up to him and said, "Okay, well that was a bumpy start to our relationship as a potential voter and a leader, but here we are. That was a little rough; I didn't expect to be in handcuffs."

And he said, "Do you like handcuffs?" As soon as he said that, for the second time that day, I went, "Okay, we have our piece. The prime minister just asked a woman if she likes handcuffs."

In fairness, I am critical of many aspects of Stephen Harper's leadership and government, but in that moment, I think he was probably as overwhelmed as I was. I think that was his attempt at levity, and I think that's just what came out.

MARK MULLANE

I was in the back of the room with Soudas beside me, and when Harper said that comment that was really gross—about, you know, "You like handcuffs?" I mean, that was a perfect thing for him to say—for us, not for him. And I'm thinking, "Okay, that's, that's great! That's going to make all the news. That's perfect!"

When he said that comment, which was not funny at all, Dimitri Soudas fell down onto his knees and started punching the sofa. Like, fake laughing.

Oh, it was just gross. It was just like, "Yeah! Everything you say, Boss, is hilarious!" So he falls down to his knees and I'm looking over there, thinking, "I wish we were filming this, too, because this is ridiculous."

And then Geri gets her bit, says goodbye. Everyone was in decent spirits.

GERI HALL

Peter and Mark and I just started walking toward the door, and we started walking faster, and we were whispering, "Just keep walking until we are out of this building."

MARK MULLANE

It was like, "Don't take our camera; don't take our tape. Let's just keep walking until we get to the parking lot!" which is normal with all those things. I would just grab the tapes, put them in my bag, and just be like, "Okay let's get out of here!"

GERI HALL

By the time we got to the parking garage—I'm reticent to even say this, because it seems a little too self-congratulatory, and I mean this in the spirit of lauding what a great support Pete and Mark were to me—but Pete turned to me in that moment, and he said, "That was amazing! Mary and I have gotten ourselves into some trouble sometimes, and this felt just like that!" It was so sweet.

MARK MULLANE

And then we went back to the office to the adulation of the crew.

STEPHEN REYNOLDS

The material, as we're sitting in the editing room with it, we're like, "This couldn't have been better!"

JENNIFER WHALEN

What I mostly remember about that was just being creeped out by Harper, when she actually did talk to Harper. He sort of spoke to her—you know when guys do the, "I'm gonna talk to you in a slightly more gentle voice because you're a woman" thing? I wasn't a fan to begin with but, when he did that, I was like, "Eww."

MARK MULLANE

Geri was absolutely amazing—never broke character at all, except for maybe two seconds in the elevator going up to see Harper, when she was like, "Well, I just got arrested."

But she was such a great person to work with. She was so quick on her feet in those situations, even though those are very uncomfortable situations to be put in, for sure.

STEPHEN REYNOLDS

She had a little bit of Second City. She could step into that world. So, here she is—one of her first real sojourns out into that world, and wham! She just responded so well, so perfectly. And it came from a core of natural reactions that just flew out of her.

GERI HALL

My brain was in a million places, but I thought, "Is that how a road piece is supposed to go?" And it was just so comforting that as soon as we were out of earshot, Pete was like, "That was great." He was so supportive. So we got back to the studio, and Mark [Farrell], the showrunner, met us at the door. "Are you okay? Tell us what the hell happened in there. We saw it on the news and Pete and Mark have been texting us."

I said, "Listen, I'm okay. Am I shaken up? Absolutely. I've never been in handcuffs in my life. And I've never really been in trouble in my life, and that kind of walked the line for a couple of minutes. But it was also really fun, and I think the piece we got says what it should say right now. But I have to run and call my husband, because if he has seen the news, he is probably peeing himself."

So I called my husband and I said, "Hi, Honey. You working?" He said, "Yeah, just working away." I said, "So you're not watching the news?" and he said, "No. Why?" And I said, "Put it on CBC, but just know that I'm okay."

And of course, that, oddly, became the news of the day. Everybody was talking about it.

But definitely one of the top five craziest days of my life.

STEPHEN REYNOLDS

These pieces are not just satirizing the news, they become the newspieces themselves. And *22* has been very fortunate, over its history, to have nailed a bunch of those. They do transcend the show itself.

GERI HALL

There were all kinds of interesting perspectives on it. People started saying, "Yeah, this is what *22 Minutes* does; this is great." And then there were people like, "*22 Minutes* has no business commenting on politics."

It's a debate that continues on why satire is so important.

But what was it about Stephen Harper that didn't want to engage with a show like ours? The show had a history of having these really great, I would say iconic moments, and I mean the people before me. Gavin and Mary and Rick Mercer and Greg Thomey—these iconic, wonderful moments between these brilliant comedians and these real politicians. They were real and charming and very human moments that, I would say, actually helped a lot of political careers. And I say that completely separate from my participation on the show. I'm talking about the people who did it twenty years before me.

If you ask Canadians about Mary Walsh storming around in her Marg, Princess Warrior outfit, people are really proud of that part of Canadians, both the performers and the politicians. We don't take ourselves too seriously. Even with important political issues, we are still okay with seeing the lighter side of things, or seeing an alternate perspective on things for levity. So it just astonished me that that was the response.

. . .

GERI HALL

That was the first day Single Female Voter ever stepped out of the house in her search for the leader that would make her dreams come true. And I think the next day, the phone started ringing at *22 Minutes*. All of a sudden, Jack Layton's people called and said, "Jack is going to be in Halifax and would love to give Single Female Voter a rose. Do you want to meet in the lobby of the hotel and we can do a little thing?"

Then we get a call from Gilles Duceppe's camp: "Gilles is going to be at this place in Québec, but if Geri can meet him there, he'd love to ask her to dance." So I went out, and we didn't plan anything with these people, they just invited us, because, unlike the moment with Stephen Harper, in my opinion, I think these party leaders understood what a great opportunity it was to poke a little bit of fun, to shine a little bit of levity, onto the process of that election—and especially after what the Harper experience had resulted in. Anything they did with me would look so much more open and lovely than that, so I went and did these amazing fun pieces.

It was such an amazing year for me, to meet these people that formed and shaped our country, and to realize that most of them were really fun, and really willing to walk down that road with me. Doing Single Female Voter was my favourite experience at *22*.

. . .

Geoff D'Eon had stopped going on the road in 2003, when he was made executive producer of Arts and Entertainment for the Atlantic region—a management job that he admitted was much less fulfilling than his previous hands-on role. So when an opportunity arose in 2008 to work with Mark Critch in China, he leapt.

GEOFF D'EON

The Olympics were on in Beijing. Shaun and Mark had been brought to Beijing to do comedic pieces for CBC Sports—"brighteners." I got a call from the person who was in charge of the show at CBC, who pointed out to me that Shaun and Mark were going to be in Beijing, and wouldn't this be a great opportunity for *22 Minutes* to gather some material?

I like to think that I'm not slow on the uptake when an opportunity like that comes across my desk, so I volunteered within seconds, and found myself in Beijing. Shaun and Mark were winding down their sports commitments. Shaun had to return to Canada, but Mark stayed. So Mark, myself, and Peter Sutherland became a comedy crew on the loose, in a country where we didn't speak the language, and nobody knew who we were.

What a perfect opportunity. Mark came up with the idea that he should become Danny Williams. Danny Williams, at that time, was the "king" of Newfoundland—could do no wrong—so we thought, "Wouldn't it be fun if Danny Williams was in Beijing?" Mark Critch did a dead-ringer impression of Danny Williams, so he became Danny Williams, accompanied by his personal assistant in a suit—that was me—and our own personal cameraman, who was there to record Danny Williams's official visit to the People's Republic of China.

DANNY WILLIAMS

He's game for anything. To go into another country—and especially that country—and do that, it's risky. And to get away with it—to have the guts to try and pull it off—I was just glad he wasn't arrested!

GEOFF D'EON

We worked at it a little bit. We had business cards printed. We dressed appropriately. We rented a limousine. And we made an appointment for an official visit to the Lao She Teahouse in Beijing.

The Lao She Teahouse is an immense facility. It's 28,000 square feet. It's classical Chinese architecture. It's one of the most famous teahouses in Beijing, and it's also a performance space. They perform classical Chinese opera as you sip tea. It's also really well known because of the grand catalogue of celebrities who have visited over the decades. I think Richard Nixon went there. Certainly, American presidents have visited. Many heads of state have been to the Lao She Teahouse. It's a highly prestigious venue, and it's on the must-do list of many celebrities who visit Beijing.

We had a fixer in Beijing by the name of Kyle who spoke fluent Mandarin, and he made the appointment for us. We arrived at the Lao She Teahouse in a limousine, flying the Newfoundland flag, and we were greeted by the staff as if we were royalty. We were ushered up the grand, red-carpeted staircase and shown into a private room, where we were served very expensive tea by our own private server, while water fountains trickled and soft classical Chinese music played.

Peter shot everything, as befits a visiting dignitary. And then we were ushered into the performance area and given the VIP table at the front, where we were served Chinese delicacies, and this extraordinary Chinese opera unfolded in front of us. We were waited on hand and foot.

At the conclusion of the performance, the staff made a big fuss of coming over to us and giving us gifts. They wanted Danny Williams to sign the guestbook as one of the visiting dignitaries. Of course, Mark obliged, and signed it "Danny Williams, Premier of Newfoundland and Labrador." We then posed for photographs with official photographers, made our way down the stairs, and got the heck out of there in our rented limo, laughing all the way back to the hotel.

Mark has a really tight relationship with Danny Williams and couldn't wait to tell Danny Williams that we had done this. By Mark's account, Danny Williams thought this was hilarious—just the b'ys having a laugh.

DANNY WILLIAMS
Exactly. He puts himself in situations, but he always comes out unblemished.

GEOFF D'EON

The whole thing was wildly amusing. It was audacious, cheeky, saucy. There's no question we took advantage of the incredible hospitality afforded by the Chinese people to visiting dignitaries. I felt a little bit of guilt about that, but it was all for a good cause. You're trying to make a funny television show, so liberties are taken.

DANNY WILLIAMS

I do remember seeing it. It just shows how brilliant he is. It was hilarious.

GEOFF D'EON

The piece is not as memorable as the experience of shooting it, I'll say that. I'm not sure that it was clear in the final piece the extent to which we had duped everybody. The viewers had no idea of the elaborate preparations we'd made, and for all the viewer knew, there was a Westerner in a suit, having a good time at a teahouse. The piece did not translate as well on television as I hoped it would have, and I take responsibility for that.

But hey—if it wasn't a home run, it was at least a double, possibly a triple, and the experience was unforgettable.

• • •

Meanwhile, another controversial moment was in the offing for Single Female Voter. In March 2009, Geri and her team would take a lot of heat for an ambush of Ontario premier Dalton McGuinty that was perceived as tone-deaf. The impetus for the piece had been McGuinty's order that journalists should maintain a distance from him of at least five feet.

GERI HALL

Our show was fascinated with—why is there this distance put between the press and the party leaders? Dalton McGuinty, just before we went to do this piece, was starting to get frustrated that, in scrums, the press was starting to get really close to him. So we had a little idea. Why don't we go see Dalton McGuinty and, at last question, we will just try and get everybody in the scrum to sing the Carpenters' song "Close to You"?

The plan was to just do a little thing in the Single Female Voter voice about, "How will people fall in love with you, Dalton, if you don't let them near you? You can't put walls up if you want people to come to your heart."

MARK MULLANE

It was actually the press crew at Queen's Park who had said, "This is such garbage. He can't do this to us. You should just come up and ambush him."

So that's what we did. And that one did not go well. That one kind of shook Geri from doing some of those types of shoots.

GERI HALL

Because of the layout of Queen's Park, they unfortunately had to house me downstairs. So I was not anywhere within earshot of the scrum and the questions. Arguably, at almost all of those things, there are serious questions, there are lighter questions, there are questions that are sort of more emotional.

As it turns out, a lot of people at the Stelco steel plants in Ontario had been laid off, and were facing the horrible prospect of unemployment. Unbeknownst to me, [Ontario MPP] Peter Kormos had just raised that question with Dalton McGuinty. That was just before last question. I got the signal on radio: "They are going to wrap this up. You need to go in there." So I walked in, not knowing that this heavy question had just happened.

MARK MULLANE

We didn't know what he was talking about. We were all backstage, in a place where we had been told to wait. The whole thing had been set up as an ambush—for all of us to pop out at the same time, and just go for it.

GERI HALL

I've been asked a couple of times: "If you'd known that was the question, would you have continued with the piece?" It's an interesting question, because maybe we wouldn't have, maybe we would have. But I would argue that there's never a day in politics when there's not something tragic happening. And if *22 Minutes* or Jon Stewart or Sam Bee or anybody—if they wait until a day in the news when there's nothing sad or terrible happening, then we could never do it.

So it was an unfortunate circumstance where I had no idea, a) that the question had been asked, or b) that Mr. Kormos was so upset. And rightfully so. He was obviously a very empathetic man for these people who were going through this hard thing.

MARK MULLANE

Yes, he was talking about something that was very sensitive, but we had no idea what he was talking about. Had we known, I think we probably would have stopped the shoot, but it was literally, like, he's doing the press conference, we come out a door—BAM!—you're into it. There's no time to really sit down and digest what he was saying.

GERI HALL

So I stepped up, trying to get this little Carpenters bit out, and all I heard was screaming. At first, I didn't even know who it was; I didn't find out until later that it was Mr. Kormos. But there was screaming—"Get the hell out of here! You have no right here!"—and we realized, this is no longer an environment where anyone is going to want to sing the Carpenters.

MARK MULLANE

Not the best time to be goofing around! But it happened, and you know, those kinds of things were bound to happen in our line of work. But I will say that it was not our call to go in then.

GERI HALL

We wrapped up and left the building, and all of a sudden people were rushing over to me, saying, "Do you want to make a comment about what just happened?"

As the next twenty minutes unfolded, I realized what we had stepped into. It was really unfortunate, and to be completely honest, it was disappointing and upsetting because—I can say on behalf of the whole show—we never intend harm. We never go into these things wanting to hurt anyone's feelings. Our piece had nothing to do with that horrible situation; it was a completely separate thing. But it just blew up into this thing.

MARK MULLANE

Again, had we known, obviously, we would have pulled back and tried another time. But, yeah, it was just unfortunate timing. And comedy is timing.

GERI HALL

It was a shocking day for all of us, because we went in with the best of intentions. It was the explosive anger—there was no chance to even mitigate that, to back out gently, because it just went from zero to a hundred. It was really unfortunate. That was a sad day. A sad day for Stelco workers, and for me and Pete and Mark, who just wanted to go do this little thing.

MARK MULLANE

She totally bore the brunt of it. I mean, she's the face, and it was totally not her fault. She was put in that position. We were all put in that position, but it is her image and her face that's out there, and it just didn't feel right on so many levels.

GERI HALL

That was near the very end of the season. We wrapped soon after. I think that was the last time Single Female Voter went out that season, and then the following season, we had a brand new showrunner, Tim McAuliffe. So Tim came in and was trying brand new things as a showrunner—he wanted to put his own imprint on the show, because that's the way it happens.

So they still wanted me doing road pieces, but because the election was over, there was not as much call for Single Female Voter.

• • •

In 2009, field producer Mark Mullane hit the road with Mary Walsh, who had returned to make a guest appearance in pursuit of the former Republican vice-presidential nominee, and governor of Alaska, Sarah Palin. Palin was on tour, promoting her newly released book, *Going Rogue*.

MARK MULLANE

One of my favourite *22 Minutes* shoots of all was of Mary doing Sarah Palin, because of the ridiculousness that we went through to actually get what we got.

The whole idea was to get Sarah Palin at her book signing, and there were two signings in one day—one in Cincinnati, and one in Columbus, Ohio.

We flew into Cincinnati and we randomly picked a hotel—just out of the blue. As much as I liked picking some of the hotels, I don't think I did, in this case. We ended up staying at this place in downtown Cincinnati.

Sarah Palin had a book signing that morning, and she was doing the other one in Columbus that evening. So we get to the hotel, and Mary's rehearsing her lines. I would always go up into her room and she would run the script with me, and we would just sort of rehearse it.

So, Mary being Mary—she's loud. She's a huge presence. And she's up there saying all of her Sarah Palin jokes, like, super loud.

The next morning, we were walking around and Mary's like, "Mark, just down the hall from my room there's a sign that says, 'Sarah P-A-C.'" And I was like, "Oh! That sounds to me like Sarah Palin's Political Action Committee." I realized, "Oh, my gosh! They're probably staying in the hotel, and they're having a meeting down here, probably before the book signing. This could be the easiest shoot of all time—all you've gotta do is jump out of your room and we'll just get her in the hallway, and it's gonna be perfect!"

We go down to Mary's room, and it clearly looks like this little conference room is where they're going to have this meeting. So, we went into her room and she got dressed and we were all getting ready to do it, but I literally think that Sarah Palin was in the next room. I'm almost certain that either she was, or her team was, but Mary was being pretty loud with going over the script. And Pete and I were both going, "Shhhh! Tone it down; they can hear us!"

PETER SUTHERLAND

Mary used to rehearse out loud. It would be hard to get her to be quiet. Her voice would go right through the hotel walls.

I got this feeling like Sarah Palin was close, so I looked outside Mary's hotel room—and there goes Sarah Palin down the hallway for a breakfast meeting. So we started chasing her, but they wouldn't let us into the meeting.

MARK MULLANE

The hotel people got wind of it, and they were like, "What are you guys do-ing?" And we're, just, "Oh, we are actually guests of the hotel. We're just wait-ing here." They kicked us out, and we were actually hotel guests. They were like, "No, you've got to get out of here."

So we waited outside. Sarah Palin did come out of the hotel. We tried to get her. She kind of went through a side door and into her bus, and then off she went. I thought that was too bad—we almost got her right away.

• • •

MARK MULLANE

We ended up having so much downtime on that shoot, between events. I remember sitting in the car with Mary, and she had written this really, really, really long script. Like, way too long to ever get out in the time that you would be allotted before you got grabbed and escorted out of there.

This was one of my first shoots with Mary; maybe it was my first. I was sitting there with Pete and Mary in the car, and Mary's in the back, and she's going over her thing, and I was, like, "Mary, I don't think you're gonna have enough time to say all of that stuff. We need to cut this down, because you're not going to get all these points across in this short amount of time that we have in there."

PETER SUTHERLAND

She wouldn't use a computer; she always wrote things down on notepaper, and inevitably her scripts were way too long. So she would voice her scripts in the car, or wherever we were, and every time it was like, "That's way too long; let's cut it down."

MARK MULLANE

I remember her saying, "Well, what the hell are we doing this for? If I can't say what I want to say, then why the hell are we doing this?"

I was like, "It would be great if you could say all of this, because it's all awesome, but we're definitely going to have to pick out some stuff and really concentrate on just getting the best one or two lines out that we possibly can."

Then she got mad and left the van. I was sitting there with Pete and I was like, "What should we do?" He's like, "Well, if she comes back, basically, you were right. If she doesn't come back, then we're fucked."

I said, "Well, let's hope she comes back."

She came back. She was like, "Okay, Mark. Sorry about that. I agree; we will cut this down. I probably won't have much time," and I was, like, "Okay, great." So the three of us sat there and just cut it down to the raw essentials.

But that was the road team. Everyone had input on what happened. Most of the time, we couldn't control what happened, but we tried to, as best we could. And it was interesting, because sometimes the writers would send you jokes, and there'd be pages and pages upon pages of jokes, and you'd have to sift through them. A lot of the hosts, rightly or wrongly, they would almost—they wouldn't dismiss them, but they would be writing their own, too.

That's what we did on the planes when we were flying somewhere. We had these pages and pages of jokes, and we would go through them, picking out the ones that we liked. There was a lot of material that was given to us, which was great. But sometimes it wasn't really used, which was kind of a bummer, too.

• • •

MARK MULLANE

Then we go to the book signing in Cincinnati, and there's a big long line and they're not letting anybody up; only cameras are allowed up. It's only B-roll, no sound—there are no questions to be asked. So we're in this Barnes and Noble type of bookstore, and Sarah Palin's on the second floor, and the camera people are allowed up for a certain period of time, and then they're told to pull back. So we were like—this is not going to work. We need sound.

We thought, "The next book signing is going to be just like this. This is going to be a nightmare. We're probably not going to get her." So we decided that we would just go rent a small little video camera, like, a Sony PD150.

PETER SUTHERLAND

We went to a video outlet and rented a camera, so Mary could become a photographer.

MARK MULLANE

We call ahead to a camera store in Columbus. We get in the car, drive the couple hours to Columbus, go to this place, rent this camera, and then we're like—we will put this in Mary's hands, and that way, she'll be close, we'll have her miked, and Pete and Mary can walk in. And as long as she has a camera in her hand, then she'll be able to get up close enough to Sarah to ask a question.

So that's what we did. The camera people were not allowed to be in the lineup with the book-signers. They were off to the side. And what blew my mind—there's Mary in this ridiculously large red coat, these ridiculous glasses, and the makeup and the whole thing. Didn't look out of place at all in Columbus, Ohio!

She's got a PD150 in her hand that has no battery pack attached to it. It's nothing; it's not on; she's just got it in her hand. What security guard would not notice that there was no battery on the back of this camera? But they let her in.

PETER SUTHERLAND

I was in line with her. There were security guards around. She had the trench coat on, and the beehive hairdo, the Marg Delahunty look, and underneath the trench coat was the armour, and she had this camera. And I said, "Mary, when it's our turn, we are going to run through those two goons and just keep on going and don't stop."

So she dropped her coat and ran through, and we got a little footage of her and Sarah Palin, until we got pushed back and manhandled out.

MARK MULLANE

She's all miked up, Pete follows her in, and then she actually gets to ask some questions. She's pulled back by security immediately—as soon as she starts talking to her. But, you know, she does get some questions in, and Palin, to her credit, answers her—yells across the room. It was like, "Great! We got something. This is awesome."

We go back to the van and we're, like, "Well, you know, we've come all this way, and that was okay. We did get some questions in, but it wasn't stellar."

PETER SUTHERLAND

Mary expects the world, and if she doesn't get it, she gets pissed off. You try hard, and if you don't get it the first time you go again and again.

MARK MULLANE

So we waited, I don't know, I think four and a half hours, something like that. We waited for her to be done doing the book signing. She'd parked her bus at the back of the mall, and we decided to walk down and hide in the loading dock.

We hid in the loading dock for probably twenty minutes. And then, we could tell that things were wrapping up, and sure enough, she comes out of the building. There are no lights on at the back of the building, but we have our camera light on, and Mary is yelling at her from the loading dock, behind a dumpster.

PETER SUTHERLAND

We were hiding. You know how a loading zone goes down and there is a railing? We were peeking out through the railing, and Mary yelled. "Ma'am! We're the Canadians!"

MARK MULLANE

Palin walks straight over to the loading dock, you know, probably much to the shock of her security team. They were probably saying, "What are you doing? There's somebody yelling at you from the loading dock, and you are walking over there?"

And Mary's basically, "We tried to ask you a question earlier. We're from Canada. We just want ask you a question."

So Palin comes over, and Mary is about eight feet down in this loading dock, and Palin is above, bending down, and they're having this interview.

It was totally surreal, and Mary says, "I was trying to ask you these questions inside." She got to get a couple of questions and answers in, and then Palin was whisked away and we were like, "Yeah, this is awesome! We did it!" We did not settle, we did everything that we could on this trip. And that was that. Mary was exhausted after this. I mean, it was a long, long day.

Pete and I went out and had a few beers to celebrate. But it was just the fact that we stuck to it, and the fact that the whole thing was so ridiculous from start to finish. That was super fun.

• • •

22 Minutes was now in its seventeenth season, and showrunner Mark Farrell, who had been an executive producer on the show since Season 7, was nearing the end of his tenure.

JOHN DOYLE

I had a good chat with Mark Farrell when I was there. Mark is very shrewd. He's a good writer and he knows when to be a good boss, too. In general, I like Mark, and one of the things I gleaned from that conversation, and from just being there in their home office, is that he was probably a tough boss, in the way that some people can bring discipline to a show which has many disparate, different kinds of personalities and types within it.

STEPHEN REYNOLDS

In my tenure there, I introduced the idea of bringing the executive producers into the director's edit at night. Henry had refused to do this, but I have always promoted the notion that any television or film project is collaboration, and working in a vacuum is a problem.

So I invited Mark Farrell to sit in, I think it was during my fourth or fifth season. It made it more efficient, and easier to make changes the next morning. At the same time, it also created conflicts inside the room, and we would fight through whatever those issues were at the moment.

In my last season, Mark and I reached a point of creative differences—enough that there was a comfort factor that had dissipated. Agreeing to disagree was not an unusual position to find ourselves in. I don't think either of us fell out of line in terms of delivering the show, but he had the creative say.

At the end of that season, Mark left, and Michael reached out to bring in one of the part-time writers—a fellow by the name of Tim McAuliffe. But before Tim is in, Ed Macdonald is in. He does the first half of the season, while Mark is doing some other show. And Ed and Gavin Crawford have a massive difference of opinion about much of the creative work they are both doing.

ED MACDONALD

Mark had ten weeks off, because he was working on something else, so Jenipher Ritchie called me. I guess they had thrown names around, and because I knew the drill, they figured it would be not so much of a learning curve.

Showrunning sucks. It's like a twenty-four-hour thing. I knew what I was in for, but the show had changed a lot. When I was just starting out, if it wasn't political, it didn't get on. Everything had to have teeth. Even though Cathy was doing "softer" stuff, it was still out of the news; it had to be tied to something in reality.

I found that the show had gotten a little more—I don't know, not toothless, but pretty soft. And it did need a shakeup, but I don't think that's what I did. I think I just tried to bring it back to what it was. And I don't think that was possible, I realize now.

I'm an actor, so it's hard to deal with other actors because you know what they need, and you know what they're going through—but also, you can't really care that much, because you have these other billion things to worry about. It wasn't rocket science, but it wasn't easy either.

I was glad to be done. I certainly wasn't after Farrell's job, that's for damn sure.

STEPHEN REYNOLDS

So, in the second half of the season, Mark Farrell is brought back. Mark is creatively invested, but not as personally invested as he had been in the past. This is not going to make or break his career, at this point. So he is in to make a fix, but he's not sure if he's interested in coming back again.

At the same time, Michael Donovan is reaching out to find somebody else, and Tim McAuliffe is invited in. So I've gone through a disruptive season with a new showrunner, Geoff and Jack are gone, and it's Jenipher and I in the leadership chairs—the supervising producer and the director.

Tim McAuliffe had left the writers' room in 2009, and had worked as a writer on *Late Night With Jimmy Fallon*, among other shows, before he came back as showrunner for Season 18. But the show's ratings had fallen drastically in Season 17—at one point, down to 468,000—and in 2010, the CBC ordered just thirteen episodes for Season 18, down from eighteen in the previous season and twenty in the season before that—a sign that the network's confidence in the show was wavering.

STEPHEN REYNOLDS

I never got a sense, until that thirteen-episode season, that the show was in crisis at any point. I always had a sense that the machinations of Michael's work—it had been Salter Street, becoming Halifax Film, becoming DHX— that he was always like, "This is my bread and butter. It's not going anywhere. I'm going to make sure that I can make this go—this is what's paying for my office downtown."

TIM MCAULIFFE

Because I had been there before, I understood the world. And I had worked for Mark, who is literally the reason why I write comedy now. He was such a nice guy to give me the job. So I don't know. People always get upset. There's always something going on. But to me, it seemed great. It didn't seem like anything really bad was going on.

STEPHEN REYNOLDS

The show's numbers had dipped a little. They were still good, but Farrell was on his way out, and the CBC has a limited amount of resources, and every year they're looking at—how much can we spend on this, that, and the other thing? I can't place the time, but there might have also been some regime change at the top—a senior-management shift that was questioning whether we should refresh, or redo, or put this money somewhere else.

So, in the questioning of it, they said, "Well, okay. Let's hang on. We can't kill it; we'll put money elsewhere and only give them X amount of dollars."

That season, the show skyrocketed, so that turned it around. The numbers were massive. We would get pieces of paper and write down the ratings—758,000, 803,000, 813,000. On the Monday morning, or on the Wednesday morning after the Tuesday showing, we'd hang them from the ceiling and say, "Look, we're doing it! We're doing it! We're bringing it back! We're relevant again."

TIM MCAULIFFE

I think we did a few things that kind of went viral, like Gordon Pinsent reading Justin Bieber's memoir. That really helped launch the show.

A YouTube clip of that sketch has drawn close to 300,000 views to date. TV columnist Bill Brioux reported in November 2010 that an episode that aired that month had drawn 925,000 viewers, and he credited the many appearances of Gordon Pinsent with helping to attract viewers.

TIM MCAULIFFE

The best thing that season was when we went to Newfoundland and filmed with Gordon Pinsent. Danny Williams had just retired, so we filmed a bit with Gordon and Danny and a couple of guys from *Republic of Doyle*. It was kind of fun, and that really generated a lot of interest and a lot of viral elements.

STEPHEN REYNOLDS

That was, in fact, one of the very few field pieces that I actually went out and shot.

I had a relationship with Gordon Pinsent, but Mark Critch has always had a relationship with him, and, being a Newfoundlander, he came up with this idea of, "Okay, Danny, you're retiring. But you can't do anything until you meet the Codfather."

The premise was this: Mark Critch was reliant on Danny Williams for comic fodder, so he insisted that Williams have his plan to retire from politics approved by the "Codfather"—the supreme Newfoundlander and Labradorian—who was played by Gordon Pinsent. When the Codfather granted his approval, Critch panicked and took both Pinsent and Williams hostage, until they were rescued by Allan Hawco, in his *Republic of Doyle* persona.

STEPHEN REYNOLDS

It was a brilliant sketch, and unlike most field pieces, there was a narrative. It was a scripted piece. We were going to shoot it like a drama.

Republic of Doyle was just starting up, and its first season was kind of a hit. So, Critchy had Allan Hawco in his back pocket as this little punchline that was kind of scripted, but he didn't know how it would go. He hadn't approached Alan and said, "Okay, well, we'll do it this way."

So, off to Newfoundland we go, and we've got three hours. Danny's going to give us an hour and a half, and Gordon's going to give us an hour and a half. And then, as they meet, they decide that, "Oh, yeah—we'll hang out." I had designed the shooting to not include them both at the same time, because of their busy schedules. But they had so much fun, they all hung out.

DANNY WILLIAMS

To be in a room with Critch and Hawco and Gordon Pinsent, it was a big deal for me. I was honoured to be involved in it. This thing was just on the heels of my resignation, and it was a lot of fun.

STEPHEN REYNOLDS

So we block the scene. Danny doesn't really know what blocking is, but we let the scene play. We get a master, and they go a little extreme, physically. You can see, in the cut, that there is a little bit of a continuity issue around the tying up of Danny, in particular. But it didn't really matter.

The hardest part was actually getting the beat finished without breaking into laughter.

DANNY WILLIAMS

That was one of the more lengthy skits, with several different pieces in it. Critch handed me the script and said, "Here's where we want to go with this. Let's go ahead and roll." So we just played it out. He took the lead, and it was just a matter, then, of responding to him. Sometimes you've got to give as good as you get with Critch, and it's not easy to keep up with him, to be quite honest with you. But as long as you can get a few counterpunches in once in a while, it doesn't hurt.

STEPHEN REYNOLDS

Danny really got into the acting. He is a Newfoundlander, and probably grew up acting as a kid. I don't know, but he found the muse.

DANNY WILLIAMS

[*Laughing*] No, not at all! The acting came in when I was a politician.

But seriously, I was in the typical high school plays like *Macbeth*, but I had a supporting role, to be quite honest with you.

But I like a bit of fun. I like to laugh. I love humour, and I think that's probably true of most Newfoundlanders and Labradorians—not that it isn't for anybody else in the country, but we love our humour down here. So you do grow up with that.

STEPHEN REYNOLDS

One of the things about that piece was that we were never sure that Allan Hawco was going to show up. He showed up at the last minute, right in the nick of time—but he also showed up with his costume designer, and she had these costumes from the show, so he could play the character of Doyle, so it was really wonderful.

It was one of those sketches where, before the edit, I knew we had a great little piece. In every set-up, there was the comic-dramatic hit that was needed.

DANNY WILLIAMS

It was a lot of fun, it really was. You adapt things on the fly, and for whatever reason, they just seemed to work.

STEPHEN REYNOLDS

At the end of the shoot, Hawco said, "Well, we're having a wrap party, but we're doing a supper at Raymonds. You guys should come." So we all end up going. Tim McAuliffe is the showrunner that season, and Critchy and I and Tim and Peter Sutherland all wind up going to Raymonds, and Hawco has already invited Gordon Pinsent to join us.

Raymonds is an incredibly good restaurant, but it ended up that Gordon, umm, provided the Scotch. And Gordon was teaching us all how to appropriately drink single malt Scotches all night long. And it just got way out of hand, way loud. Eventually, we stumbled our way out of there with an incredibly monstrous bill that, down the road, became an issue. Who was paying for what? Tim and Mark and I wound up with some astronomical number on the thing, going, "Oh, my God! What has Mr. Pinsent done?"

TIM MCAULIFFE

We started really partying down and drinking a lot, and the next thing you know, the bill comes and it's $4,000! I was just like, "Wow, that's amazing!" So Critch and I split it. It was so crazy. We had had so many drinks. It was insane, but it was really fun.

STEPHEN REYNOLDS

Anyway, our numbers were huge that season. Tim just got it, and we had our biggest year since Mary and Rick had left. The numbers were in the 800,000s consistently; there was just joy and a newfound breath of life in the show.

• • •

TIM MCAULIFFE

After that season ended, my wife and I moved to LA from New York, and basically I got a job on a sitcom in LA.

STEPHEN REYNOLDS

Tim would not return, and then Michael reached out and found Peter McBain.

McBain had been a writer on *22 Minutes* from 2000 to 2003, but had moved on to work as a writer on CBC's *The Hour* with George Stroumboulopoulos.

STEPHEN REYNOLDS

He worked with George Stroumboulopoulos for a few years, and then he went into news and became a news producer. Michael found him, and pulled him out to come and be the showrunner.

So Peter comes in during my last season. He knows how an executive producer in the newsroom operates, and he shifts the systems just enough to keep us on our toes.

By this time, I'm fairly confident about my choices. I know how to edit, but by the end of the season, Peter and I end up butting heads over the edit—over creative content; the pace of the sketch. His expertise, at this point, is all around news and butting things together—bang-bang-bang-bang-bang. And to this day, my biggest complaint about the show is how brutal it looks in the pacing of the pieces.

GERI HALL

When Peter McBain was there, that was my final year on *22*. I left at Christmastime—I think it was December 2011.

Leaving a show is never easy. As an actor, particularly a Canadian actor, there's always that moment when, if you are lucky enough to be employed, you've got to decide—is it time to go, or is it time to stay? For me, there were a few factors involved.

The most pressing one—and this is quite personal, but I made a vow that I was going to share this kind of stuff, anytime it comes up in an organic way—my husband and I, the whole time I was at *22 Minutes*, had been trying to conceive, with no luck whatsoever. By year four-and-a-half or five, what started out as a little bell in the background, reminding us that we'd better keep on it, turned into a full five-alarm fire. "If you guys don't make some big choices soon, you're going to have to accept a life without a family."

We had been going through fertility treatments during all of our break periods. So any time a season ended, we would jump right back into fertility clinics and keep doing treatments, right up until I got on the plane again for Halifax. But then I would be in Halifax, and not doing it there, so we were putting this other dream on hold so I could live this acting dream. So for the last year, we were talking about—how long does this go on? What is our choice? What is our path?

At the same time, just to speak completely honestly, I was getting a lot lighter in the show. And that happens. It's a part of the organic ebb and flow of what happens in an ensemble cast. But it meant that I was not on the show very much anymore, even though I was out in Halifax, and not at home doing this very important thing that we should have been working on.

So as my opportunities on the show got less and less, and we were talking more and more about what we were going to do, it just became very clear to us that it was time for me to leave the show—to call it quits. It became a choice of—be on the show, or come home and try and make a baby. So we came home. And a year and half later we had twins! So it all turned out in the end, despite all odds.

• • •

And then there was Rob Ford. In 2011, the then-mayor of Toronto, known for his belligerent behaviour—and a notorious video that showed him smoking crack cocaine—was about to become the target of an ambush by Marg, Princess Warrior. Once again, the ambush itself would become the subject of some media attention, drawing criticism about whether it was fair to ambush the mayor outside his own home.

STEPHEN REYNOLDS

When there are problems in the democracy of the world, or when there's shit going down—when there's a Rob Ford—that is when the show is really relevant. When there's nothing going on, the show relies on current affairs, or it relies on cultural commentary: "Oh, yes! The new Note 7 blew up on a plane!" We can make fun of Samsung, but it doesn't have the currency of drug footage of the mayor of Toronto, who's denying it.

In my tenure, there were a few seasons where that stuff was going on, where everything we did felt vital.

MARK MULLANE

The whole idea behind that one was that Rob Ford was sort of hard to get to. We debated just doing it at City Hall, but we really didn't think that was our best opportunity to get a nice long time with him. I forget whose idea it was to go to his house; it very well could have been mine. We were thinking about the best way to get somebody who's not expecting it. Some people said it wasn't fair to go to his house, but we did learn a lot about him that day, that's for sure.

STEPHEN REYNOLDS

There'd been a reporter who had already come to the backyard, or down the public fence and the other property, and looked over, so there was this little controversy going on.

MARK MULLANE

So basically it's me and Mary and Pete again, and we decided that we would go there pretty early in the morning. It was October, so the sun was coming up a bit later, and we decided we would drive down the street, park close enough so we could see his house, and then just wait for him to come out.

When we pulled up, it was dark. The TV in the main room was on. It must have been on all night, probably. We waited and waited and waited a long time—like, a ridiculously long time. And we thought, "Well, surely he has to be in the Council Chamber at nine o'clock; what is going on here?" I can't remember the exact time, but it was well past the time where you could be driving into downtown Toronto [and get to City Hall on time]. And we were like, "What is he doing in there?"

One thing that we totally discussed beforehand—because my son was just about to be born—was: if he's with his kids, we don't do this. That was 100 per cent clear. I mean, the whole team was like, "Yeah. If his kids are there, this is not going to work. We'll just go to City Hall and we'll get him there."

So Rob Ford's in-laws, or maybe his parents, I can't remember—somebody pulled up, and it was bright at this point. They went inside, presumably to take care of the kids, and we waited some more. Still nothing.

And then, finally, Rob emerges from the house, closes the door behind him, and starts walking towards the car.

That's when we said, "Go." We saw that there were no kids with him, there was clearly somebody inside with them, and we just said, "Go."

So Mary gets on the sidewalk, and I'm still in the car, because I'm driving the—basically, the getaway vehicle. I'm in the car, and Mary and Peter start walking towards Rob, and Mary just starts going into her bit, saying, "Rob! Come here!" Very friendly, very friendly, right off the bat. But then he gets upset—as you would, if you were trying to go to work. We didn't expect him to greet us with open arms.

But also we didn't expect the more violent reaction that he had, either. So I was watching it all unfold from the driver's seat of the van. I wasn't hearing any of it. I just saw them talk to him; I saw Mary go around the other side of the van, so I couldn't see him pulling the door on her, until I saw the footage afterwards. And then after it was all said and done, he's on his front lawn with his phone, presumably calling the cops. That was when he called 9-1-1.

STEPHEN REYNOLDS

He's pacing on his stoop, and he hides behind a bush, and he's saying, "I'm calling the police," and the mother is in the window, and he says, "You're terrifying my kids!"

MARK MULLANE

I remember Mary—she was yelling at him. I can't remember exactly what she was saying. I don't think this is on film, but it was something to the effect of, "Come on, Rob. Don't be such a coward."

STEPHEN REYNOLDS

So, he calls her out on it and she's just like, "I'm terrifying your kids?" He goes in, gets his coat on, then he comes and tries to go to the car. And Walsh just commits, and says, "Well, frig this! Wait a second! I'm not terrifying." And she walks right up and has this joyful little confrontation that ends up as being a part of *22 Minutes* history.

Footage of the encounter shows Walsh approaching Rob Ford in his driveway, in daylight, hollering, "Mayor Ford, it's me, Marg Delahunty! I gave up the Princess Warrior stuff, but when I saw what was happening to you…I came up all the way from Newfoundland to talk to you," as Ford attempts to get into his van. "One good thing about being stubborn, Mayor Ford, is you always know what you're gonna be thinking the next day. God love ya; take care of yourself now," Walsh says, as Ford walks away.

Ford later told reporters that it was dark, that his daughter had been frightened and had run back into his home, and that he didn't know who they were…"and obviously I've had death threats and there was a camera and a mic."

MARK MULLANE

Mary's whole thing, back in the old days, was to get up close to somebody and kind of lock their arm. She would put her arm in between them so they couldn't go anywhere without pushing away, which is a great move. I mean, that's such an awesome move, if you're ever doing this kind of comedy, to just lock their arm, like—"Hey, what's going on?" And then they can't leave without looking like a bully.

RICK MERCER

Anyone who has ever worked with Walsh will tell you this: if you have a scene where you have to waltz together, she will bruise you! It won't look like she's bruising you, but she will bruise you. She will hurt you.

I used to feel bad for them. You could see in their eyes, "This woman is going to break my arm!" Like, physically, he would not get out of those clutches. There's no walking away from that.

MARK MULLANE

So Rob was looking at our van, and trying to take down the plate number. We weren't fleeing the scene, but we were just kind of, "Well, we got what we wanted out of this." And he went back inside. He was not coming back out, obviously. And we were like, "Well, that, that was weird. That really didn't go according to plan."

Not that there was a real plan, because you never know when you're ambushing somebody. But, you know, he said his kids were there; they 100 per cent were not there. They were probably inside his house, but they were not with him. He said it was dark outside. It was bright, light of day. I think it was 8:30 in the morning in October, so the sun was up—completely up.

But we didn't do anything out of the normal *22 Minutes* handbook. She definitely had her microphone that says "*22 Minutes*." He said, "They didn't identify themselves." But it's like, how can you miss a media icon with a *22 Minutes* microphone? It was pretty obvious.

I don't know if anything ever happened with those 9-1-1 tapes, but I think he said some pretty disparaging comments to the 9-1-1 operators—that they weren't getting there quick enough, and that sort of thing. This is all hearsay from people. But something later came out that he had called them every name in the book when he was on the phone. That's when the whole "Rob-fucking-Ford" thing started. "Don't you know I'm Rob-fucking-Ford?" That's what he was saying on the phone. I mean, he was getting pretty worked up on the lawn, I can say that for sure.

So we drove back to the city and I called Peter McBain at that point and I just said, "This is what happened." We went straight to the CBC. I got the tape transferred and sent back to Halifax, probably within a couple of hours from when we shot it. And then we went off to City Hall to try to get him again [*laughing*].

By now, Michael Donovan was spending less and less time on *22 Minutes*. In 2006, The Halifax Film Company had merged with Decode Entertainment of Toronto to create DHX Media, which, at this point, was becoming a major global player in the production and distribution of kids' television. The demands of running DHX meant he had less time to be hands-on with the show.

STEPHEN REYNOLDS

I did eight seasons, and over the course of the eight seasons, Michael Donovan visited less and less and less. He would try to make a point of getting to the read-throughs, and make a point of getting to the taping of the show, and, of course, come to the final cut. His company expansion made further demands on his time. It became more and more difficult; it was never that he didn't want to. "Okay. I can't be to the read-through today, but I'll put in my two cents worth," you know, from London, or from Mexico—wherever he was in the world.

At the end of my tenure with the show, DHX had been born, DHX had begun to explode, DHX had required a CEO that would operate the business, report to the board of directors, and he couldn't be hands-on.

So, he was trusting the show to Tim McAuliffe and then to Peter McBain. And then, with Peter, I think he was—"Okay, great. There's a guy who knows news, there's a guy who knows the system already." The previous two or three trials of showrunners, in my tenure, were people who didn't know the system, and relied on me and Jenipher.

I found myself in my last two seasons being overly taxed. I said to Jenipher that maybe we should consider letting me split my duties, given that there's no Jack, there's no Geoff. I said, "Why don't I share it, and we give the studio directing to somebody like [associate director] Michael [Lewis]? He knows it, and that's what he wants to do. Why don't we let him do the studio work and then I can help execute the rest?"

I pushed that in my last season with Peter—and that might have been my undoing [*laughing*].

I did eight seasons with the show, which was just year to year to year. At the end of each year, it was, "Thanks very much; we will let you know." The season ends the first week of March; by the end of April, they were booking me for the next season. And that happened up until 2012, at which time they said, "We are going to refresh and go after somebody new."

I was not invited back after my eighth season in 2012.

Season 20 saw the arrival a new cast member: Susan Kent, a native Newfoundlander with a background in theatre, who had spent some time in the *22 Minutes* writers' room before graduating to an on-camera role.

BILL BRIOUX

She came at a point after Geri. I know they were trying a few people, and she just sort of stepped into it and became that face. She brought her own characters and another look. I think she made the transition very smoothly. It didn't seem to rock any boats. She is very good at the desk.

JOHN DOYLE

I visited again in 2013...I talked to the new showrunner, Peter McBain, at that point. It was very different from talking to Mark Farrell. I was not writing a big piece about the show; it was mainly to go and talk to Susan Kent and do a profile of her, but I got the sense that there was a very different atmosphere in this space, you know, in the room—at the whole production at that point. They were much more careful in dealing with me. They were wary of me. They were perfectly polite to me, but in the way that you can sense that things are not working perfectly here, and they don't want me to have a sense that things are not going perfectly smoothly.

At that point, I think Susan Kent had been with the show for a year, or it might have been her second season. But she was a sort of the new star. So there was a lot of interest and curiosity in who this Susan Kent woman is. We had a good chat.

Kent told John Doyle during that 2013 visit that her contribution to the show was to bring "misfits, weirdos, and skinny people. And Céline Dion. A long time ago, someone told me I look like her, which I don't. But I started to do an impression of her. And when I came here they asked me what impressions I did. That was it—Céline Dion. But you have to able to do an impression of somebody on this show. I'd say I'm still building that muscle that does political satire. You need that muscle here."

But with Kent, Critch, and Majumder on the news desk at the start of Season 21, Cathy Jones—the longest-running cast member on the show—had her role scaled back when she was told that she would no longer be appearing on the desk, although she could continue to perform in sketches.

BILL BRIOUX

As someone who watches the show, I don't think that was necessary. I think Cathy could and should be part of the desk, if that's what she wants. She's always funny.

I'm guessing the reasons were because they wanted fresh faces, and that the series was evolving, but personally I was happy to see her on the desk, and I would still be that way.

Nonetheless, Cathy's characters continued to leave an indelible mark on the show, and in Season 22, she tapped into the zeitgeist with "Angry Yoga"—a sketch in which she guides a class through a sequence of yoga poses as she gently lists her frustrations—"man buns," clear-cutting, and "apple-butter-vegan terrorists." The sketch led to several spinoffs, and the original sketch on YouTube now has well over one million views.

BILL DONOVAN

I marvel at their ability to renew themselves. When I first saw Cathy's "Angry Yoga" I thought, "There is no end to it. What a genius idea." Where did that come from? Probably from Cathy. It may have been somebody else's idea, but the execution is just remarkable. And this is not in year one, it's in year twenty-two of the show.

Twenty-five Years and Counting

Twenty-five years on, *22 Minutes* continues to evolve. Writer and actor Meredith MacNeill became a recurring cast member in Season 24, and Season 25 saw the arrival of a new face: stand-up comedian Trent McClellan.

GEOFF D'EON

That's a good cast they have now: Majumder is a funny guy. Susan Kent is a gifted comedienne. Mark Critch—a brilliant mind. It turns out that Mark is one of the most gifted performers in the Canadian talent pool. So it has survived this turnover of cast.

DANNY WILLIAMS

They are multi-dimensional, that cast. The people who have gone through that show over the years are very talented individuals, and I think that's what gives them such longevity.

BILL BRIOUX

I think the show is approaching another crossroad. Mark Critch has been "the guy" for a long time now—for half the life of the show. I think, right now, it's all firing and working. If Mark decides there are other things he wants to work on, I think that will pose a challenge for the series. What would it be like after him? I'd be interested to see how the show would weather that transition.

GEOFF D'EON

I'm sure Mark has had opportunities to work in the States. I know he's worked as a writer on *Just for Laughs* in Montréal for John Oliver. Mark is well-connected in comedy circles. It wouldn't surprise me if Mark one day popped up on American television, but I'm not convinced that Mark is driven by that need for the big Yankee bucks. In some ways, it's more fun being a big fish in the small Canadian pond than it is being a Canadian trying to make an impression on the giant US market.

STEPHEN REYNOLDS

22 Minutes was successful because of Rick and Mary in a big way—because they attacked the political climate of the day. Then that was handed over to Mark Critch. So the show will carry on, I'm sure. I think Michael Donovan's goal is to outlive *Front Page Challenge*, which ran for something like thirty-eight years, because it is an ideal format. If you've got somebody who can sit in a chair and make fun of current politics every day, there's always a ferocious appetite for that, 'cause we're all pissed off.

BILL BRIOUX

I think the idea of a news parody is a well that never goes dry. I just think it was a smart idea that Mary had, way back when. It's one that keeps giving. "Weekend Update" has been part of *Saturday Night Live* for forty-two years, and people seem to like that more than ever. And I do think swapping the cast in and out has revitalized it at times. Gavin Crawford was really a great addition to the show—very talented and funny guy who brought different characters, a different look and energy. So they've had jolts when they needed them, by making cast changes over the years.

IVAN FECAN

I admire very much the skill that it has taken to keep it fresh, and to keep regenerating it as cast members come and go, and writers come and go. The idea of keeping a show fresh for that long is quite a skill and a challenge, and hats off to Donovan for doing that. Michael's really done an amazing job.

ED MACDONALD

It's the structure. It's kind of fill-in-the-blanks. It's like, here's the show, this is what we do. We have the headline news at the top, we have sketches related to the news and stuff like that. You know pretty much out of the gate what the parameters are. They've changed a little over the years, but it's still kind of the same thing.

GEOFF D'EON

I thought, for the longest time, that this show could only be done by these four people: Rick, Mary, Cathy, Greg. I thought that was it, and if they were ever going to be replaced, it would have to be by another Newfoundlander.

And that was not the case. The format is incredibly resilient. If you have a news desk with four people on it, you can, in fact, take one of them off and replace them with someone else. That's not to say that everyone who filled in was as good as Rick. Clearly that's not the case. But the show endures. It has a very durable format, and it will never run out of raw material, because it is topically based.

BILL DONOVAN

They have managed to keep the essence of the show. The key creative ideas have sustained through a virtually complete change of cast, writers—and probably on the production side, as well. I think that's remarkable. I don't know if you could say that about any other show of any kind.

GERALD LUNZ

Our show, *22 Minutes*, was unapologetically by and for Canadians. Everybody else tries to make these shows that you can sell in America for export, and they become these watered-down versions of kinda-Canadian, quasi-North-American shows. We just didn't do that, because we had come from a place where the regional voice was important.

HENRY SARWER-FONER

I think it has been able to connect with viewers because it reflects Canadian culture back to Canadians, kind of like a funhouse mirror. It's topical, it's raw, it's smart. Canadians are also news junkies, and here was a show that kind of satisfied that itch. The cast gives voice to whatever bugs the nation that week, and they're very saucy and insightful, and never afraid to take a shot at authority. I think people find it cathartic. Like any good comedy or drama, it's catharsis.

GERI HALL

I love that we are a country that makes fun of itself, even on the highest level of government, and I'm proud that this show gave that sort of phenomenon to us as a part of our identity.

Mary Walsh with that sword in her hand—that is something that makes me proud to be a Canadian. That's who we are. We are still politically savvy and conscious of what's going on, but we don't take it too seriously, and I love that.

JOHN DOYLE

I do think there has to be a satiric news outlet in a Canadian environment. There will always be an appetite for a satiric news show, and that's one of the reasons why *22 Minutes* is still there. It has a core audience that is curious about how the team is going to treat whatever Justin Trudeau did last week, or even whatever Trump did, or whatever else happened in the Canadian news.

But one big question mark hangs over the show's future: where will *22 Minutes* live? For the entire history of the show, it has been produced out of CBC Halifax's Bell Road studio. In late 2014, all television and radio news production moved from Bell Road to a new building across town—all except *22 Minutes*. The new plant doesn't have the space to accommodate the show and its production team, and the building that has always been home to the show is up for sale.

For now, *22 Minutes* is the only production left in an otherwise abandoned TV station, and there's no guarantee that the space will be available for the show's twenty-sixth season. By 2018, the show could be homeless.

GEOFF D'EON

I know anecdotally that [production manager] Jenipher Ritchie has explored different scenarios in Halifax. Where could they get studio space in Halifax? How much would it cost to equip a soundstage in Burnside [Industrial Park in Dartmouth, NS] with a control room and dressing rooms and writing rooms? I'd be very surprised if that tentative planning did not go ahead, because at one point, it was declared that Bell Road would be closed, so it would have been on Jenipher Ritchie's to-do list to find out where they could do this show in Halifax, and how much would it cost.

No question it's doable: it's time and money. You find a suitable space in an industrial park, and you build sets, and you put up a lighting grid, and you can make a television show anywhere.

I'm personally glad that it's still emanating from a CBC building, because the CBC has contracted out so much of its programming in recent years; it's become less of a producer of programs and more an acquirer and a broadcaster of programs. So I personally find it very satisfying that *This Hour Has 22 Minutes* started in the same studio that *Don Messer* started in, and to this day comes out of a studio that is thirty metres from where Don Messer plied his trade, producing the most popular show in Canada at the time. There's a certain poetic symmetry to that for me.

Over the past twenty-five years, hundreds of individuals, from cast to crew to writers to executives, have stepped into that Bell Road studio to play their part in the fate of *22 Minutes*, and for many of them, being part of that team has had a lasting impact on their lives.

GEOFF D'EON

In 1993, I needed a change. I was burnt out on daily news. I had two young kids that I never saw. My wife always reminds me that when my kids were really small and the phone would ring, they would point to it and go, "Dada." I was doing eighty or ninety hours a week running a newsroom, which I loved; it was my life, I was obsessed with it.

But I really needed a change. I had supporters in that unit, but I also had detractors, and I was just sick of it. I was sick of the politics, and I wasn't having enough fun. I wanted more fun; life is short.

So in 1993, when *22 Minutes* came along and they needed a news guy— that was serendipity of the greatest kind, and I will appreciate that serendipity for as long as I live. It was just the right show at the right time.

HENRY SARWER-FONER

I got to work with all these talented people, which gave me the opportunity to direct many different styles—albeit very quickly. Still, you get to play around, and that's kind of why I got into it in the first place—that little endorphin squirt you get when you create something from scratch, either writing something by myself, or working with a team. I mean, that's a joy.

EDWARD KAY

It was an education. I learned how to write faster, and under a lot of pressure. You realize you really don't need as much time as you thought you needed. There would have been a time when I would stew over something all day. But on that show, you had to do that, and three other things, in the next hour. So that was good.

I also loved meeting everybody. I thought they were really great. They were really interesting people, and fun and funny. It wasn't one of those shows where you have to pretend everything's awesome. Like sitcoms? "Last week's show was brilliant!" No it wasn't! But on that show, we felt like we were doing something—like it mattered.

COLIN MOCHRIE

I got this writing lesson from amazing people. Mark Farrell, who I really can't say enough about, sort of taught me how to write sketches and how to get to the point right away—keeping it short, and keeping it funny. So it was like a really fun school.

It's not too often in an actor's life where you get a chance to be on something that is a classic, so I am always grateful that, although my time there was short, I was part of a Canadian classic. It's something I have always been proud of, and I'm glad they had a little breakdown and hired me.

GERI HALL

I feel like I found my place on that show. Eventually, I earned my place on that show. But there was never a day that went by when I wasn't very cognizant of the fact that I was very lucky to be there. There are literally thousands of actors in this country who would have loved to have taken my place. So my heart was full of gratitude at all times.

It was the craziest of times, it was the most amazing of times. And it's a fun memory now.

GAVIN CRAWFORD

For me, it was just a giant thrill to be able to step into that environment and work with Cathy and Greg and people that I had watched—not my whole life, but when I was in my twenties for sure. It certainly taught me how to be a faster writer. It taught me how to be creative and commercial, in a weird way. To sort of bridge the gap between what I think is great, and what resonates with the largest number of people—not necessarily in a sellout way, but how to tweak it to make it speak to this percentage more people, if I just shift this tone. I don't always do that, but it's a good skill to have.

JENNIFER WHALEN

The show kind of had a lovely, weird sense of family, because it is a weekly show and you're all in the same building. From the props and costume people, the writers, all of the administrative office people—it was kind of fun. You kind of became like a weird little pirate crew, all together.

It definitely made me a better writer because of the volume of material that you produce. You have to kill all your darlings. Writers can be very sensitive and precious about their material, and you just learn not to be. Every once in a while, there'll be a "No" that really hurts, because it's something that you really liked. But you get better at being like, "Okay, you didn't like that. I'll write something else."

I think a lot of people who are interested in writing have a real problem with putting their bum in the seat and doing it. Now, if I need to write, I can sit down and write. I used to be like, "I have to be wearing my special bathrobe. I must sit at my desk at a certain angle, and then I must have the proper muffin and coffee," or whatever it was. And now I'm just like, "Whatever. I can sit in this chair in a lobby and write, if I have to."

PAUL BELLINI

I now teach a news desk course at Humber College, and it's basically what I learned at *22*. I'm teaching a course in how to write the copy gag, how to manipulate footage, how to do double-enders, and I'm bringing all that experience I have from *22 Minutes* into the classroom, which is great, because, let's be honest, news satire is bigger now than it's ever been.

I said to Humber, "This is where most of your students are going to get jobs in the future—on shows like *22* and *The Beaverton* in Canada, or *The Daily Show*, John Oliver, Samantha Bee. This is what's happening now in terms of comedy—not so much sketch, but a lot of news satire. So, I'm really glad my experience at *22* gave me something I've been able to turn into a career.

GEOFF D'EON

In one's life, there are always these giant forks in the road. And you know what they say: when you come to a fork in the road, take it. So I did.

What would I have done had I not taken it? I honestly don't know.

JACK KELLUM

It was a pleasure to go to work. I enjoyed my time. Nineteen years, I think it was. And I still believe in the show.

GERALD LUNZ

It was the most fun I have ever had, working with this group of great artists and producers, and the collective thing we did—working together and living on top of each other to create something that was a huge success, and still is. So that's like real legacy stuff.

PETER MANSBRIDGE

Those of us in our business, even in the news business, never know how long things are going to last. To a degree, your fate is established by the way the audience relates to you. Twenty-five years is a long time for a program to last. You know, nothing is automatic in our business. It's tough. And it's even tougher in the entertainment side of things.

That they've stayed relevant, and have made a success of that—a continuing success—is a tribute to the talents of not only those on air, but the Geoff D'Eon types, behind the scenes, who have taken a particular kind of—not just Maritime or Atlantic Canada humour, but Canadian humour—and made it something that's popular from coast to coast to coast, and that distinguishes us from others. We have visitors to the country who watch the program and go, "What? I don't get it." But we get it, and that's what's important.

I just think they're terrific and there's no reason why they can't go for another twenty-five years.

RICK MERCER

That day in the boardroom, I knew it could last forever. I really did. I thought, "If this doesn't work, I know nothing."

Now, in hindsight, I think a lot of great TV has been made by different people that hasn't captured the imagination of the king, and the audience was not there for it. But I just knew it was going to go for a very long time.

ED MACDONALD

I'm thinking it could go on another maybe six hundred years? Roughly. And I'll still be saying, "It's not as funny as when I was there!"

GEOFF D'EON

You've got to tip your hat to Michael Donovan and Mary Walsh and the team of people who got that show off the ground, because I think they created something that is truly meaningful—as much as a television show can be meaningful.

In the grand scheme of things, it doesn't amount to a hill of beans, but if you look at it through the prism of television shows that have actually made a difference in Canada, *22 Minutes* is, I would argue, one of the brightest shining examples. And it's testimony to the skills and passion of people over the years who have gone through that show.

I think it's an extraordinary accomplishment. I'm very proud to have played a part in it. I give thanks that I was able to work with such a talented group of people.

RICK MERCER

It was a difficult birth, but no one ever really talks about the difficult birth if it all works out in the end. And it did all work out in the end.

GEOFF D'EON

This, I think, is one of the secrets of the strength of *22 Minutes*: really good ideas, excellent writers, brilliant performers, small crews, knowing what they are going to get, and just getting that.

And then executing it in simple and straightforward ways. Never forgetting that people need to laugh. And for all the horrors in the world, people have heart. The world is full of really good people.

22 Minutes just has the hugest audience of great Canadians.

VIDEO LINKS

- Want to watch the 1993 "conga line" election hit?
  Go to goo.gl/WA8qDo and fast-forward to the fifty-minute mark

- To see episodes from the entire first season, go to: goo.gl/j6gJ9K

- Rick Mercer's "Raise a Little Hell" video: goo.gl/iMZ31s

- A montage of clips with Jean Chrétien and Stephen Harper, including
  Rick and Chrétien at Harvey's, Mary in Chrétien's office, and Geri's arrest
  at Harper's news conference: goo.gl/VSHQA4

- Rick's Stockwell Day petition: goo.gl/rK6S9k

- Watch a (grainy) version of Rick's "We're Here for a Good Time" video
  from Bosnia at: goo.gl/47ZF5D

- *Talking to Americans: The Special* can be found on YouTube in three parts:

  - Part One: goo.gl/VbDpmW

  - Part Two: goo.gl/bAf5Kq

  - Part Three: goo.gl/jwEIUp

- Gavin's Mark Jackson retires: goo.gl/LdVzYh

- Mary Walsh ambushes Sarah Palin: goo.gl/wgMIkb

- A CBC News item about Geri Hall's ambush of Stephen Harper: goo.gl/
  PjZpq3

- Geri Hall's ambush of Dalton McGuinty: goo.gl/0YrYgc

- Mark Critch, Gordon Pinsent, and Danny Williams—the Codfather: goo.gl/B1f52o

- Gordon Pinsent reading from Justin Bieber's memoir: goo.gl/Z4JsvQ

- Cathy Jones's Angry Yoga: goo.gl/2CfR1R

ACKNOWLEDGEMENTS

They say it takes a village, but really, when "it" involves writing a book, it's mostly just you, sitting in a poorly heated office, shivering under a blanket and staring at a blinking cursor.

But it does take momentum to get a project like this off the ground. And for that, I have to offer my most heartfelt thanks to Geoff D'Eon—my first interviewee—who immediately embraced this project with gusto, and who very generously opened his personal archives and shared his wonderful stories over many hours with me. I knew, after interviewing Geoff, that there was a book here, even if it only turned out to be a volume of his wonderful stories.

And on the subject of momentum, a positive nod from Gerald Lunz meant access not only to his gleefully unvarnished stories told at breakneck speed; it smoothed the way to critical interviews with many other people, including Rick Mercer. So, thank you, Gerald.

I owe Rick my most sincere thanks for being so generous with his time ("In for a penny, in for a pound!" he said cheerily, somewhere around the two-and-a-half-hour mark in our conversation). Rick is that rare breed who is truly as decent in "real life" as he appears on TV.

Thanks, also, to the folks from long ago at the CBC in Halifax—Jack Kellum and Bill Donovan, both now enjoying well-earned retirements; Penny Longley, who was once my boss when I was an associate director there, and who once kindly allowed to me quietly sob in her office when she handed me a layoff notice; and Fred Mattocks, invariably described as "the smartest guy around," who is now having big impact at the CBC in Toronto.

And speaking of mucky-mucks, thanks to George Anthony, Phyllis Platt, and Ivan Fecan for sharing their perspective on and insight into the CBC's higher echelons.

Thanks to Cathy Jones for inviting me into her home to be interviewed and for making me a nice cup of tea. Her sweet (and often tearful) stories didn't end up in the book, but that's not because she isn't a key player in this story.

Also very generous with her time: Geri Hall, who opened up in ways that were very intimate and honest, and who made me feel like her "bestie" the whole time we spoke. Gavin Crawford was loquacious and frank (but not too frank); and the modest Colin Mochrie kindly squeezed me in between his usual million other things.

I'm grateful to the writers who shared their stories: the ever-cheerful Paul Bellini; the kind and insightful Jen Whalen, now a star of *Baroness von Sketch Show*; the ever-dry but sweet-like-fine-wine Ed Macdonald; the logical and level-headed Edward Kay; and happy dude Tim McAuliffe, who totally went the distance by taking my call on his way to play golf in LA.

Thanks also to directors Henry Sarwer-Foner and Stephen Reynolds, and to field producer Mark Mullane, who very generously shared their stories from their days on the show, as did cameraman Peter Sutherland (who was surprisingly laid-back about all the historic moments he'd played a huge part in).

And thanks to Alan MacGillivray for sharing the Salter Street side of the story; to Danny Williams for being a great sport; to Peter Mansbridge for having a sense of humour about his satirists; and to TV columnists John Doyle and Bill Brioux for sharing their perspectives on the show.

I owe a big debt of gratitude to the folks at Nimbus Publishing: to my publishers, Terrilee Bulger and Heather Bryan—thanks for your faith in the idea and in me; thanks for supporting me through the challenges posed by this book, and thanks for giving me my first author credit. To my editor, Elaine McCluskey—your input and advice was invaluable.

For help with transcribing, thanks to Terri Strickland—your aid was greatly appreciated when I was elbows-deep in interviews, and your attention to detail was exceptional.

A big thanks to my sister, Jocelyn Mombourquette, for being my "first reader" and for providing a very detailed and helpful (and, surprisingly, not-too-painful) critique.

And most especially, my deepest gratitude goes to my lifelong partner, Wendy Purves. I should have bought stock in a greeting-card company, given how many "You can do it!" cards you gave me over the course of writing this book. Also, you get extra bonus points for riding out the emotional roller coaster that was the ongoing Quest for Interviews. I promise to provide the same support for you very soon, while you write your long-awaited novel.